Oxf
to
Princes Risborough

A GWR Secondary Route

by
C.R. Potts

THE OAKWOOD PRESS

© Oakwood Press & C.R. Potts 2004

British Library Cataloguing in Publication Data
A Record for this book is available from the British Library
ISBN 0 85361 629 9

Typeset by Oakwood Graphics.
Repro by Ford Graphics, Ringwood, Hants.
Printed by Pims Print, Yeovil, Somerset.

'61XX' class 2-6-2T No. 6106 (now preserved at GWS, Didcot) arrives at Thame with a 2-coach down train.   *N. Simmons/Hugh Davies*

Title page: On Sunday 26th September, 1953 '41XX' class 2-6-2T No. 4149 passes Tiddington with the diverted 9.20 am Sheffield-Swansea service. This usually ran via the former Great Central route to Woodford Halse, then Banbury, Oxford and Swindon. It was normally scheduled to arrive at Oxford at 1.20 pm.   *John Spencer Gilks*

Front cover: On 2nd April, 1965 'Britannia' class 4-6-2 No. 70052 *Firth of Tay* passes Blackbird Leys *en route* to Oxford with a car train. The higher level line is a siding to Q block in the car works (the 1955 sidings), this ground is now Sandy Lane Sports/Tesco's.
John Hubbard

Rear cover, top: In the last summer of passenger operation (1962) a prairie-hauled train (thought to be the 5.44 pm Princes Risborough-Wheatley) stands in Wheatley's down platform.   *Doug Nicholls*

Rear cover, below: On 9th May, 1984 class '58' diesel No. 58014, the first to have traversed the branch, passes the site of the old station, hauling passenger stock. This was one of three trips from Oxford ferrying VIPs to the opening of F.C. Bennett's warehouse (Cowley Freight Terminal) by Minister of Transport David Mitchell. The Terminal lasted 13 years until Rover wanted the ground for expansion. The photograph was taken from the overbridge used by new cars driven from the factory to the railway yard for loading.
John Hubbard

Published by The Oakwood Press (Usk), P.O. Box 13, Usk, Mon., NP15 1YS.
E-mail: sales@oakwoodpress.co.uk
Website: www.oakwoodpress.co.uk

Contents

	Introduction and Acknowledgements	6
Chapter One	The Wycombe Railway - Some Defective Legislation	7
Chapter Two	The First Stage - High Wycombe is reached	11
Chapter Three	Extending the Railway	22
Chapter Four	Opening to Thame and then to Oxford	45
Chapter Five	Financial Difficulties and the End of Independence	65
Chapter Six	Swallowed up by the Great Western	71
Chapter Seven	A New Century brings improvement	95
Chapter Eight	Into the Motor Age	123
Chapter Nine	War and Nationalisation	149
Chapter Ten	Timetables and Operations	169
Chapter Eleven	Closure as a Through Route	205
Chapter Twelve	Only a Stub remains	239
Appendix One	Coaches in Through Narrow Gauge Trains - June 1880	249
Appendix Two	Authorised Staff Establishment - 1925	250
Appendix Three	Private Sidings for the car trade at Morris Cowley	252
Appendix Four	Station Masters on the Line	253
	Bibliography	255
	Index	256

Thame station, with its distinctive overall roof, looking towards Oxford, 16th October, 1960. The 10,000 gallon water tank can be seen behind the line of trucks. *Philip Kelley*

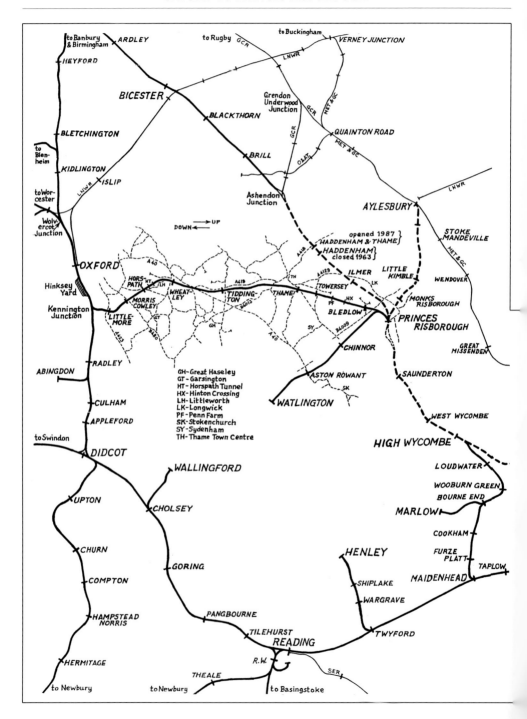

GH - Great Haseley
GT - Garsington
HT - Horspath Tunnel
HX - Hinton Crossing
LH - Littleworth
LK - Longwick
PF - Penn Farm
SK - Stokenchurch
SY - Sydenham
TH - Thame Town Centre

BR Standard class '4' No. 75000 coasts towards Kennington Junction with the 11.30 am Princes Risborough-Hinksey yard freight on 4th December, 1965.   *E. Wilmshurst*

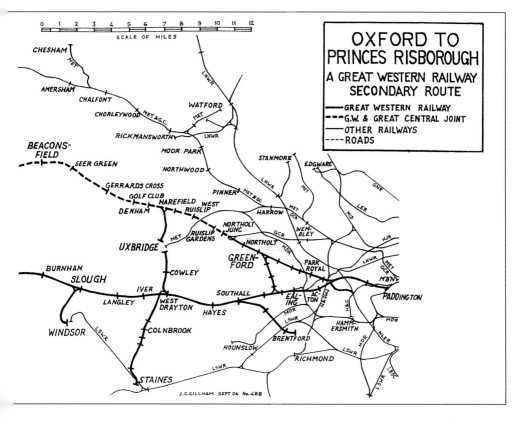

Introduction and Acknowledgements

There is no shortage of archive material relating to the Wycombe Railway Company at the National Archives at Kew, and I was lucky enough to have access to more at the BR Records Centre which now may be at Kew. But it is still the case that that which is preserved is only a tiny fraction of the day to day business of any railway company. As the reader will find, even a well-documented company did not record embarrassing facts, and quite frequently only one side of correspondence has been preserved. So an author has to piece together and interpret details of events of over a hundred years ago as best one can, assisted by other sources such as local newspapers. I do not pretend that everything there is to know about the Oxford-Princes Risborough line is contained herein; much of the daily detail of working the line was not recorded at all.

Having said that, I feel that this is a comprehensive history of a line opened in 1854, a short portion of which remains open for freight traffic today. But I would be delighted to receive any further information, for use in any future edition and this should be sent to the publisher. I have tapped many sources, personal and impersonal, in my search for information, but one is always aware that there will be as many more 'out there', unknown to the author. Fairly late on I came across the British Motor Industry Heritage Trust, at Gaydon in Warwickshire, an unexpected source of railway photographs. Because of the close association of the Morris and Pressed Steel works at Cowley with the railway the Trust does hold a few valuable railway pictures, some of which are included.

Mentioning Cowley works, one of my chief unsolved mysteries is unravelling all the work that took place there in World War II. As Chapter Nine explains the place played a huge part in assisting the war effort and there were frequent expansions of the railway facilities inside the works. These are listed in Appendix Three, details being obtained from the various submissions to the GWR Board. But the files seen did not have plans attached, and separate plans held in a different location did not quote the Board reference and authority date! The fact that the locations were private sidings, outside GWR territory, and it was wartime has not helped to throw light on the darkness. If you hold information that will help clear this up, please write to the publisher.

My thanks to the following who have helped me with information or by lending material which has helped with research or for inclusion as an illustration: A.D. Ayres, David Castle, Tony Cooke, Ian Coulson, Larry Crosier, John Edgington, P.R. Forbes, John Gillham (for his maps), John Glanville, Gordon Gresly, Michael Hale, John Hubbard, Gerald Jacobs, Colin Judge, Philip J. Kelley, Tim Loakes (British Motor Industry Heritage Trust), Brian Matthews, John Norris, the late Harold Purser, Peter Treloar, Chris Turner, John Yoxall. All known photographers are credited under their pictures. Mowat Collection, and all other Brunel University Transport Collection prints, are available from: W.R. Burton, 3 Fairway, Clifton, York, YO30 5QA.

Finally my thanks to my wife Sue for allowing me the peace and quiet to complete the task and for typing the manuscript.

Christopher Potts
January 2004

Chapter One

The Wycombe Railway -
Some Defective Legislation

Princes Risborough to Oxford via Thame, the subject of this book, was part of the Wycombe Railway, from Maidenhead to Oxford. This had started life as an Act for making a railway from Maidenhead to High Wycombe (9 & 10 Vict. cap. 236) receiving its Royal Assent on 27th July, 1846. So the early part of the book will, of necessity, include matters *not* relating to the part of the line which is its real subject, because the building of the Oxford line was the second and third stages of the Wycombe Railway Company (WRC), and we cannot miss out the first stage. But once the line was open to High Wycombe (1854), thoughts very soon turned to extension first to Thame, and then Oxford and from the opening to Thame in 1862, this book will not deal with the detail of running the railway between Maidenhead, High Wycombe and Princes Risborough. For many years the entire railway was run as one section Maidenhead-Oxford, just as intended when it was built, but early in the 20th century the Great Western Railway (GWR) started treating Princes Risborough-Oxford as a separate branch.

The promoters of the Wycombe Railway (originally 'Great Western & Wycombe') reached agreement with the Great Western Railway in October 1845 for the latter to lease their railway from Maidenhead in Berkshire to High Wycombe in Buckinghamshire, 9¾ miles. The terms were an annual payment by the GWR of 4 per cent on the capital of £150,000 (=£6,000) and half of the profits.

An early shot across the bows of the Wycombe Company came in a letter dated 30th January, 1846 from the GWR Engineer, I.K. Brunel, to the Wycombe Secretary, W.H. Wilson. It read:

> I have communicated the subject of your letter of the 26th to the Directors of the GWR. I regret that more time was not given to the selection of the line, in the economical construction of which the GWR is so deeply interested. Under the circumstances, however, the Directors will not raise a point which apparently would be fatal to the Bills - and authorised me to consent to your abandoning at present the lower line but it must be clearly understood that they reserve the right to apply or to call upon your Company to apply to Parliament in another Session for any deviations or any improvement which they may think necessary ... this should be clearly understood between the Directors of the two Companies.

As the Minute books of the Wycombe company were not commenced until 12th August, no other information regarding the 'lower line' has been found. But note particularly that Brunel was not happy with the proposed route.

The Bill to authorise the October 1845 agreement and to incorporate the Wycombe Railway received much opposition in the House of Commons from the projected London & Oxford Railway which intended to run through Uxbridge, High Wycombe, Thame and Oxford. Of 14 days' duration, this hearing caused considerable legal expenses to be incurred by the company. However, the Bill was passed, the Royal Assent being given on 27th July, 1846. (The London & Oxford, defeated, was dissolved.) The Act allowed for 12 Directors of the company, required that the (single track) railway should be finished within five years and required the company to provide a double line

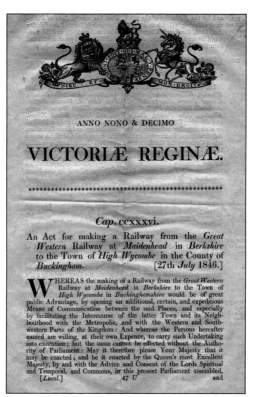

First page of the Act for the Wycombe Railway, 27th July, 1846.

after 12 months of opening if the Board of Trade felt it necessary. The line would be built with trackbed and bridges to allow for double track in the future.

At the first Board meeting on 12th August, 1846, the Directors reduced themselves to eight persons; Frederick Pratt Barlow (Chairman), Robert Wheeler (Deputy Chairman), A.F. Paull, G. Emery, William Rose, F. Parker, C. Venables and J. Neale. William Henry Wilson was to be Secretary, he would also be Secretary of the Great Western & Uxbridge Railway which shared six of the same Directors. The appointment of the Engineer was deferred.

Already the Directors had decided it would be better to sell their concern, rather than lease it to the GWR. The Act, however, only gave power to lease not sell the concern (S.46) and a further approach to Parliament would be necessary. As they told their proprietors at the first AGM on 26th October, when seeking their authority for such an approach:

'The lease which had been agreed for with the GWR Company, advantageous as it was during the abundance of unemployed capital, did not promise, under the altered circumstances, to give a sufficient permanent value to the shares to enable the Directors to carry out the measures [of constructing the railway] promptly and successfully.' The altered circumstances referred to were the (second) 'Railway Mania' which began in 1844. At first railway shares were in great demand, but as speculators moved in some increasingly optimistic, even a few fraudulent, schemes were floated and eventually the market reacted against railway shares. Even firmly based companies found difficulty in raising funds. Over a third of the mileage authorised between 1844 and 1847 was not built.

The October meeting of shareholders agreed that the GWR should be approached with a view to selling the concern, and to make application to Parliament for permission to do so. The Board felt it would be 'useless' to make calls (ask for the next instalment) on their shares in the present financial climate. At this time some £9,732 had been received as £1 deposits on the 9,732 £15 shares issued and, with interest, assets stood at £9,856 11s. 3d. Of the £9,526 16s. 8d. liabilities, the bulk had gone (as ever) in legal fees, mainly in connection with the Parliamentary work (£6,267 7s. 10d.), most of the rest in engineering surveying and 'traffic charges' (estimating traffic levels) (£2,376 17s. 6d.) and the remainder on 'sundries' including rent, salaries, furniture and travelling expenses (£882 11s. 4d). This left a balance of £329 14s. 7d., cash in hand. Messrs Barlow, Emery, Paull and Parker were appointed to deal with the GWR.

At the next Board in December, it was reported that the GWR had offered £20,000 for the purchase of the Wycombe and Uxbridge companies. This the Board approved, subject to the GWR paying all Parliamentary expenses *and* advancing £12,000-£14,000 to enable shareholders' £1 deposits to be returned (this figure includes the Uxbridge shareholders), the balance (10s. per share) being supplied after the Act of Parliament was obtained.

Some of the Directors had formed a Committee of Management (CoM) which met in between Board meetings. On 20th January, 1847 the WRC solicitor told this body that the GWR had introduced additional clauses into the sale agreement of which he could not advise acceptance. Four days later Messrs Barlow, Emery and Paull met the GWR Directors and were told that 'misunderstandings between the relevant solicitors had been resolved'. However, on 13th February, Mr Rose, WRC solicitor, said that the GWR solicitor would still not 'expunge one of the objectionable clauses which they averred was inserted by Mr Saunders' [GWR Secretary and General Superintendent] special instructions'. The Chairman went straightaway to see the GWR's solicitors and arrangements were made to see Mr Saunders on 16th February.

This meeting duly took place and agreement was reached, the CoM approving the agreement on 19th February. On the 22nd the Board met, after which a shareholders' meeting took place and what was intended to be a final set of accounts was presented. Receipts were £9,850 16s. 2d. and payments were about 90 per cent of this, so a cash balance of £986 15s. 6d. existed. Miraculously a reduction in legal charges had been achieved! The Board advised that the sale to the GWR would be known as the GW Amendments and Extension Act 1847. The meeting agreed the terms of sale, outlined above. The Act of Parliament was obtained on 22nd July, 1847.

The next entry in the Board's Minute books is dated 22nd May, 1851 - over four years later! What happened in between? The Agreement for sale approved in February 1847 does not seem to have survived, but a helpful précis of the situation can be found in a legal brief dated 1st May, 1852 [RAIL 768 8, National Archives, Kew].

The February 1847 Agreement called for £1 per share to be returned to each shareholder immediately providing they transferred their shares to Messrs

Charles Russell (GWR) and George Emery (WRC) as trustees. The balance would be paid once Parliamentary sanction to the sale was obtained. In the meantime Messrs Russell and Emery were to hold the shares in trust, their subsequent action being dependent on one of three possible events:

1. If the transfer to the GWR was concluded by 31.12.1850 and the balance of the purchase money had been paid, then after 31.12.1850 the shares to be held in trust for the GWR.
2. If the transfer and the payment of the balance had NOT been concluded by 31.12.1850 then either the Wycombe or Uxbridge companies, or both of them, could within three calendar months, refund the £1 per share advanced, plus 5 per cent interest, and re-transfer the shares to the original shareholders.
3. If 2 (above) applied [no action by 31.12.1850] but the Wycombe-Uxbridge companies had not reimbursed the GWR within 3 calendar months, then the shares would be assigned to the GWR for disposal as they should direct.

The document continues:

It therefore appears that until the expiration of 3 months after the 31st December, 1850, namely until the 1st April, 1851, unless the sale was completed in the meantime, the shares transferred to Messrs Russell and Emery were impounded subject to be reclaimed by the Wycombe and Uxbridge shareholders, and until the same period the Great Western were legally prevented either from disposing of the shares or availing themselves of the powers of carrying out the line. In fact both parties were held fast and nothing could be done.

In the Great Western Act of 1847 in which powers were sought to be obtained for carrying out the sale the introduction of the clause [S.46] in pursuance of the sessional order requiring half the capital to be called up and actually expended, prevented the completing of the sale and rendered the fulfilment of the Agreement impracticable.

So the lawyers had thoroughly tied themselves up! A meeting of the Wycombe company had been held in February 1848 (reported in *The Railway Times*) and the WRC Directors had attempted to untangle the situation by suggesting that perhaps the GWR might like to advance the money equal to the shares being half paid up, and expend it upon construction. [With 9,732 £15 shares in issue, only £1 paid up, this would have cost the GWR £63,258.] Not surprisingly, the paper reports, 'The Great Western, however, very naturally feel indisposed in the present state of the money markets to become voluntary parties to an immediately outlay of money . . .' A suggestion that the WRC shareholders might raise the money to proceed with the works was voted for by holders of 525 shares and against by 5,030. The Directors therefore concluded that all they could do was apply to the Railway Commissioners for an extension of time to conclude the building of the railway. This they did in 1849, extending compulsory purchase powers from three to five years and extending the powers for construction from five to seven years.

The aforementioned précis document says that just before the April 1851 deadline, in February 1851, the Wycombe Directors contacted the GWR, through Mr Brunel, to negotiate fresh terms. On 9th April an 'arrangement was actually concluded between the Wycombe and GWR company for a lease or sale of the line at £3,600 a year'. Having, at last, resolved the lawyers' 'own goal' a fresh attempt could be made at building a railway to High Wycombe.

Chapter Two

The First Stage - High Wycombe is Reached

The WRC Directors met formally, for the first time in over four years, on 22nd May, 1851. The solicitor had written to the GWR suggesting a revival of the original terms of leasing the line to the GWR 'in case the line were constructed'. The latter had offered to lease the line, when constructed, at a rent of £3,600 pa and to work the line at prime cost, paying 'over the surplus proceeds after recompensing themselves the actual expenses . . .' These terms were accepted. The Board had asked I.K. Brunel to act as Engineer. J. Neale, former Director, had died during the long interregnum.

Brunel (or his staff) surveyed the line during June and July, providing plans in connection with Notices of Compulsory Purchase and these notices were served to landowners and occupiers before the 27th July deadline for execution of compulsory purchase powers.

During July there was a flurry of activity within the directorate. A draft agreement with the GWR was approved. Captain Bulkeley, a GWR Director, was proposed as a Director and elected at the next meeting vice F. Parker who resigned. At the same meeting Randolph Crewe of Wycombe was elected a Director vice J. Neale, deceased. Later in the month A.F. Paull resigned as a Director and was replaced by Captain George Young of Wycombe. (Were Parker and Paull getting out while they could, or perhaps they had been asked to resign to bring in fresh talent?) At the September Board, Brunel provided an estimate of the cost of construction, not quoted in the Minutes, but they do include the statement '. . . assuming the work will not exceed £65,000 . . .' In November the Board noted that Brunel's specifications were ready but they could not yet proceed as the GWR's Agreement had only just been received from their solicitors.

Terms with the GWR were agreed at a meeting on 17th December, but then at a meeting a fortnight later, on 31st, the Minutes note 'some disagreement with the GWR wanting to carry forward any surplus in one year over and above the £3,600 rent to make up a deficiency in another year'. The WRC was unhappy about this. However, on 14th January, 1852, the Agreement was approved. The WRC also agreed to side with the GWR in opposing the Oxford, Worcester & Wolverhampton Railway's (OWWR) proposed line to Brentford. On 28th January Brunel reported that the contractor he had in mind to build the line would not consider the job until the 'proprietary was increased' - accordingly more shares were taken (presumably by the Directors).

The shareholders came face to face with the Directors for the first time in five years on 25th February, 1852. The Report stated that the GWR had inserted a clause in the 1847 Act authorising the sale of the company that prohibited that sale until one-half of the capital had been subscribed and expended on the works, 'a provision wholly incompatible with the terms of the arrangement and which resolved its fulfilment impracticable'. The GWR had paid over £12,000*

* As stated in Chapter One this was part payment for both the Wycombe and Uxbridge companies.

but this clause prevented the balance being paid (a further 10 shillings for each share), and everything had been in limbo since then. Some 9,250 Wycombe shares (at £1 per share) had been transferred to the two trustees appointed. The Directors said that 'the recent revival of railway enterprise' had led them to reopen negotiations 'with view to construction on the basis of a guarantee' but stated that the Agreement with the GWR was not yet finally concluded. A Bill would be placed before Parliament to legalise the Agreement. Finally, there were no accounts with the Report because the auditors had resigned; new ones were appointed by this meeting.

A lengthy petition was presented to the House of Commons by the OWWR opposing the Wycombe's Bill to legalise the Agreement with the GWR and to obtain an extension of time for completion, etc. The OWWR contended that neither the GWR nor the Wycombe (which it considered was really the GWR anyway) intended to build the line and there were many examples elsewhere in the Kingdom where the GWR had proposed lines to stop other companies building them. It saw the proposed line as a crude attempt to stop the OWWR from building a line from Oxford to Brentford via Wycombe (which they had announced in November 1851 and was now before Parliament) by buying land at Wycombe which the OWWR would need. Furthermore, the capital needed by the WRC could not be reused without the guarantee or security of the GWR, 'which guarantee the GWR are not authorised by law to grant and therefore such authority ought not to be granted'. At the shareholders' meeting in February the Directors had spoken about a guarantee - had the OWWR had spies there?

Much of what the OWWR said was borne out by a letter from Brunel (who, remember, was also the Wycombe's Engineer) to the Chairman of the GWR, dated 26th March, 1852. Unfortunately, as so often seems to happen, his letter has been preserved in isolation, even the reply not being in the WRC file at Kew. Mr Rose was either William Rose (WRC Director) or, more likely, Philip Rose (WRC solicitor). Mr Hunt was the GWR solicitor (or one of them). The implication is clear, a contractor would build it and then the GWR take it over, at less than cost, and its main *raison d'etre*, as far as the GWR was concerned, was to stop the OWWR extending its line to Brentford.

My dear Sir,

I am afraid that you will begin to believe that the Wycomb Railway is an evil spirit haunting you for some past crime if you have any such upon your conscience and that I shall be the embodiment of this nuisance in your mind, but having a strong belief of the great importance of this little outpost in the country the enemy is attacking, I have persevered in attempting to remove the difficulty of carrying out the arrangement which you sanctioned and I think I have at last succeeded. As Mr Rose's letter points out and more particularly as Mr Hunt can tell you there are legal difficulties in the way of our carrying out the arrangement in the exact form proposed and this in fact is the impediment - we have at last devised a plan by which without our becoming answerable for or liable to the payment of any capital sum the Gt.Westn.Ry.Co. buys the line *when made* for certain perpetual annual payments amounting to the sum before agreed upon, there would be a trifling saving in fact in the annual payment and G.W.R. would get the whole receipts and profits of the line. The machinery of the arrangement is as yet rather clumsy but Mr Hunt says it is at all events strictly & correctly within the powers of our Acts & requires no fresh powers. The principle is simply this, a contractor is found to *buy up all the shares* & to complete the line - the Gt.W.R.Co. undertaking to buy it when complete at a *nominal* sum to be made smaller than the real value so that the Company shall be safe - and the contractor undertakes to receive and the Company undertakes to give in lieu of that sum, when the line is made & handed over to them, 36 annual payments of £100 each. I believe this will effect everything and involves the G.W.R. in no liability for the payment of a 1*d*. piece of capital.

I assure you that the importance of getting this branch made is not thought more of by me than it is by all our legal advisers in our coming Parliamentary contest - of course you know that the construction of the Wycomb not merely destroys the principal local case of the Oxfd. & Brentford but actually renders its construction all but impracticable as they go over our ground and through our station and I assure you that all the company's professional advisers look upon the Oxfd. & Brentford fight as a very uphill one which wants every assistance.

May I hope that I have at last got the Wycomb into a shape that you think at least worth considering - I mean as a way of carrying out that which you had consented to.

I am my dear Sir
Yours very truly
I.K. BRUNEL

We do not know how much these sketchily - described proposals changed in the next few weeks, but a lease was drawn up between the two companies on 22nd April, 1852. A Board meeting was held on 21st April (the first for six weeks) and all the Minutes of this meeting said was that an entirely new agreement had been submitted by the GWR 'following many meetings between Philip Rose, I.K. Brunel and Messrs Hunt'. There would be a limit of £90,000 for construction and the GWR would lease the line at 4 per cent (£3,600 pa). (The previous capital was £150,000.) I.K.B. said that a contractor would construct for £62,000, leaving £28,000 for land and other liabilities. Brunel would take £3,000 for past and future services so as not to exceed the amount of money available. Terms would be put before the GWR Board tomorrow and this Board (the WRC) would reconvene on Saturday 24th - but, later, this had to be postponed to the 29th.

Now came a great flurry of legal documents. First came the Agreement to lease dated 22nd April. Summarised this provided (reference numbers as in the document):

1 . The WRC to acquire land sufficient for a double track broad gauge railway and stations, works, etc. to allow for completion of the railway within the laid down time limit.
2.   The WRC will complete the railway from Wycombe to a junction with the GWR near Maidenhead with a single line of rails, broad gauge and with all stations and works, etc. out of capital (excluding a station at Maidenhead junction) at their own expence [*sic*], according to designs approved by I.K.B and under his superintendence, to be ready for traffic no later than the 27th July, 1853.
3.   Arrangements for arbitration during the building process.
4.   When the railway is completed it shall be handed over the GWR and the WRC will grant the GWR a lease for 999 years, commencing on the day it opens for traffic.
5.   When this lease takes effect the GWR will pay the WRC £3,600 per year, ½ yearly.
6.   Additionally the GWR will pay one-half of the clear profits, unless within 14 days the Directors of the WRC request that these continuing profit payments be commuted to a one-off payment of £10,000.

7. The WRC to be responsible for all existing debts, or any they created in the future and if the GWR found it necessary to pay-off such debts, such money to be taken out of the GWR's rent payment plus 5 per cent pa interest.
8. WRC responsible for land tax.
9. WRC can dispose of surplus land for their own benefit.
10. Lease to be properly drawn up and could be modified with permission of Parliament.
11. Arrangements for arbitration if differences of opinion on the terms of the lease.
12. If lease needs to be modified before it is implemented, both sets of Directors to agree.
13. Arrangements for a more formal agreement, if required.
14. This agreement to be submitted, as soon as practicable to GWR shareholders for approval.

Next, dated the same day, came a Deed of release between the Wycombe and Uxbridge companies and the GWR, releasing the latter from the purchase of the former as 'impractical to carry into effect . . .' The sum of £1,250 was paid to Philip Rose on account of expenses and liabilities (the lawyers always made sure they got their money!). Furthermore, the 9,660* £1 shares in the Wycombe company standing in the names of trustees for the GWR could be disposed of and transferred back to the WRC who must arrange for someone to buy them within 14 days. As no sale of the WRC had occurred, that money would have to be returned to the GWR. Finally all parties were released from any claim by one of the other parties.

Finally on 29th April, came an Agreement between the parties concerning payments. There seems to have been a change of mind about the 9,660 shares, probably the WRC had said they couldn't sell them so quickly. It would remain as an outstanding loan from the GWR for a further 6 months, on which 4 per cent interest would have to be paid. Additionally the WRC must issue to a person appointed by the GWR a further 1,000 paid up shares to act as security on the loan, and if the loan was defaulted on, the GWR would keep these shares. (As will be seen this matter would drag on for years!) Not surprisingly, the WRC had elected to take the £10,000 lump sum, in place of continuing profit payments, and this document said that it would be paid in instalments, as the WRC required to purchase land, the conveyances for such land to be passed to the GWR to hold as security. Already the so-called independent company was not looking very independent.

The WRC Directors met on 29th April and approved the Agreement to lease to the GWR, and its £10,000 one-off payment in lieu of profits. On 7th June the Minutes briefly note that Mr Peniston had been approved as contractor to build the railway. A shareholders' meeting was held immediately after the Board and approved a Bill placed before Parliament 'to extend the time for completion of the railway and reduce the company's capital and to approve the Agreement with the GWR.'

The Wycombe Railway Amendment Act 1852 received its Royal Assent on 30th June, 1852, its chief provisions were:

---

* No explanation is given as to why this is higher than the 9,250 figure previously quoted.

1. Subject to agreement of 60 per cent of the shareholders the share capital to be reduced from £150,000 to £100,000 and borrowing powers to £33,600.
2. Powers given to issue Preference Shares.
3. Powers to pay preferential or fixed dividends on any new shares issued, out of the GWR rent payment.
4. Powers for compulsory purchase of land extended for a further year to 30th June, 1853.
5. Railway to be completed within two years, i.e. by 30th June, 1854.
6. The Agreement dated 22.4.1852, and any subsequent lease drawn up, to be binding between the two parties. The lease would not, however, be granted unless the Board of Trade was happy that one-half of the share capital of each company (WRC and GWR) had been raised and expended upon their respective undertakings.

The Directors noted, no doubt with some satisfaction, the passing of this Act at their meeting on 7th July. The Minutes also record that Mr F.R. Ward had been appointed as an additional Director, making nine.

A special meeting of shareholders was held on 29th July, as required by the Act, and the meeting duly resolved to agree the reduction in share capital and the value of each individual share from £15 to £10; they also approved the increased number of Directors (F.R. Ward being duly elected).

On the same day an Agreement was drawn up between the WRC and the contractor, William Michael Peniston. He must comply with all the terms of the 22nd April Agreement between the WRC and the GWR, and build the railway for the sum of £60,000. This sum would be totally paid *in shares*. When the contractor brought his plant to the site he would receive 4,000 shares, each of £1 value, a further 2,000 shares being transferred to him when authorised by Brunel. As the work proceeded, the value of the work undertaken would be credited as extra paid-up value to the shares. When the works were complete, the shares would have reached their full value (£10) except that 5 per cent of the total value (£3,000) would be retained by the WRC for a year as security upon the maintenance of the line, for which period the contractor remained responsible.

The Agreement stated that the WRC share capital must not exceed £90,000 without the agreement of Mr Peniston, who would be far and away the largest shareholder with 6,000 shares, so long as he continued to hold at least 1,000 shares. The share capital included the 1,000 shares to be held by a person appointed by the GWR as security against the £9,660 owed them by the WRC. The Agreement also restricted the borrowing powers, etc., of the company without the consent of two Directors previously selected by Mr Peniston.

The final paragraph of the document said that Peniston undertook all the liabilities of the WRC in constructing the railway, and would indemnify them against all claims, loss and damage in respect of non fulfilment of the requirements of the 22nd April Agreement. So one of the requirements of Brunel's letter of 26th March (see earlier) seems to have been fulfilled - a contractor would build the line at no risk to the GWR.

A few days later, on 5th August, an Indenture was drawn up between the contractor, the WRC and the GWR, transferring 260 fully paid up shares, worth £2,600, from the WRC to Peniston. On the basis that no contractor could be expected to build a railway on the strength of payment in shares alone, it permitted the *GWR* to advance him £1,733 13s. 4d. (two-thirds of their nominal value), on the security of this package of shares, which would be transferred into the names of Charles Russell (GWR), Frederick Pratt Barlow (WRC) and Thomas Bulkeley (GWR & WRC) and held by them as trustees as security on the loan. Interest at 4½ per cent per annum would be paid by Peniston on the loan which must be repaid by 1st January, 1854. The Indenture allowed for similar advances to be made as required, on the same terms, noting the amounts on the document. An Indenture issued after the WRC's winding up, dated 1st January, 1868, showed that Peniston eventually had 3,957 shares, of which the GWR had an interest in 3,407. If they lent ⅔ of the nominal value of these shares to Peniston, this will have cost them £22,690. A first call of £3 per share was made upon the shareholders about a week later.

The Board Minutes have nothing much to say (only one intermediate meeting was held) until 22nd December when they noted the decease of George Emery, Director. Between the latter part of August and December the contractor had been spending just over £2,000 every four weeks. The greater part of the earthworks was now complete, with the remainder being finished within three months. I.K.B. had been paid £1,000 in paid-up shares on account of his charges to date (£1,209). A further call of £3 per share would be made on 31st January, 1853.

The next Board, on 28th February, 1853, preceded the annual shareholders' meeting both of which were chaired by Captain Bulkeley. The Board noted the demise of another Director, deputy Chairman R. Wheeler. The Report to the shareholders explained the contract with Mr Peniston, £60,000 payable in shares, and considered that there was 'every reason to believe the line will be open for traffic in May next . . .' The accounts showed expenditure of £22,763 (mostly land purchased £9,283, contractor's account £12,600) and receipts £22,856, giving a small surplus of £93. The Engineer's report said that all the necessary land had been obtained and taken possession of and more than ⅚ of the earthwork had been completed.

Unfortunately this optimism of an early opening did not last long. On 16th June the Directors met specially to ascertain the cause of delay in completion of the line. I.K.B. had submitted a report, but the Directors regretted he had not attended in person. Brunel blamed the late acquisition of some of the land for the delay, not the contractor. Mr Peniston was there, but as he did not even know if the rails had been ordered, the Directors decided to make a site inspection on the following Monday. I.K.B. would be asked to let them know, before then, when the line would be ready for opening.

The Directors met again on 20th June, at the Bear Inn, Maidenhead. Brunel had not replied to the Secretary since 16th June. The site inspection had revealed that no permanent way had been laid and Brunel would be asked to instruct the contractor to commence the permanent way 'forthwith' and report back by 28th June. On a more minor matter, the Secretary's salary was to be increased to £200, backdated to 1st April, 1851, and Wilson agreed to take £100 of the increase in shares.

On 28th June when the Directors next met, Peniston was there but still no I.K.B. However, he had sent a letter confirming that the rails had been ordered, the delay was caused by a query over the price. Their next meeting, on 15th August, at Maidenhead, noted that another £2 per share would be payable on 15th October and that a further £4,100 had been paid (in shares) to the contractor.

Now things began to go badly wrong. Payments to the contractor in shares must have seemed a good idea to the solicitor and accountant but it didn't work in the real world. On 12th October the Directors met at Park Street, Westminster with Captain Bulkeley in the chair and I.K.B. in attendance. Mr Ward, Director, made a long statement re the contractor who was unable to carry out his contract without 'some understanding from his creditors . . . and he would require the assistance of the WRC to pay 2 weeks wages and tradesmen's small bills due on Saturday next by an advance . . .' The Board agreed to pay £350 if necessary (in shares) on account of Brunel's next certificate. Did they suppose that the navvies and tradesmen would accept their payments in shares?

There was now a flurry of Board meetings. On the 20th it was agreed to pay another £150 (in shares) to Peniston. A deputation of Peniston's creditors waited upon the Board and were told it was intended to complete the line, provided the *GWR* would make further advances upon the security of the WRC shares. On the 25th further unspecified advances were made to Peniston. On the 9th November the Board were informed that Peniston had transferred his shares to Director F.R. Ward. These shares were subject to be claimed by the GWR to whom they had been mortgaged. (The Indenture of 1.1.1868, previously mentioned, tells us that by November 1853 some 3,820 of Peniston's shares had been assigned to F.R. Ward. Some of these he had paid for (no cash amounts are mentioned), others had been issued as security upon the amounts he had paid Peniston for the shares. For all but 550 of the 3,820 shares the GWR had first claim on any cash raised by selling them, to reimburse itself for its own cash advances to Peniston. By assigning the shares to Ward, the latter would obtain any remaining cash value, after the GWR had had its portion, which otherwise would have gone to Peniston. Even at this early date Ward could probably see that the GWR would eventually take over and would have to buy out the WRC shares. Peniston, in his present state, could not afford to wait for this event.)

On 17th November Brunel wrote to Wilson suggesting that 'provided you exercise a due discretion in paying only such labour and materials bills as appear really to have been necessarily and properly incurred that it would be desirable to make a further advance to the contractor but . . . this must be the last'. And on 25th November, Brunel wrote again saying that he had heard that men were collecting barrows and planks and removing them with a view to selling them - these items formed part of the company's security (against the contractor defaulting) and they should not be removed without permission.

The Minute book is silent from November until 25th January, 1854 when the Directors met with I.K.B. in attendance. Although the contract specified that the contractor paid for the rails, the Directors decided, in the circumstances, to stump up the cost of rails, delivered to the site, provided they cost no more than £10,000. Brunel would enquire and report back. The solicitor required a further £4,000 for land purchase and it was resolved to issue company bonds, or debentures, worth £5,000 payable in 3 years with interest at 5 per cent per annum, to pay for this.

On 8th February the Board heard that Messrs Glyn Mills bank would lend £4,000 upon security of £5,000 debentures at 5 per cent but the company had now decided they would need to issue £6,000 worth of debentures and would therefore want £5,000 from Glyn Mills. Two of Peniston's creditors attended the meeting and reported work had stopped; they were meeting Peniston shortly and would report back to the Board the following Tuesday. The Board approved payment of £500 in shares to I.K.B. on account of charges.

An important Board meeting was held just a few days later, the 14th February. First of all Brunel reported that the contractor was removing materials from the line and the company's solicitor had issued a letter forbidding this; the Secretary had backed this up verbally 'on the ground' and was told that only damaged sleepers (value £15) had been removed. Next, Mr Peniston attended the Board to agree terms for the abandonment of his contract. It was agreed that he give the company immediate possession of the line, all plant and equipment on payment of £750 (in shares!) in full settlement; the solicitor would draw up a legal agreement. I.K.B. estimated the cost of completion as £13,600 and was authorised to arrange for this, the cost not to exceed the unpaid balance of the now collapsed £60,000 contract.

How much the shareholders knew of all this is a matter for conjecture - probably most of them living locally were fully aware of the problems. On 27th February, 1854, at the annual shareholders' meeting, all was revealed. The Report said, *inter alia*, that the 'Contractor fell into serious pecuniary difficulties . . . long time spent in fruitless endeavours to recruit his position or induce his principal creditors [to complete] the contract . . . your Directors have been compelled . . . to enter upon the task of completion for themselves'.

Some £45,590 had been spent (out of £60,000) and Brunel considered that the balance should be sufficient to complete the line; the work remaining 'is of small amount and consists chiefly of permanent way'. The company now owned the plant and the line. It was intended to exercise its borrowing powers to complete the line, and to borrow, on mortgage, a sum not exceeding £33,000. They anticipated opening the line on 1st May next. [Readers may recall that something similar had been said exactly a year ago.]

The appended accounts showed receipts of £55,255 (in share purchases plus the GWR's £10,000 in lieu of profits) and expenditure just £81 less than this. The bulk of the expenditure had been on land purchase (£12,330), the contractor (£39,570) and the Engineer (£1,200). At the Directors' meeting immediately following the AGM F.P. Barlow was elected Chairman and William Rose deputy Chairman.

The Directors met again on 7th March with I.K.B. in attendance. Messrs Crutwell of Cwm Celyn & Blaina Ironworks near Abergavenny had undertaken to supply iron rails at £10 per ton with a credit period of eight months on each transaction [which seems exceedingly generous]. Brunel estimated 670 tons of rails were needed; the Board agreed this arrangement. Brunel reported that he had accepted a tender from Messrs Orten & Child to complete the line for £3,214 (in *cash*). On 6th April, 1854 former contractor W.M. Peniston was adjudged bankrupt.

At most future Board meetings Mr E.F. Murray, an engineer on Brunel's permanent staff, attended instead of Brunel. On 11th April the Board decided that there should be a valuation of all surplus land with a view to disposal. On 3rd May (with both Brunel and Murray in attendance) the Board heard that the supply of rails had been delayed 'owing to [the contractor's] execution of foreign orders'. Brunel agreed to supply 80 tons of Barlow rails from the GWR to enable completion to Loudwater, these to be replaced within one month. The rails would be delivered from Slough station. On the 17th May the Board authorised construction of a coal siding at Cookham and gave notice to the Board of Trade of their intention to open the line within one month of 20th May. On 9th June Murray advised the Board that 393 tons of rails had been delivered by Crutwell's to the South Wales Railway for onwards transmission to the WRC. Ten tons of bridge rails would be ordered.

At the next Board meeting, on 6th July, it was decided to defer giving the Board of Trade the necessary 10 days' notice of readiness for inspection until the next meeting, although the GWR had been told a month before that it had been intended to open by 8th July. Brunel would give this notice 'the instant we are ready'. Just a few days later, on the 12th, the Board resolved that the line would open on the 1st August.

The Board of Trade having been notified, Captain Tyler carried out an inspection on 20th July. Whilst satisfied with the permanent way and bridges, 'work appears to be sufficiently substantive and in satisfactory condition', he was not happy with the junction arrangements at Maidenhead.

Distant signal required on main line towards the east; desirable that this, as well as the other junction signals, be worked from some point at which the levers should be collected. Under present circumstances, the junction signalman is obliged to cross the main line and branch to work the three main signals; he has also to go a further 310 yards to work the switches communicating with the main line which may, perhaps, be avoided.

Captain Tyler had not been able to contact the GWR re the working of the junction (and he was on his way to Derby immediately after this inspection), nor had he been advised of the method of working the single line, so he was unable to pass the line for opening.

The WRC moved speedily and on 28th July Brunel wrote to the Board of Trade that a new down line signal had been ordered and that the other signals would be connected up as required by Captain Tyler. The method of working of the branch would be 'One Engine in Steam'. On the basis of this reply the Board of Trade withdrew their objections to opening.

On the 26th the Directors had decided to 'go over the line', just prior to opening, on the 31st, with opening to the public on the following day, the 1st August, 1854. At last after nearly nine years of trying, High Wycombe was connected to the main line and the first section of the Wycombe Railway was complete.

After this 'high', the Minutes revert back to the necessary matters of administration, particularly financial. On 7th September the Secretary was authorised to sell plant and materials used for making the line at not less than £500. There would be a call of £1 per share on 31st October. Brunel reminded the Directors, in November, that there were some 20-25 tons of rails on site belonging to the GWR and these must be returned, not sold.

The next Board was just before Christmas, on 21st December and the Directors heard some bad news. A Mr Taunton had promised a loan of £10,000, on the security of the company's debenture bonds, but for some unstated reason had withdrawn his offer. The company needed £1,115 urgently to pay for rails. An unlikely lender, in the shape of the GW Hotel at Paddington, had offered £1,200 at a rather high 6 per cent, repayable on 1st March, 1855. The Board thought that if funds were not available then they would have to earmark £1,200 out of the GWR's first rent payment (£1,500 for 5 months, payable on 1.1.1855) for that purpose. However, just after Christmas the Board learned that the GW Hotel could not now make the loan and accepted a loan of £1,500 from a Mr Stevenson*, upon security of £2,000 of the company's debenture bonds.

About a month later, on 24th January, 1855, the Directors met at Park Street, Westminster. A statement of costs and receipts showed that loans were becoming a large part of the 'receipts' accounting for £13,600 out of a total of £74,169. On the costs side, land accounted for £17,893, the contractor £50,165 and the Engineer £2,043. A large bill for rails was becoming due and the Directors decided to ask Messrs Crutwell, the suppliers, who held 308 shares, if their representative, Mr Simpson, would agree to be nominated as a Director. Messrs Glyn Mills' £4,000 loan was due for repayment and the Directors were looking for an extension to 30th June. A couple of weeks later, on 7th February, the Board learned that Messrs Glyn Mills had agreed to extend the loan, and Messrs Crutwell had extended the repayment period for the £1,500 bill for rails by four months at 6 per cent, but their Mr Simpson had declined to be nominated for the Board!

Next came the annual shareholders' meeting on 27th February. They learned that the construction accounts were not yet closed because of the contractor's failure and the considerably increased costs of labour and materials. It was still hoped to complete within the authorised £90,000 capital. But for the difficulties, a 4 per cent dividend would have been paid, but now it would be 3 per cent, 2s. 6d., on each £10 fully paid up share (for 5 months). Some 1,000 shares had been forfeited as their holders had not responded to all the calls for instalments to be paid.

At the Board on 28th March, Mr Ward said that no dividend should be paid on 550 shares transferred to the GWR by Mr Peniston in September 1853. The Directors would investigate the matter further; in the meantime no dividend would be paid. (Once again the Minutes are silent as to the reason for this decision.) This event led to the GWR taking legal action against the WRC and the matter was in the Court of Chancery by November.† The Board would not agree to Brunel's request for fencing at Cookham, saying that this was now the GWR's responsibility. Sale of materials, etc. had raised £440 after expenses.

There was no Board meeting now until 18th July, when the Board declared a 3s. dividend on the shares (equivalent to 3 per cent per annum). Mr Ward paid

---

* Might this have been the GWR's Financial Secretary (see Chapter Five)?
† I have no details of the outcome but the helpful Indenture of 1.1.1868 states that the GWR had not advanced any money to Peniston on security of these 550 shares, and they were therefore assigned to Mr Ward in 1856 and not subject to any prior claim by the GWR. (All of the shares assigned to Mr Ward by 1853 were affected by the bankruptcy and were in limbo for a period but were reassigned by the Bankruptcy officials in 1856.)

over £1,000 as a loan to the company, for which he was issued a debenture at 5 per cent pa interest, repayable in 3 years. However, the most important business concerned a letter from Brunel who said that just before Peniston went bust, he (I.K.B.) used his personal influence with the firm of Peto & Betts to obtain rails so that the work should not be badly delayed. The WRC had paid Peniston in shares with the intention that the money therefrom be used to pay the costs of rails. However, as soon as the shares representing the second payment were paid, the contractor went bust leaving the bill for rails unpaid. I.K.B feeling personally liable to Peto & Betts paid the amount due himself and was advised legally to claim the amount from the contractor's estate. This was making no progress and he was out of pocket to the tune of £6,078 (equal to about £295,500 at 2002 prices). As he was acting entirely in the interests of the WRC he looked to them to reimburse him. He would be quite happy to accept payment in 'shares, bonds of any shape convenient to the company' and would repay them if paid subsequently from the bankrupt's estate.

How this was resolved is not clear. The Minutes say this was to be deferred for discussion at the next meeting but this has been crossed out in the Minute book. At the next meeting (in October) there is a reference to the balance due to Brunel to 1st August, 1854, to be settled by a debenture bond at 5 per cent for 3 years, but it does not say that this included the £6,000 for rails, in fact in November the balance due to Brunel to 1.8.1854 is shown as £1,068 16s. 9d.

At the end of the July Board meeting Mr Philip Rose submitted that it would be highly desirable to extend the line to Thame, and was authorised to open negotiations with the GWR. One does wonder why after their experience with the first section, and with Mr Ward having to make a large personal loan, they should want to enlarge the concern, but they did (Mr Ward loaned another £2,000 a year later in July 1856). At the October Board the Directors learned that only £500 remained to be paid to Messrs Crutwell (next February) and this would close their account. In November a bill from Brunel for £250 for the year up to 1st August, 1855, was not entertained and would be referred to the GWR.

The last recorded event in the life of the original Wycombe Railway, before expansion beyond High Wycombe, was the annual shareholders' meeting held on 26th February, 1856. The Report stated that nearly all claims against the company for constructions costs had been settled. 'Unfortunately times are unfavourable for procuring loans from the public upon the securities of Railway Bonds at a low rate of interest.' The dividend would continue at 3s. per share. The accompanying statement showed cumulative receipts of £86,793 (shares £51,113, GWR payment £10,000, GWR rent £3,300 and loans £22,380 - up from £13,600 last year) and costs were just £60 less than this with the main constituents being land £18,162, construction £55,774, legal charges £3,570 and the Engineer £3,107.

At the following Directors' meeting Francis Ridout Ward was elected Chairman (F.P. Barlow had died since the last AGM) and William Rose deputy Chairman.

Chapter Three

Extending the Railway

Since about 1830 Thame had been served by an Oxford-London stagecoach which ran via the town thrice-weekly (and continued to run until 1860). In its 29th July, 1856 edition the *Thame Gazette* carried a front page item agitating for a railway ('We must have a Railroad') which brought in a shoal of letters, too many to print in the next edition ('What is wanted is energetic action'). The *Thame Gazette* was first issued on 11th March, 1856 and cost 1*d*.

At their next meeting on 14th November, the Board resolved to issue notices, deposit plans and take the necessary steps to bring a Bill before Parliament to extend the WRC to Princes Risborough and Thame. The Minutes noted that Mr Tredwell, the new contractor, thought highly of the scheme, would subscribe to the cost of the Parliamentary proceedings, and would make good the deficiency of the company's resources, necessary to accomplish the work. The WRC had at present £45,000 'unexhausted resources', money not expended from the authorised capital and borrowing powers.

The *Thame Gazette* on 18th November carried news of the proposed extension. On 4th December a meeting was held in the 'Spread Eagle', Thame, attended by the WRC Secretary W.H. Wilson. Those present pledged to 'use every exertion to assist the promotion'. In an editorial on 9th December, the *Thame Gazette* said that to secure the line, Thame was asked to subscribe £30,000 (about £1.47 million at 2002 prices). Surely, it asked, 'our well-to do town, surrounded as it is by so many of the gentry, and large landed proprietors, to whom railway accommodation is of as great importance as to the town itself, a call for aid will not be made in vain'.

A further meeting was arranged in the Market Hall, Thame on 16th December, at which the Earl of Abingdon presided. This was well attended. Mr Ward, WRC Chairman outlined the reasons for extending to Thame. The line to High Wycombe was yielding large profits; the GWR had got a good bargain and was earning far more than the shareholders. Extending the line would improve its earning potential further, and should enable the WRC to earn an increased revenue. The 'unexhausted resources' were quoted as £50,000 and as the line was estimated to cost £110,000, a further £60,000 was required. A Committee was appointed to canvass the town for money. The Engineer described the route of the line; that from Wycombe to Princes Risborough need not concern us but after leaving Risborough it would run near Lower Horsendon, Holly Green and Penn Farm, near Towersey, to the south end of Thame, where a station would be built in the fork of the roads leading to Stokenchurch and Chinnor. A similar meeting was held at Princes Risborough at the end of the month, where another committee was set up and a number of shares were immediately subscribed for.

A Subscription Contract was published on 24th December, 1856 in connection with the intention to apply for an Act of Parliament to enable the Wycombe Railway Company to construct and maintain:

Firstly, a railway to commence by a junction with the Wycombe Railway, at or near the terminus thereof, in the Parish of Chipping Wycombe . . . And passing there in such a direction as is or shall be determined upon by the Directors for the said WRC, and terminating in the Parish of Princes Risborough, on the east side of the road leading from Culverton Mill and Park Mill, and about 20 chains south from the said Park Mill.

Secondly, a railway to commence by a junction with the said railway at its proposed terminus, in the said Parish of Princes Risborough, and passing thence, in such a direction as is or shall be determined by the said Directors, and terminating in the Parish of Thame . . . in a field at the east side of the turn pike road leading from Thame to Stokenchurch near the junction of the said road from Thame to Chinnor.

Appended to this was a printed list of subscribers and their subscriptions totalling £45,270, plus several more handwritten sheets totalling several thousand pounds more. Most of these subscriptions were for £100 or less, but prominent were Thomas Treadwell [sic], contractor, who had promised to subscribe £30,000 and Solomon Treadwell, contractor, £5,000. Francis Ridout Ward, Chairman of the WRC, had promised £500 and the Secretary, W.H. Wilson, £1,000. Daniel Ponting, ironmonger of Thame, had promised £500, whereas the Earl of Abingdon had subscribed just £100. A tenth of the total had actually been paid over, £4,527, of which the Tredwells had contributed £3,500. It would seem that the contractors' money was treated separately in the accounts because those issued in February 1858 showed only £910 received for Thame shares.

A legal Agreement was drawn up between Thomas Tredwell and Philip Rose (WRC Solicitor) dated 31st December, 1856, 'in the event of his obtaining the contract' for the construction to Thame in the sum of £85,000, requiring him to take £30,000 of the payment in shares. He had paid £1 per share, and the shares (which he himself was paying for) would reach their full value by being credited by the company on account of work performed. He undertook not to sell any of these shares until £15,000 worth had been issued to him. Had the Act only authorised construction to Princes Risborough a proportional reduction would have been made to the contract and his subscription. He also agreed to contribute up to £375 to the Parliamentary costs. Attached to the Agreement was a schedule of construction prices signed by Brunel and Tredwell. For the construction of the permanent way, exclusive of rails, switches and crossings, £1,600 per mile was allowed. The rails themselves were purchased by the company. The Agreement allowed the company to cancel it within six months, in which case they had to pay £4,000 compensation to Tredwell and return his £3,000 deposit.*

The *Thame Gazette* kept plugging away the case for the railway, in February 1857 advocating shareholders to urge friends to buy shares. At the shareholders' meeting at the GW Hotel, Paddington, on the last day of that month, the usual dividend of 3s. per £10 share was declared. The decision to extend to Thame was formally stated, 'which will bring a large and populated

---

* Although the contractors were Messrs Tredwell, it would seem that Thomas Tredwell was sometimes considered almost a separate entity, probably because of this legal agreement. The official paperwork (and therefore this book) sometimes refers to contractors (plural), sometimes contractor (singular), in the latter case Thomas Tredwell is being referred to.

agricultural district into immediate connection with the GWR, and increase the value of the shares'. The balance sheet showed £91,653 had been expended so far on building the Wycombe Railway, only a few hundred had been spent on construction since the last AGM, but, of course, dividends had now to be paid and interest on the loans, which at £23,880 accounted for over a quarter of the receipts. Arthur T.P. Barlow was elected a Director, vice Capt. Young who retired; £100 was voted to be paid to the Directors.

In May the offices of the company were moved from Park Street, Westminster to Victoria Street, where they would be joined by their solicitors, Messrs Baxter, Rose and Norton. A special meeting of shareholders unanimously agreed to the presentation of a Bill to Parliament to authorise the extension to Thame.

The Bill passed its second reading in June. In its 7th July edition the *Thame Gazette* announced, joyfully, that the Bill had passed the House of Lords Committee 'notwithstanding much opposition' and now only awaited its third reading and Her Majesty's assent.

An internal document dated 15th July, 1857 by Mr Baxter, solicitor, sought to limit expenditure on stations on the extension to between £8-£10,000 in total (including permanent way and fittings but excluding land purchase). This element of the construction the WRC saw as a legitimate cost for the GWR, as tenant, to pay, either directly, or by the WRC putting up the money, say £8,000, on which the GWR would pay them interest. The document assessed the *other* costs for building the single line of railway at between £135-£140,000. At the WRC's request Brunel wrote to the GWR confirming that he considered £8,000 the appropriate amount for stations on the extension.

A further dividend of 3s. per £10 share was declared on 31st July.

Royal Assent was given to the Wycombe Railway Extension Act 1857 on 17th August. This authorised an extension from a junction with the Wycombe Railway at High Wycombe via Princes Risborough, Towersey, and terminating at Thame near the turnpike road leading from Thame to Stokenchurch. The works must be completed within four years and constructed on the 7 ft gauge. The estimated cost of construction was £108,000 [*sic*] for which it was necessary to raise a further £60,000 capital by creating new shares. Additionally the Act authorised the company to borrow not more than a further £20,000.

A Working Agreement with the GWR was signed on 13th August, 1857 which Mr Rose concisely (for a solicitor) described as follows:

The GWR out of the Gross Receipts of the line to Thame - (for which separate accounts would be kept) - first to pay the interest on the Debenture debt (£40,000) - secondly to hand over as rent to the WRC 40 per cent of the residue of such receipts, retaining the balance for working expenses, and in addition to this the excess receipts on the Wycombe line between Maidenhead and Wycombe in respect of traffic which will be brought over that line by means of the extension to Thame are to be appropriated to increase the 40 per cent paid to the Extension Co. so as to make up a dividend of 4 per cent on the whole Share Capital of the WRC including the extension. The (actual) share capital was £60,560 for the original line and £110,000 (intended) for the extension, £170,560.

One side of the correspondence in October 1857 between William Parker, a Thame solicitor, and the Secretary of the WRC, W.H. Wilson, has been preserved, showing that at this time interest was flagging in Thame. The canvassing committee had been a failure, members being unwell or too busy to be active. Potential subscribers were concerned at the solvency of the WRC and Parker was urging Wilson for the arrangement between the GWR and the WRC to be made public.

The Directors did not meet between July 1857 and 4th January, 1858. On the latter date the Agreement of August 1857 with the GWR was confirmed and the solicitor instructed to prepare a legal document embodying the terms. The outstanding loan of £9,260 [sic], which had never been paid back to the GWR, would continue for a further four years. The Directors decided to obtain powers at the next shareholders' meeting to issue Preference shares against capital authorised by the 1852 Act sufficient to pay off the existing Debenture debt. Brunel would be asked to resurvey the extension with a view to reducing construction costs. It was also pointed out that Mr Tredwell's compensation clause expired next month (i.e. the ability of the Board to terminate the contract with £4,000 compensation). Two Director's vacancies were to be filled by Samuel Turner, barrister of Gray's Inn and Edward Griffin, farmer of Towersey. The former was probably a friend of the Chairman; he had subscribed for shares to the value of £1,000.

A fortnight later, the Directors learned that Mr Turner had declined the opportunity of becoming a Director - too busy - and Mr Griffin had asked for more information as to his duties. The company's broker had stated that the time was not right for the issue of Preference shares. The Board were not happy with the contractor's prices which they felt could be reduced by at least 15 per cent if paid in cash. Brunel was asked to try and get a reduction or find out what Tredwell would want if paid in shares alone. Finally, if no agreement could be reached, what penalty would Tredwell accept upon the abandonment of the Agreement (i.e. less than £4,000)?

Meetings now came thick and fast. On 16th February Brunel said that he should have met Mr Tredwell that morning to discuss prices, but the latter had not turned up. However, he thought Tredwell would be prepared to accept £1,500 in compensation if the Agreement was abandoned. The matter was deferred for the present. Mr Griffin had accepted his directorship.

On 27th February, 1858 the Directors met at Paddington, prior to holding the annual shareholders' meeting there. Mr Ward would continue as Chairman, Captain Bulkeley as his deputy. At the AGM the shareholders were told about the August 1857 agreement with the GWR. The Chairman said that work would not start on the extension to Thame 'until the whole or the greater part of the land has been agreed for'. He hoped that land owners would take their purchase money in the form of perpetual 4 per cent Rent Charge stock, as affording, in his eyes, 'an excellent permanent investment'. The Chairman floated for the first time the likely possibilities of extensions to Oxford and Aylesbury - 'a glance at the map will show the certainty of their ultimate construction'. The financial statement issued with the Report showed the balance sheet now standing at £95,045 1s. 5d. but there had been no increase in Share Capital. The usual dividend of 3s. per £10 share (original capital) was declared. Deposits of £910 had been received (@ £1 per share) towards the extension. A special meeting followed which authorised the issue of Preference shares, as mentioned earlier.

The AGM at Paddington having been poorly attended, the Directors convened a meeting of shareholders at the Spread Eagle Hotel, Thame on 13th April. Mr Ward, Chairman of the WRC, presided. He said that, as long as the landowners were reasonable in their prices, the company needed £140,000 to make the extension [the 1857 Act had stated £108,000] and that a new subscription list would be opened, with a view to raising a further £15,000 of new money locally. If this sum was not raised, then the extension would not go ahead. Speaking specifically of Thame, he considered that they should raise another £6,000-£7,000 (to get up to the figure of £30,000 he had previously asked of Thame). It was noticeable that, so far, large landowners were almost entirely unrepresented on the Subscription lists.

Mr H. Lupton was called upon by the Chairman to move a resolution to this effect: that a further subscription list would be opened; unless £15,000 was raised the extension would not proceed. He did so, saying that he would double his initial subscription [£100] and hoped others would do so. A second resolution set up a committee to canvass the district, to include Edward Griffin (Director of the WRC) and with Mr Parker, solicitor of Thame, as secretary. A member of the audience said that some people objected to the proposed siting of Thame station, but Mr Murray, WRC Engineer, pointed out that this was located with a view to further extension to Oxford in mind. After a vote of thanks to the Chairman 'many of the proprietors followed Mr Lupton's example and enrolled their names as subscribers towards the further capital required'.

In May 1858, the Directors accepted a loan of the large sum of £8,000 at 4½ per cent interest for seven years from Mr C. Ward of Bristol (a relative of the Chairman?), the bulk of which was used to pay off Debenture Bonds which were due or overdue for redemption. In July the Directors declared the usual dividend, 3s. per £10 share. Further loans were secured 'through' Mr Ward (Chairman) of £500 in November and £2,451 in January 1859, both at 4½ per cent over 5 years.

An almost illegible internal document written by Mr Ward in September 1858 showed that 'local' subscriptions had raised only £17,000 and after adding in the contractor's contribution (£30,000) and the amounts to be raised by issue of Rent charge stock (£20,000) and Debentures (£40,000) there was a deficiency of some £43,000 to arrive at the now desired capital of £150,000 (the document is amended from £140,000). It was hoped to make good this deficiency by the issue of Preference shares and the document expressed a belief that the supplier of rails, estimated to cost £13,000, would take some £5,000 in payment in Preference shares. By some complicated arithmetic, the document concluded that some £43,500 would be available to make cash payments to the contractor, and Mr Ward hoped that he would take the balance of the contract sum in Preference shares.

Brunel was asked in January 1859 what he would be charging for the extension to Thame. The Directors also decided that an Agreement should be drawn up with Mr Tredwell which would specify the maximum amount he would be paid prior to the opening of the new railway. Twenty-three acres of Sir George Dashwood's land would be purchased for £4,000, 'provided the company require the land for the railway'.

At the next AGM on 28th February, 1859, the shareholders were told that work on the extension should start early in the Spring 'the eminent contractors Messrs Tredwell having agreed to construct the line taking payment to a large extent in Extension Shares. The large resources of these gentlemen as well as their well known energy . . . afford the surest guarantee of the speedy completion of the undertaking . . .'

The Directors still expected the Thame Committee to obtain a considerable increase in local subscriptions, and to assist the company in obtaining land on reasonable terms. The accounts showed that deposits on Thame shares had increased from £910 in the last accounts to £4,108 this time.

The usual dividend, 3s. per £10 (original) share was granted, and after the report was given the meeting passed a vote allowing the Directors to obtain the £20,000 loan authorised by the 1857 Act, secured by the issue of Rent Charge Stock, once one-half of the authorised share capital was paid up. This was not implemented until 1860.

After the AGM, the Directors met and Messrs Ward and Bulkeley were approved to continue as Chairman and deputy Chairman respectively. The solicitors were asked to finalise an agreement with the contractor, on the basis that he did not require more than £40,000 before the railway opened, and that he took £40,000 in shares of the Extension Railway as part payment of his contract.

Hardly surprisingly, the Finance Committee were told in April, the eminent contractor's solicitors had told the company that their client would not accept these terms 'unless the financial state of the company was more satisfactory' (!) As the contractor's solicitor had failed to attend the Finance Committee meeting, the matter was deferred.

At a meeting of the Finance Committee (which consisted of Messrs Ward and Barlow) on 9th August, the company's solicitor told them that a draft Agreement with the GWR for working the extension was ready, but the GWR refused to seal it. The latter asked that the WRC agree to submit to arbitration a GWR claim for charges incurred by them in the first year's maintenance of the Wycombe line (the WRC was responsible for maintenance the first year), and a further claim 'for the first time brought forward' of the cost of constructing the junction at Maidenhead.

Over the proverbial barrel, the WRC had no choice but to agree 'but without thereby in the slightest degree admitting the existence of any claim which ought to be a matter of reference'.

Now there came a flurry of legal documents. On 10th August the lease of the WRC by the GWR was signed. This was for the Maidenhead-High Wycombe section and applied for 999 years from 1st August, 1854 at an annual rental of £3,600. On 11th August came the Agreement between the two companies re the Thame Extension Railway [RAIL 768 40 at Kew]. The copy held by the author is 22 pages of closely written manuscript, the first 6½ pages of which recite the preceding legal history of the WRC. The key features of the remainder are:

1. The WRC would acquire the land required for construction of a double line broad gauge railway from Wycombe to Thame.
2. The WRC would complete the Extension Railway with a single line of broad gauge rails together with all station and siding accommodation, station accommodation not to cost more than £8,000, the expenditure (to this limit) being under the control of the GWR as lessee but at the expense of the WRC.
    To be ready for opening to traffic by 17th August, 1861.
3. Any differences between the parties re construction and completion to be determined by an impartial Civil Engineer as Arbitrator.
4. When ready, and having been passed for public traffic, the Extension Railway to be handed over to GWR who will work at their expense as an extension of the Wycombe line and will provide all 'rolling stock plant superintendents police porters and other servants necessary' . . . [sic] and keep and rend accurate traffic accounts to the WRC.
5. The Extension Railway to be leased to the GWR for 999 years from the date of Royal Assent of the Bill.
6. From hand-over day, the GWR will pay the WRC (by ½ yearly payments) - first out of the gross receipts, £2,000 pa to pay interest [at 5 per cent on £40,000] on bonds or mortgages issued for the Extension Railway, second, 40 per cent of the remaining gross receipts; third, when the gross receipts of the *original* Wycombe Railway exceed £7,200 pa, the excess amount to be paid to the WRC to enable them to make up a dividend of 4 per cent on the total share capital (£170,560) (after certain other payments had first been made).
7. If the GWR have to step in and pay for something the WRC should have paid for, such debt to be deducted from the ½ yearly payments due, with interest added at 5 per cent.
8. The WRC are liable for cost of maintenance in the first year, after which the GWR would bear the cost and keep the line in good repair.
9. Deals with Land Tax.
10. Deals with surplus land.
11. Legal.
12. Accounts.
13. Terminal charges, subject to Clearing House rules.
14. Rates and charges to be agreed between the two companies.
15. Financial.
16. Any modification to Agreement to be agreed by both Boards of Directors.
17. Legal.
18. Either company may apply for the Agreement, or any subsequent modification to be confirmed in a subsequent session of Parliament [this Agreement was confirmed in the 1861 Act, see later].
19. The WRC may, if thought fit, apply for additional capital, but only on condition that this should not subject the GWR to any further liability , over and above those expressly provided for in this Agreement.
20. Arbitration on matters in the Agreement, or the lease.
21. The Agreement to be confirmed by the proprietors and Directors of the GWR as soon as possible.

On 12th August the two companies signed an Agreement extending the 'loan' of £9,660 (figures 9,260 crossed out) made by the GWR in 1852, for a further four years. The Agreement noted that the GWR had only received 925 £10 shares as security against this loan, instead of the 1,000 (then £15 each) intended by the 1852 Agreement. It also noted that instead of interest at 4 per cent on the £9,660 loan (totalling £386 pa) it had received dividends on the 925 shares (totalling £277 pa) and the difference between these two figures had not been paid by the WRC.

Finally on 22nd August the contract between Thomas & William Tredwell and the WRC was signed. This 17 page document covered all the legal aspects of their employment as contractors. It stated that the line must be open for all traffic on 1st July, 1861. The line must be modelled on the Maidenhead-High Wycombe branch. The contract was in the sum of £85,000, of which £30,000 payment must be taken in shares. £5,000 worth of these shares would be held by the WRC as security upon the contractors completing the work.

On 23rd August some of the Directors, with the Secretary, met the local committee at the Spread Eagle Hotel, Thame. They were brought up to date with recent events and told that it was intended to complete the extension by July 1861. Of the £30,000 hoped to be raised in the neighbourhood, only £15,000 had so far been forthcoming. Harry Lupton, chairman of the local committee, reminded Mr Ward that at a meeting last Christmas he had said that construction work would start in March. The company Chairman replied that he acted on the principle that 'never commence work until the contract is signed and sealed, and this is now done' (the contract was passed round for inspection). He said that the act of cutting the first sod on a piece of land belonging to Mr Thomas Malins at Towersey would take place shortly. This act was duly recorded in the *Thame Gazette* as happening on 5th September.

A much fuller account of the sod-cutting appeared in the 20th September edition occupying the best part of three columns of the paper. The first sod was cut by Director Edward Griffin, 'in a most workmanlike manner', followed by four other worthies, and last of all the juvenile Master Griffin. Afterwards 'the majority of those present repaired to Mr Griffin's house where they were most hospitably entertained and sat down to a sumptuous dinner, with well-iced champagne and other wines in excellent order'. Mr Venables, a Director, who was acting as Chairman for the occasion, in a long speech hoped that the extension line would pay the shareholders 8 per cent. There was still a lack of interest on the part of the 'noble lords and gentry resident in the district, who had not done what they ought to have done in aiding the project'. They would still like to raise another £12,000 in this area. If the extension to Oxford took place, he undertook to invest another £1,000 himself. Mr Wilson, the WRC Secretary, emphasised that Thame was to be only their resting place, not their terminus.

The Directors met briefly on 11th October, where the Secretary reported the death of their Engineer, I.K. Brunel, on 15th September. Messrs Bereton (Brunel's assistant) and Murray (Resident Engineer) had written on the question of succession, but the matter was deferred until 18th October.

Meeting on that date, Mr Bereton's letter dated 29th September was read. He said that had Brunel decided not to accept the engineership of the extension railway, he would have recommended to the Directors that Mr Murray be appointed engineer-in-chief. For the present, Bereton would carry out Brunel's duties for all the companies for which he was Engineer. In a separate letter dated 5th October, Mr Murray wrote that he was aware that it was probable that

Brunel might decline to act as Engineer for the extension, and that he intended to recommend Murray for the post. Murray had 22 years' experience, and had acted as Resident Engineer for the Wycombe line. He said that since Brunel's illness, most of the work on the extension and the extra management of the engineering work had devolved to him.

The Board decided to appoint Murray as Engineer, but there was a dispute over payment for the extra work (he was already Resident Engineer). The Chairman proposed that he be paid £1,600 cash plus 400 shares. Mr Venables proposed a cash payment (only) of £1,500. The six Directors voted three each for the different proposals. The Chairman gave his casting vote for his own proposal. Mr Murray was given until the end of the week to accept or decline these terms. The Secretary was told to express the Board's condolences to Brunel's relatives.

Murray wrote back on 22nd October (which letter does not seem to have been preserved) and again on 24th October. In contrast to his 5th October letter which had been written in copperplate by a clerk, his 24th October letter is extremely difficult to read and in places illegible. But it seems he was not happy with the terms and proposed £1,600 in cash over the two years in quarterly instalments, and undertook to subscribe for a few shares after some months. In the event of an interruption in the work, because of a cash problem, he would accept a reduction to £150 per quarter with three months' notice. The Chairman wrote back on 25th October proposing:

> Employment for 2¼ years from 30th September, 1859, at £1,600 cash plus £200 in shares, paid quarterly, the last payment to be made in shares.
> The employment to be subject to three months' notice.
> If engineering work is postponed, the 2¼ year period would exclude the gap but Murray was not obliged to return if he did not want to.
> If work exceeds 2¼ years, terms are subject to renegotiation.

The Board agreed the Chairman's proposals, except that the shares should be divided equally with the cash payments, i.e. £180 plus two fully paid up £10 shares per payment. Mr Murray accepted his appointment as from 30th September.

The first report of work on the extension appeared in the *Thame Gazette* of 1st November. The works were 'progressing favourably'; at Wycombe a cutting of about 35 ft depth was in 'a forward state' (*but see below*). A large number of men were levelling the ground at Horsendon and at Towersey a bridge was being erected over the road to Sydenham.

A meeting with the local committee at Thame on 8th November revealed that £10,000 was still needed to complete the capital required. At a meeting of the Finance Committee on 14th November an offer from S. Beale & Co. to supply rails at £9 7s. 6d. per ton, 'to be made after their own method with hammered iron', was considered. The manufacturers would replace any defective rails within four years of delivery and would take payment in ½ shares/½ cash. This was considered a good deal and Messrs Murray and Rose were asked to check that the GWR Engineer would accept the rails. At a subsequent meeting of the committee, a price of £10 10s. per ton delivered to High Wycombe was accepted from Messrs Beale.

The first fatalities on the extension occurred at Bell Field cutting, High Wycombe, on 28th November. At about 5 pm a report reached the town that the cutting had fallen in and five men were buried. It took until 10 pm to get all the bodies out, by which time no less than 2,000 onlookers were observing the ghastly scene. All the men were single, except one who had a wife and three children. At the ensuing Coroner's inquest the jury gave the verdict: 'Accidental death, but the jury are of the opinion that the proper precautions demanded by the nature of the soil and the depth of the cutting have not been adopted and the attention of the contractors is called to the necessity of greater care for the future'.

The annual shareholders' meeting took place on 29th February, 1860. Mr Ward told the proprietors that the lease with the GWR for the original line had been signed, as had an agreement for the extension the terms of which were spelled out. The original line was estimated to be earning £7,200 a year. Following the sad death of Mr Brunel, Mr E.F. Murray had been appointed to succeed him as Engineer-in-chief, and works were proceeding well (he made no mention of the slip at High Wycombe). The usual 3s. dividend for original shares was declared. At the end of the meeting a vote would be taken to authorise the Directors to issue Preference shares (this was passed).

Mr Murray's report was attached. This stated that work had begun on 13th September, starting with the 'heaviest portion of the line between Wycombe and Bradenham' but work was also taking place between the latter and Risborough, and at several important points between Risborough and Thame. He said that 'although the extraordinary rainfalls of the last few months had materially retarded . . . the earthwork . . . the general progress has been satisfactory, nearly one-third of the total earthworks required having been executed'. About half of the public road bridges on the line had been completed or were in progress. He saw no reason to doubt that the line would be completed on time.

The accounts for the extension line showed receipts of £8,801 3s. 9d. (including a loan of £3,010 3s. 9d.) while expenditure had been £500 less than this. The biggest outpayments had been £3,764 7s. 6d. Parliamentary expenses, £3,157 to the contractor (a third of this in the form of shares) and £420 to the Engineer. Ward and Bulkeley continued in the top jobs in the directorate.

Most of the subsequent entries in the Minute book for the year were dealing with financial matters. In March the Secretary was told to bring the company's borrowing powers into operation. Also he was required to supply a list of share deposit/first call defaulters to the solicitors. The latter were asked to negotiate with Messrs Tredwell to try and persuade them to accept £13,000 worth of 5 per cent redeemable Preference shares, in the proportion of half cash/half shares, presumably in lieu of £13,000 of pure cash. In April the Chairman said he had £2,500 to lend once the borrowing powers were in force; in May he advised he could similarly supply a further £3,600 from clients of his in London once the borrowing arrangements were finalised and another £400 immediately. In June a £2,000 loan from Messrs Osborne & Ward of Bristol was accepted and £2,500 actually handed over by the Chairman as a loan from himself, Mr Charles Ward of Bristol and two other gentlemen; both of these loans were secured by the issue of Debenture Bonds at 5 per cent interest. At the same meeting it was reported that £8,000 had been paid to the contractor (probably this was the total so far this year) and the latter had returned £8,000 to the company 'on account of calls on his shares'. The second £2 call on the other shares had raised £1,882 at the end of May, showing that there were still only about 900 shares issued, other than the contractors', on the extension railway.

Later, in June, the Directors met at the Spread Eagle Hotel, and the Minutes noted that the borrowing powers of £20,000 under the 1857 Act had been confirmed, £10,400 to be borrowed at 4½ per cent, the remainder at 5 per cent. A cheque for £3,000 was drawn in favour of the contractor. In July, as well as £3,000 and £2,000 cheques for the contractor, a dividend of 3s. per share was declared, and John Theobald Wilson (son of the Secretary?) was appointed clerk at £50 pa. In September Mr Rose was asked to negotiate for the purchase of gravel for ballast from Messrs Skrine & Rogers. The contractor continued to receive an average of £1,200 a month during August, September and October.

In September, a year after work had begun, progress must have been quite well advanced (although opening would be a year late, as will be seen) and shareholders' thoughts turned to the possibility of extension to Oxford (and Aylesbury). The Thame local committee, who now seem to have been very active, arranged for a meeting the Spread Eagle on 4th September. The usual comprehensive reporting by the *Thame Gazette* occupied two columns. Railway historians must be grateful to these early local papers, as, generally, far more can be learned from them than Directors' minutes which are brief and to the point, and usually miss out embarrassing facts.

The key facts to come out of this report of the meeting, in a crowded Assembly Room, are that 'rapid progress' had been made in construction of the extension. Following communication by the committee with the principal landowners and residents, replies received were supportive and unanimous for extension to Oxford. The price of coal locally would be reduced by 5s. or 6s. per ton (to Oxford prices) if brought in by rail and farmers would be able to reach more distant markets with their corn and other produce. Mr Murray described the route for the extension, via Albury, Tiddington, Wheatley and Horspath.* It would join the GWR near Iffley and the 12½ miles 'ought to be made for £10,000 a mile'. A land surveyor from Oxford, in the audience, said that the line should come into Oxford from the north, rather than the south, which he thought would attract opposition from the University. A Dr Adams, Fellow of St John's College, in reply said that he thought the line was laid out in a way to avoid opposition. 'It must not be supposed that the University, as a body, was so beknighted as to oppose a railway merely because it was a railway (applause). There was a time, he was sorry to say, when Heads of Houses, Doctors and Proctors, had no sympathy with railways and opposed the system, but, like many others, they had seen the errors of their ways . . .'

The paper concluded by saying that the meeting was one of the largest and most influential ever to be held in Thame, and there was an earnestness

---

* At this time Murray had surveyed the route via Garsington rather than Wheatley but he must have known it was to be altered, although the decision was apparently not taken until 17th November (*see later*).

exhibited which gave every promise of success. Incidentally the Revd Elton of Wheatley was in the audience and he seconded a resolution that the Wycombe Railway should be extended to Oxford. He kept a diary of railway progress which we shall see later. A new Committee was formed to liaise with the Directors.

The committee wasted no time and on 20th September sent a petition for the extension of the line to Oxford to the WRC. The Directors met the committee at Thame on 16th October and resolved to apply to Parliament for a Bill to extend from Thame to Oxford and Princes Risborough to Aylesbury. The local committee was asked to take the most active measures to obtain local subscriptions and to secure the support of landowners and residents and report to the Board from time to time.

This news must have reached other ears, although it was not a public meeting, because the *Thame Gazette* of 23rd October carried two letters complaining strongly that a railway to Aylesbury should be made from Thame, not Princes Risborough. However, the 6th November edition of the *Gazette* carried an advert for a public meeting to be held in Oxford on 10th November to enlist support for the extension to Oxford, and advising that the WRC Directors would be present.

On 13th October, Mr Murray had written one of his almost illegible letters to the WRC Chairman, which boiled down to the fact that he wanted more money. The outgoings for which he was responsible hardly left anything for himself, and there had been a particular problem with ballast 'of which the Board could not have been conscious at the time of my agreement with them'. The Chairman's reply is not preserved in the papers, but from Minutes of a Board meeting the following February (in fact the next Board meeting) it can be established that his request was declined.

The 27th November, 1860 edition of the *Gazette* carried a lengthy advert for an intended Aylesbury & Thame Railway, giving notice of intention to apply for an Act of Parliament. The advert gave no clue as to the instigator of the proposal, nor of the amount of money required to be raised. In the same issue, another advert announced that, following the withdrawal of the Oxford, Thame and London Coach, Mr C. Simmons of Thame was commencing to run the 'Eagle' leaving the Spread Eagle at 7 am daily to connect with the 9.30 am train from High Wycombe. This arrived in London at 10.55 am and day passengers could leave there by the 5 pm train, connecting with the 'Eagle' at Wycombe and arriving back at Thame at 9 pm. Fares were 3s. 6d. inside and 2s. 6d. outside.

In November the WRC Board initiated a series of meetings and letters with the GWR regarding the proposed extensions. Not all the relevant paperwork seems to have been preserved so it is not possible to explain every nuance of the matter. Following a meeting at Paddington and receipt of a letter from the GWR dated 3rd November (no details of either in the file), the WRC's solicitor wrote to the GWR on 5th November stating that if the GWR intended to make arrangements for leasing the new extensions under the same arrangements as for Thame, then the WRC would not proceed with them. They were concerned that the rental contemplated would not pay sufficient interest on the new shares to make them attractive, and that there would be no extra money to pay the existing shareholders anything for the extra risk to their shares brought about by the extension. The main thrust of this first bid was that the GWR pay them 1 penny per ton per mile for all through goods traffic which it suited them to route over the Maidenhead-Oxford line; that they allow the WRC to keep a higher percentage of the gross receipts from through passenger and local traffic at the start, reducing as the traffic developed; that they be released from an old debt of £9,250 or £9,260 (both figures quoted in documents) and 'all minor disputed claims' and that the minimum amount of rental required by the WRC to pay dividends and debenture and rent charge stock interest would be £13,250 (i.e. £2,000 existing Thame debenture interest, plus £11,250 on new debentures and shares). The 'original' Wycombe shareholders got their dividends paid out of the £3,600 annual rent payable by the GWR for that portion of the line. The new line brought no benefit to them, but additional risks; the release from the £9,250 debt would, however, be of benefit to them which is why the WRC requested it.

An internal WRC document dated 17th November, 1860, showed that they would need an annual income of £20,900 just to pay the debenture interest, rent charges and dividends on shares of *all* the capital required (£460,000), including that proposed to be raised for the Oxford/Aylesbury extensions.* The company hoped that they would be allowed a higher percentage than the present 40 WRC/60 GWR division while traffic was building up. The entire system, when built, would total 44 miles. They requested that the 40 per cent threshold not be introduced until the system was earning £19 per mile per week, at which time their proportion of traffic receipts would earn them £14,400 pa. The papers noted that the decision (taken that day, it later turned out) to route the Oxford line via Wheatley rather than Garsington had increased costs by £20,000.

A Preliminary Agreement dated 'December' 1860 was drawn up between the two companies. The main points were:

The WRC to apply to Parliament for a Bill to authorise the extensions.
The GWR to lease the lines and pay a fixed rental of £11,500 pa, payable half-yearly.
(In the event of only one line being constructed, rental to be £7,700 for the Oxford line or £3,800 for the Aylesbury line.)
The GWR to postpone for seven years the repayment by the WRC of their debt of £9,260 (they would not waive the 'minor disputed claims').

The solicitors for the WRC were forced to write an embarrassed letter to the GWR Chairman on Boxing Day, 1860. Mr Murray had estimated the cost of the

---

* The capital figure shown as needed (£460,000) does not agree with capital actually authorised in 1861 which was £420,000:

Authorised capital

Date of Act	1846	1852	1857	1861
Original	£150,000	£100,000	(£100,000)	(£100,000)
Thame			£ 60,000	(£ 60,000)
Thame				£ 20,000
Oxford/Aylesbury				£240,000
	£150,000	£100,000	£160,000	£420,000

new lines as £240,000. When the company submitted its proposals to the GWR prior to the drawing up of the Preliminary Agreement, Mr Murray had not been present and the Chairman had decided to split the costs £160,000 Oxford and £80,000 Aylesbury. On sending the estimate to Mr Murray for his signature the latter had replied:

> I have had your estimate and hope sincerely that the apportionment for each line of the gross sum therein set down has not been acted upon, or allowed to form the basis of any agreement . . . The sum for the Aylesbury line is too large and that for the Oxford line too little. Any Engineer will see on the most cursory glance that the cost *per mile* of the Oxford line will be some thousands in excess of the Aylesbury and I have always said so . . . I hope there is nothing to prevent the error being corrected . . .

In a subsequent letter Mr Murray estimated the Oxford line would cost £175,000 and the Aylesbury £65,000. He said there would be a difference of nearly £4,000 per mile between the two lines (probably Wheatley tunnel had a major bearing on this).

This only had a consequence for the Agreement if only one line were made, as there would be insufficient money for the Oxford line on its own. The Chairman also asked that the proportional rent income for the two lines be altered from £7,700 for Oxford to £8,380 and Aylesbury from £3,800 to £3,120. The subsequent Working Agreement dated 29th April, 1861 incorporated this change to the proportional rent increase , but with slightly different figures.

On 14th December Mr Murray had submitted one of his regular certificates. The cuttings near Wycombe were all finished, but those at Thame 'could not be proceeded with' because of the weather. There was, however, a problem with the contractors and ballast (*see later*). He wished to know if Messrs Beale might start rolling the rails and delivering them, but this depended on the ballast being laid first.

At the next meeting of Directors, 4th February, 1861, Mr Murray put in a written report. Except for one embankment, all the earthworks between Wycombe and Bledlow, 10 miles, was complete. Between Bledlow and Towersey they were not yet in possession of all the land required. From Towersey to Thame cutting the line was finished, Thame cutting would take another three or four months to finish. All the brickwork for bridges had been built and all the iron and timber work fixed. The ballasting and laying of rails had not yet started and could not have been done anyway, because of the weather. Satisfactory arrangements had been made with the contractor and the owner of a ballast pit at Cookham, and ballasting would commence and proceed rapidly. He asked permission to order 200-300 tons of rails. Stations at Princes Risborough and Thame could not be started until the result of the application to Parliament (for the Aylesbury/Oxford extensions) was known, but these could be completed at the same time as the permanent way.

Mr Murray was authorised to order 300 tons of rails. The Board decided that a Consulting Engineer was needed to work in conjunction with Mr Murray to work up the engineering case for the extensions. John Fowler would be invited to act in that post. Mr Ward also reported that he had drawn up an agreement with Messrs Tredwell for them to accept £20,000 of their cash payments in

Lloyds Bonds paying 6 per cent interest for 2 years [less risky for them than shares, but still not cash!]. The Board approved this.

The Chairman, reminding the Board of Mr Murray's request for more money last October, which they had declined, said that a further letter had been received from their Engineer, asking for all his payments in cash in future. This the Board agreed to do 'but must consider Mr Murray bound by the arrangements on which he was appointed Engineer for the Extension Works' [somewhat contradictory?].

Also dated 4th February, Mr Murray submitted an estimate of the further sums required for construction works.

Messrs Tredwell's Contract

	£	£
Contract amount	85,000	
Certified to 11. 1.61	39,066	
Remainder on contract	45,934	
Estimated amount of		
Extras (accommodation works for landowners)	800	46,734
Estimated amount payable to GWR for tolls, signals,		
guards etc. [for movement of ballast]		1,200
Rail contract say 1,450 tons @ £10 10s.		15,225
Stations (as per agreement with GWR)		8,000
Total required for works		71,159
	(say)	71,500

The Directors met again on 28th February, as a prelude to the AGM. John Fowler had accepted the Consulting Engineer's appointment. When the shareholders met at the GW Hotel, there were insufficient to hold a meeting and it was deferred to the next day - however, a dividend of 3s. per share was declared. The next day no shareholders attended so the meeting was adjourned *sine die*! A Report, intended for the meeting, was issued as usual but there are no accounts or minutes. The report said that there had been difficulty in obtaining ballast and that a slight modification had been made in the Tredwells' contract as a result. It stated that they could 'look forward with certainty to the opening of the line to Thame within a twelvemonth' [months late, but it would be even later than this]. It also stated that John Fowler would be involved in the Parliamentary work (appearing before committee, etc.) of the new extension. Finally, a report from Mr Murray was also produced for the meeting saying much the same as his earlier report to the Directors; all the bridges, including Wycombe viaduct, were built. All the works had been severely tested by the lengthy frost following the heavy rainfall, and had stood up well and were in good condition.

None of the correspondence regarding the ballast problem seems to have survived so it is not possible to be sure why there had been difficulty in obtaining it. But on 27th March a new Supplemental Contract was made between the Tredwells and the WRC which covered the ballasting in some detail. The ballast must be obtained from a ballast field adjoining the railway at Cookham belonging to a Mr Rogers; any other ballast used without permission would be removed at the contractors' expense. Ballast would be allowed for at the rate of 4s. 1½d. per cubic yard, instead of 3s. per cubic yard in the previous contract. Just about every eventuality was covered; after being spread it must not be unnecessarily worked over by horses or men, and if it should become 'injured' it must be made perfectly good.

The new contract noted that £41,000 of Tredwells' £85,000 had already been certified by the Engineer up to the 15th March. It specified that £4,000 of the £85,000 figure must be devoted to ballasting. Any agreed extra works accepted after 6th November, 1860 would be paid for on top of the £85,000 allowed for. Recognising that things were running late, the new contract stipulated that all work must be completed with 12 months of the date of the first certificate issued by the Engineer under this new contract. Finally it noted that the Tredwells had agreed to accept £20,000 in Bonds rather than cash, as recorded in the first Board meeting in February.

Writing at this period, Edward Gibbons, a farmer from Bledlow Ridge, says, 'Six trains a day bring ballast, near 100 tons each, with a north wind we hear it distinctly'. He considered the gradients on the Thame branch so steep as to need alteration.

In April 1861, the West Midland Railway (WMR) presented a petition to the House of Commons objecting to the Oxford extension. This was lengthy, going back to 1852 in its protestations and need not be gone into in any detail here. But one of its complaints was that in 1858 the predecessor to the WMR, the Oxford, Worcester and Wolverhampton Railway, had agreed with the GWR that for a period of nine years neither company would enter into or encourage any lines competing with existing lines. This agreement was enacted in 1859. The WMR claimed that by sponsoring this line the GWR was breaking the 1859 agreement.

The Board met on 18th April and were appraised of the altered contract for ballast. At the same time Mr Murray was authorised to obtain stone from Griffin's Quarry (Edward Griffin - Director?) for use as ballast at the Thame end in lieu of gravel - at the contractor's expense. Frustratingly, no reason or details are given. Messrs Beale had submitted an invoice for £3,164 2s. 4d. for rails; they later agreed to take half this sum in shares.* Mr Murray submitted a statement of extra works required (over those contracted) costing £905. This included £213 for the access to Cookham ballast field, £321 for alterations at Wycombe junction ('to suit the permanent working') and £135 for a 60 ft siding for Edward Griffin (Director) at Penn Farm. The Board approved the cost of these extra works.

An Agreement between the WRC and the GWR for lease of the Oxford and Aylesbury extensions was signed on 29th April, 1861. It is very similar to the 1859 Agreement for Thame, except that it does not specify an opening date! The rent was £8,266 for Thame-Oxford and £3,234 for Aylesbury, total £11,500 per

---

* From two invoices in Mr Murray's papers, it would appear that a load of rails was brought from South Wales, on 16th April, hauled by the South Wales Mineral Railway (SWMR) broad gauge locomotive *Moloch*. The invoices are for stores supplied at Newport and Swindon. Apart from the obvious coke, oil and tallow at both places, at Newport it was necessary to supply fire irons, a pinch bar, a steel bar or tommy, seven spanners, a hammer, brush, bucket and shovel amongst other things! Were these removed by the SWMR crew at Newport or thought to be substandard by the GWR? An intriguing mystery, and a long haul for a Welsh locomotive.

annum. On 4th May an agreement was signed postponing the repayment of the debt of £9,660 [sic] by the WRC to the GWR for seven years. A special meeting of shareholders on 18th May approved the submission of a Bill to Parliament to extend the railway to Aylesbury and Oxford.

When the Directors met on 20th June, Mr Murray reported that the ballasting would take a long time and, if the extension was not opened until this was finished, 'would cause a delay of seven months at least'. He recommended that the GWR be asked to work the line partially ballasted, in which case it could be open by 31st December. Mr Murray was asked to negotiate with Messrs Tredwell for them to erect and complete all stations on the Thame extension (as a separate contract) and report back to the Board. As Tredwells were currently owed £8,272 2s. 4d. and a further account for nearly £5,000 was imminent, it was resolved to issue two Lloyds bonds of £5,000 each in payment, bearing interest at 6 per cent. The Chairman was authorised to negotiate a temporary loan with Glyn Mills of up to £20,000 on best terms, the company issuing the necessary Preference shares to support it.

The Wycombe Railway (Extension to Oxford & Aylesbury) Act, 1861, received its Royal Assent on 28th June. New capital of £260,000 was authorised (£20,000 of which was required for the already authorised Thame extension) and borrowing powers for a further £86,000 (£6,000 of which was for Thame). If authorised by three-fifths of their shareholders present at a special meeting, the GWR was allowed to subscribe up to £100,000 to the cost of these undertakings. (*Bradshaw's Manual* 1862, and successive issues, stated that the GWR had subscribed the £100,000.) The Working Agreement between the companies dated 11th August, 1859 was confirmed by the Act. The new lines must be completed within four years. Finally section 44 of the Act authorised a reduction in the number of WRC Directors from seven to five. On 3rd July Mr Murray submitted an account for £1,234 for his Parliamentary work. This revealed that it had been decided as late as 17th November to deviate the line via Wheatley, rather than Garsington, involving Mr Murray in seven miles extra surveying work and increasing the cost of the Oxford extension by £20,000.

At the next Wycombe Board on 18th July, it was reported that bonds for £10,000 had been issued to Tredwell. Mr Murray submitted plans for the Thame extension stations and was asked to obtain tenders from Tredwell. A dividend of 3s. per share was agreed.

Now comes another mystery that cannot be completely resolved from the paperwork still in existence. The Board decided to appoint Richard James Ward as Engineer for the Oxford and Aylesbury extension, terms to be agreed by the Finance Committee and reported to the next Board. Immediately one asks - why was Murray not appointed?

On 23rd July the Directors met again, with Captain Bulkeley in the chair in Mr F.R. Ward's absence. Mr R.J. Ward had proposed that he be paid £250 per mile, plus a superintendence allowance, not exceeding £500, to be paid in shares. Captain Bulkeley, an experienced GWR Director, thought that £200 per mile was sufficient. However Mr F.R. Ward then arriving, Capt. Bulkeley vacated the chair. Mr Crewe, seconded by Mr Venables, moved that Mr R.J. Ward be paid £250 per mile, this amount to include all charges. Captain

Bulkeley counter-proposed £200 per mile, but no-one would support this and a vote being taken, £250 per mile was carried by 4 votes to 1 (the captain), the Chairman, Mr F.R. Ward not voting.

At this 23rd July meeting, Mr F.R. Ward's letter of 18th July to Mr Murray and the latter's reply were 'laid before the meeting' but unfortunately their texts were not included in the Minutes (as one finds so often when anything embarrassing is discussed). The meeting resolved 'That the Secretary . . . inform Mr Murray that the Board were not influenced in the appointment of Mr Ward as Engineer . . . for the new lines "by any charges, statements, or insinuations" made to Mr Murray's prejudice and that nothing could be further from their wish than to "throw any slur upon his professional character and prospects"'. [Why didn't they appoint him then?]

The Directors met again, only two days later, to consider a letter received from Mr R.J. Ward dated 24th July, Westbury, Wilts. He accepted the position, but there was an interesting paragraph:

> I beg to say that these terms are considerably less than I have received from other companies, and that they will leave a narrow remuneration for my labor [sic] and responsibility but *after consideration of the circumstances under which the Board is acting*, I am prepared to acquiesce in them [my italics].

He accepted the post, on the assumption that the railway would be completed in three years from 'this date' (i.e. date of letter) and his engagement would be limited to that period. Again the Minutes give no clue to the italicised portion of the paragraph quoted above. (At their meeting of 19th September the Board amended 'this date' to the date when Mr Ward received instructions to proceed.)*

At the same meeting Mr Murray was authorised (again) to obtain tenders from Tredwells for the stations on the Thame extension and report back at the next Board on 15th August. Next a letter was read from Captain Bulkeley, who was absent. The latter must have felt that Mr Murray had been badly treated and asked for a special Board meeting in a week's time so that Mr Murray could make a statement re the appointment of the new Engineer. This was agreed, but Mr Murray, being present, elected that the matter be gone into at once, rather than wait a week (although it might have been better for him to wait until Captain Bulkeley was there). Once again, the Minutes throw no light on the proceedings. Mr Murray's no doubt passionate statement is not recorded, nor the Chairman's statement in response, the reader being laconically informed that it was 'resolved that the statement of the Chairman in reference to the appointment for the extensions to Oxford & Aylesbury, now read be and is hereby adopted'.

So why didn't Mr Murray, apparently highly thought of by Brunel, get the job? Because some important letters are missing and the Minutes lack facts, one

---

* Mr Ward was also Engineer to the Berks & Hants, Marlborough, and Weymouth & Portland Railways. Messrs Baxter, Rose, Norton & Co. (WRC solicitors) were solicitors to all these companies. W.H. Wilson (WRC Secretary) was Secretary to the Marlborough Railway. A.T.P. Barlow (WRC deputy Chairman) was deputy Chairman to the Weymouth & Portland Railway. It was a cosy club, wasn't it?

can only guess at the reason. Certainly his request for more money and that he be paid in cash rather than shares will have caused annoyance. The fact that the Thame extension was running a year late cannot have helped. Would it have helped if his surname had been 'Ward'?

At the next Board, 15th August, Mr Murray submitted his estimate for the cost of the stations. This totalled £7,606 but when 10 per cent was added on for 'extra works' and another £634 for turntables, pumps and cranes, the cost came to £9,000. Murray was told to send a copy to the GWR 'informing them that the erection and completion of the said stations . . . will occupy six months, the amount provided in the Agreement is £8,000, and that this Co. must look to the GWR for all the excess above that amount'.

At the September Board (19th) Mr Murray provided the detailed station estimates as follows:

	£	s.	d.	£	s.	d.
West Wycombe						
Station buildings	430	12	3			
General Works	417	8	8	848	0	11
Princes Risborough						
Station buildings	1,104	9	5			
General Works	824	8	0	1,928	17	5
Bledlow						
Station buildings	619	12	3			
General Works	361	3	8	980	15	11
Thame						
Station buildings	2,201	1	5			
General Works	2,137	8	8	4,338	10	1
				8,096	4	4
less permanent way included in contract				490		
				7,606	4	4
Additional works at 10 per cent				760	0	0
Turntables, pumps, cranes etc. etc.				634	0	0
Total estimated cost (say)				9,000	0	0

There is no discussion in the Minutes as to why the station buildings at Thame were so much more expensive than the others, even Risborough, but in the 'general works' at Thame 13,000 cubic yards of earthworks were required, for example, far more than the others, the next largest, Risborough, only required 1,500 cubic yards of earthworks. Thame also got allocated some of the general costs, like 55 mile posts at £1 each.

Messrs Tredwell had agreed to construct the stations, henceforth known as Contract No. 2, and to obtain tenders for the turntables, pumps and cranes etc., which were not included in Tredwells' contract, before the next meeting.

At the October Board (17th) Mr Murray presented his estimate of the amount required to complete the line and works (to Thame):

	£	s.	d		£	s.	d.
Contract sum	85,000						
Estimated amount of extras	582						
	85,582						
Less certified to 20.9.1861	68,600						
Remainder on contract					16,982		
Station Contract	7,606	4	4				
Addtl works at 10%	760				8,366	4	4
Total payments to Messrs Tredwell					*25,348*	*4*	*4*
Machinery for stations: Pumps, cranes, etc. etc. (say)					634		
					25,982	*4*	*4*
Estimated amount payable to GWR for sidings etc. at Cookham and Wycombe and for wages of men for Ballasting (say)					702		
Estimated total to complete railway [to Thame]					*26,684*	*4*	*4*

Mr Murray was authorised to make arrangements for erection of machinery for pumps, turntables and cranes, etc. at stations. The solicitors would be told to apply during the next session of Parliament for a Bill to amend the company's existing powers in respect of the issue of Preference shares. A special shareholders' meeting would be called 'at such times as the Chairman may think best' to authorise the issue of Preference shares under the existing powers.

At the November Board (21st) a letter from Mr Bell (Tredwells' solicitor), was read, but as usual not minuted. It would seem that Tredwells were being kept short of money because the company's solicitors were told to write to Mr Bell explaining the steps being taken to raise money and requesting that the ballasting be continued. Tredwells were also to be assured that the station contract would not be offered to anyone else 'providing the works are not stopped' and the company would give Lloyds bonds for the balance of cash payments now due.

A special shareholders' meeting was held on 19th December and the Directors were authorised to issue Preference shares paying not more than 5 per cent 'to such an amount . . . as they see fit and as authorised by the said [1861] Act'. Outside the special meeting, the Directors agreed that five debenture bonds totalling £2,000, now due for repayment (one was held by the Chairman) would be extended for a further five years.

On the last day of 1861 the Finance Committee, with new Engineer R.J. Ward also in attendance, met and discussed a letter from Mr Murray re terms for the continuation of his services. It was agreed to pay him £300 for services up to the opening of the (Thame) line, 'and as contained in his letter of the 30th instant'. Unfortunately the contents of the letter are not minuted, nor has the letter been found in the files extant. However, the Directors met on 9th January, 1862, when a letter from Mr Murray dated that day was discussed (and minuted):

I should be willing to go on as Engineer to the Thame Extension on the present terms of £800 per annum till the station buildings are commenced under a contract and to receive the sum of £500 for all subsequent work as now arranged including the settlement of all accounts. The sum of £200 to be paid three months after the commencement of the station buildings.

These terms were accepted by the Board.

Other relevant matters discussed on this date were all financial. First of all they resolved to issue £10 Preference shares paying 4½ per cent per annum up to the authorised amount of £260,000, as mandated by the shareholders in the special meeting of 19th December last. Payment of dividends on these would have preference over dividends on all ordinary shares other than those of the original shareholders. Next the Finance Committee was authorised to pay the contractor with 'so many [of these shares] as they shall think fit' and paying 6 per cent interest upon such shares. After the Thame Extension had been open for six months the shares would be classed as fully paid up, after which the contractor would receive dividends in the usual way. Finally offers from the Chairman 'to obtain' £5,000 to be invested in Preference shares 'upon terms he mentioned' and £3,000 on loan from Mr Rose (Director) at 5 per cent, for which debentures would be issued, were accepted.

The 1862 AGM was held on 28th February, where the 'disappointed' Directors had to apologise that the line was not yet open, but were sure it could be ready within three or four months' time. Embarrassingly, they had to defer the payment of the usual (3s.) dividend until the line opened, because the time limited by the Act for the completion of the railway (to Thame) had elapsed. This was laid down in Section 13 of the 1857 Act. They reported that, once again, they would have to obtain fresh Parliamentary powers as 'the capital authorised to be raised by the Act of 1857 required readjustment before it could be issued' and a Bill was before Parliament.

The Thame Extension account to 31st December, 1861 showed income of £101,896 only £53,307 of which was from shares bought, the remainder coming from various loans (Debentures or Lloyds bonds), including a £9,000 loan from the Wycombe 'Proper' account (i.e. money available from the original Maidenhead-Wycombe accounts). On the expense side the major costs were £10,749 in land purchases, £67,745 to the contractor for works, £9,304 for permanent way, £3,764 Parliamentary expenses and £2,880 to the Engineer. A small balance of £328 enabled the Extension accounts to remain in the black.

The meeting ended by becoming 'special' and the shareholders were asked to approve the 1859 Agreement whereby the GWR leased the Thame extension, and the 1861 Agreement whereby the GWR would lease the Oxford and Aylesbury extensions, which they did.

An interesting letter which has been preserved was written by Director C. Venables to the Secretary, W.H. Wilson, on 22nd March 1862, and read, in part: 'I am wearied by being asked *when* that event [opening to Thame] is to take place, it is a sad state after expending above £100,000 not to be able to finish' . . . Sadly, he had several more months of enquiries to face yet.

The Directors next met on 3rd April when it was noted that a loan from Miss Holdsworth of £5,000 had been received (possibly the £5,000 mentioned at the January meeting?) and had been used to pay Messrs Tredwell. At their 31st May meeting, Mr Murray was able to report that the line to Thame would be ready for opening on 1st August.

Meanwhile the Wycombe Railway Amendment Act, 1862 had received the Royal Assent on 16th May, 1862. The Preamble noted that the Thame Extension had been estimated to cost £108,000, 'but will greatly exceed this sum' [remember that the Directors estimated costs at up to £150,000 at a time when their Act stated £108,000!]. Accordingly under Section 2 and 3 of the 1862 Act the company was authorised to cancel the 1,000 forfeited shares and 2,944 shares vested in certain persons as trustees for the company and on which nothing had been paid and recreate them, hopefully, to raise £39,440 further cash. (The company's capital authorised by the various Acts stood at £420,000 and borrowing powers for a further £139,600.) Section 18 authorised the company, with the shareholders' permission, to negotiate with the holders of the *original* 6,056 Wycombe shares who had always had first call upon the £3,600 rent money paid by the GWR for the Maidenhead-High Wycombe part of the line, for this right to be surrendered in favour of the Preference shareholders. (Obviously the 'shareholders' permission to negotiate' excluded the need to obtain such permission from those who held the 6,056 shares!) With the exception of payment of rent charges and interest on loans (and the £3,600 just mentioned, unless negotiated away), any money received from the GWR in annual rental for any of the extensions could be used towards the Preference shares dividend as priority (subject first, as always, to the agreement of 60 per cent of the shareholders at a special meeting).

The *Thame Gazette* for 3rd June carried a report of a hoax notice that had been printed and distributed amongst the shareholders. This purported to call a meeting at the Market Hall at Thame for the purpose of considering 'the advisability of removing the present Directors or inducing them to open the Railway without further delay'. Apparently one or two people had turned up for the meeting. Possibly the notice was drawn up by a disgruntled shareholder who wanted his postponed dividend payments!

A special shareholders' meeting was held on 3rd July, when the Board was authorised to create and issue 5 per cent Preference shares. The Directors resolved to create and issue £10 shares up to £260,000 bearing interest at 4½ per cent.

On the 30th of that month the Finance Committee met, with Mr Ward the new Engineer in attendance, and looked at the various bids received for the Oxford extension:

	£
Messrs Rilson & Rodley	138,000
Mr Rowland Brotherhood	147,839
Mr J. Roach	125,625
Messrs Smith & Knight	134,000
Messrs Dalrymple & Finlay	129,700
Messrs W. Munro	130,000
Messrs Chambers & Hilton	119,000
Mr John Lucock	145,505
Mr H.T. Ross	138,422

That from Chambers & Hilton was selected and Mr Ward was asked to open negotiations with them. Noticeably, Messrs Tredwell did not tender!

The day before this, Col Yolland of the Board of Trade had submitted the report of his inspection of the extension to Thame. The broad gauge single line stretched for 13 miles 77.5 chains with sidings (not passing places) at the stations at West Wycombe, Princes Risborough, Bledloe [sic] and Thame. Sufficient land had been purchased for an eventual double line; all the bridges had been built for a double line and much of the earthwork. The permanent way, 'that usually adopted on the Great Western system' consisted of bridge rails on average 23 ft long, weighing 64 lb. per yard fastened to longitudinal bearers by fang bolts. The ballast consisted of clean gravel, said to be 13 inches deep under the longitudinals.

Turntables for tank engines had been erected at Wycombe and Thame. There were 2 viaducts, 7 over- and 10 under-bridges, the overbridges variously constructed of timber (2), brick (8) and wrought or cast iron (4). The underbridges all had wrought-iron girders except one which was built entirely of bricks. Col Yolland was happy with the bridges except one small one over a 12 ft opening where the rails had been placed directly on the girders without use of longitudinals, and this required strengthening. There were also two viaducts built in brick, these were well constructed, the longest span of which was 35 ft on the skew.

Col Yolland said that Mr Murray had agreed to alter the position of the signals at some of the stations. Palings at the platform ends needed moving back so they were not so close to the platform edge. Clocks had not yet been installed and gradient boards were required. Col Yolland continued:

> The line is constructed in accordance with the Parliamentary Plan which shows a junction with the Wycombe Railway 7 or 8 chains from the platform of the Wycombe station. The present station at Wycombe is to be made use of for the Extension line and this will involve the shunting or towing of every train into or out from the platforms to the junction which is objectionable - but in accordance with the practice at present followed at Wycombe for some trains and at other places on the Great Western Railway.

The line would be worked (by the GWR) with a single engine (or two or more coupled together) and Col Yolland was satisfied that the line could be opened for traffic, provided that the girder bridge over the 12 ft opening was suitably strengthened.

So as can be seen the line as opened was very basic, with a single engine providing a shuttle service between Wycombe and Thame and no passing loops constructed to enable more than one train to use the line at a time.

On Thursday 31st July, 1862 a special train consisting of an engine and 'two or three carriages' arrived at Thame about 10 am bringing the station officials, station master, policemen, porters. At 12.55 pm a special train bearing the Directors left Paddington, arriving at Wycombe at 2.10 where about 60 shareholders joined and thence onwards to Thame arriving there at 3 pm. The 3-coach train was drawn by *Sunbeam* a 2-2-2 saddle tank of the 'Sun' class built in 1840 (and withdrawn in 1870) and the engine was accompanied by Mr Murray, the Engineer. Some 500-600 onlookers had collected at the station but there were no special celebrations there. In fact the stay at Thame was the briefest possible, the special departing at 3.30 pm, but leaving behind three of its original passengers who returned to the station just two minutes too late! One wonders how long it took them to get home. Those who had not strayed received their reward at Maidenhead when the party dined at Skindle's Hotel at 6.30 pm.

Chapter Four

Opening to Thame and then to Oxford

The train service to Thame started the next day, 1st August, 1862. The *Thame Gazette* for 5th August carried a brief report of the non-event at Thame and a timetable for the first train service:

		Weekdays						*Sundays*
		am	*pm*	*pm*	*pm*			*pm*
Thame	d.	9.00	12.15	2.40	7.00			6.40
Bledlow		9.08	12.23	2.50	7.08			6.48
P. Risborough		9.13	12.28	3.00	7.13			6.53
W. Wycombe		9.25	12.40	3.15	7.25			7.05
H. Wycombe	a.	9.35	12.50	3.25	7.35			7.15
	d.	9.40	12.55	3.30	7.40			7.20
Taplow	a.	10.13	1.35	4.00	8.20			8.00
	d.	10.15	2.08	4.17	8.28			8.20
London	a.	11.00	2.40	5.15	9.35			9.35

		am	*am*	*pm*	*pm*	*pm*	*am*	*am*
London	d.	7.30	10.55	5.05	7.00	8.10	8.00	9.00
Taplow	a.	8.25	11.49	5.40	8.06	8.45	9.10	9.55
	d.	8.35	11.55	5.42	8.50	8.50	10.00	10.00
H. Wycombe	a.	9.15	12.35	6.20	<u>9.30</u>	<u>9.30</u>	<u>10.40</u>	<u>10.40</u>
	d.	9.45	1.00	6.25	9.35		10.45	
W. Wycombe		9.55	1.10	6.30	9.45		10.55	
P. Risborough		10.12	1.22	6.42	9.57		11.07	
Bledlow		10.19	1.27	6.46	10.02		11.12	
Thame	a.	10.30	1.35	6.54	10.10		11.20	

All trains were available to 1st and 2nd class passengers, but 3rd class passengers could only travel on the 2.40 pm (Weekdays) and 6.40 pm (Sundays) from Thame, and the 7.30 am and 7 pm (Weekdays) and 8 am (Sundays) from London.

No clues are given by the timetable as to whether trains ran beyond Wycombe without need to change there but an August 1862 GWR public timetable states 'Passengers may have to change carriages at Maidenhead & Taplow (the name of the junction station, often abbreviated to Taplow*). Studying the above times it would appear that quite possibly the 9 am from Thame went through to London, and possibly also the 5.05 pm from London was through to Thame. Other trains probably involved a change at Taplow (and possibly also High Wycombe in one or two cases). The Thame-based engine *may* have shuttled backwards and forwards as follows:

*The GWR station at Maidenhead from 1838 to 1871 was adjacent to the Bath Road bridge, one mile east of the present Maidenhead station. It was first called Maidenhead, then Maidenhead & Taplow (from 1854). In 1871 the present Maidenhead station was opened, that at the Bath Road bridge being closed when a new Taplow was opened ¼ mile east in September 1872.

Thame		*High Wycombe*
9.00 am	>	9.35
10.30	<	9.45
12.15 pm	>	12.50
1.35	<	1.00
2.40	>	3.25
6.54	<	6.25
7.00	>	7.35 (possibly through to Taplow arr. 8.20)
10.10	<	9.35 (possibly engine from Taplow d. 8.50)

This would have allowed scope for some goods working between 10.30 am and 12.15 pm (from Thame) or 3.25 and 6.25 pm from High Wycombe as a round trip Thame-High Wycombe did not take more than about 1½ hours. However, in the absence of a Working Timetable for the period this must remain conjecture.

John Greenaway was appointed booking porter at Bledlow at its opening, being regraded station inspector there in 1890, and finally retiring from there in October 1899 at the age of 67 - loyal service indeed. He was followed by Charles Wrighton, by now 'station master', who remained there until 1919.

At the time of opening fares from Thame were as follows:

To	Single						Return			
	1st		*2nd*		*3rd*		*1st*		*2nd*	
	s.	*d.*	*s.*	*d.*	*s.*	*d.*	*s.*	*d.*	*s.*	*d.*
Bledlow	1	0	0	8	0	4	1	6	1	0
P. Risboro'	1	6	1	0	0	5½	2	3	1	6
W. Wycombe	3	0	2	4	0	11½	4	6	3	6
H. Wycombe	3	6	2	4	1	2	5	3	3	6
Taplow	6	4	4	3	2	1½	9	6	6	6
London	10	0	7	2	4	0	16	0	11	6

Interestingly, by the time of publication of the next *Thame Gazette* (12th August), the 1st and 2nd class London fares had been reduced to 9s., 6s. 3d. single) and 15s. and 10s. 6d. return) respectively.

The seemingly vexed question of Mr Murray's pay rumbled on. The Finance Committee met on 5th August and considered a letter from Mr Murray wherein he said that he could not undertake superintendence of the maintenance of the way, etc., for less than £350 up to the end of Tredwell's [sic] contract (13th May, 1863), or £500 if fresh arrangements had to be made to extend the time to 1st August, 1864. The Committee decided to repeat the offer him made to him on 31st December last of £300 'as a liberal remuneration for the services required' [up to May 1863]. This offer Mr Murray accepted the next day, by letter. On 9th August another letter was received from the Engineer (dated 8th August), addressed to the Chairman:

My Dear Sir,
   Since my note to you of the 6th inst. I have been able to see Mr Lane [GWR Chief Engineer] and in consequence I can now agree to your proposal of the 5th inst . . . that the company will pay me £300 for superintending the maintenance to the 1st August, 1863 [the company's Minutes say *May* was offered on 5th and accepted on 6th August]

which sum is not to be reduced in the event of my being freed from responsibility . . . at an earlier period.

Of course this proposal does not affect my present Agreement [whereby] I have to wind up all the Engineering accounts, except those of the maintenance, and I quite understand that your proposal covers the settlement of those accounts in addition.

A very large proportion of the £300 will be paid away in expences [sic] and I must therefore stipulate for quarterly payments as previously.

A brief reply from the Chairman dated 9th August accepted these arrangements.

Other financial arrangements at this time involved both new and old contractors. On 5th August the Finance Committee was told that Messrs Chambers & Hilton had withdrawn their (winning) tender for the Oxford contract. Mr Roach had reduced his from £125,625 to £122,000 providing that the WRC would guarantee that rails would not exceed £7 2s. per ton. Mr Munro had reduced his tender from £130,000 to £119,750. Finally Mr Brotherhood had reduced his from £147,839 to £119,000! Without access to all the correspondence it is impossible to know how Brotherhood was able to reduce his tender by 20 per cent. But on the contract papers there are listed seven modifications to the specification on which his second (£119,000) tender was based, which were accepted by the WRC on 7th August. One of these seems quite unusual and wide ranging and may indicate that Mr Brotherhood was a bit worried that he could keep within his bid: 'That he is to have the benefit of any saving which can be made in the earthworks by altering the Contract Section; provided that such deviations be lawfully made - and do not in the judgement of the Company's Engineer prejudice the Railway or any of the works . . . thereof'. Anyway Mr Brotherhood now got the job and was present at Finance Committee on 7th August when Mr Vernon (land agent) was instructed to settle with the landowners for the land required for the Oxford extension. A contract with Mr Brotherhood dated 9th September was sealed on 29th September.

At the 9th August Finance Committee it was agreed to pay Messrs Tredwell £30,000 in respect of six Lloyds bonds (of £5,000 each) issued to them in lieu of cash on 5th April, 28th June, 26th July and 19th September, 1861 and 18th March, 1862 (2 bonds). The Minutes are not clear whether this very large amount of money was paid in cash. At the same time a further £1,494 in interest payments on the six bonds would be paid; this definitely was paid by cheque. Finally the deferred (from February) dividend could now be paid on ordinary shares.

At this time the *Thame Gazette* was carrying an advertisement for a Royal Mail coach leaving the Bell Inn, Thame, at 8 am every weekday for Aylesbury and connection with the London & North Western Railway, arriving in London at 11.10 am. It was possible to have four hours in London, leaving there at 3.20 pm, Aylesbury was reached at 5.20 so travellers would have arrived home in Thame about 6.40 pm. This competition may be the reason the GWR reduced its London fares.

Also advertised, in fact run by the same proprietor as the Aylesbury coach, Thomas Sheldon, was a thrice-weekly coach from Oxford to Thame, leaving the George Inn, Oxford at 9.45 am every Monday, Wednesday and Friday, calling at various places, including Wheatley at 10.30, and arriving at Thame in time for the 12.15 pm train to London. The coach returned to Oxford the following days (Tuesday, Thursday and Saturday) connecting out of the 7 pm arrival from London and the mail coach from Aylesbury. Oxford to Thame cost 2s. 6d. outside and 4s. inside. Charles Simmons, the proprietor of the Spread Eagle Hotel, Thame and also a WRC shareholder, advertised that he acted as parcels agent for the WRC and provided an omnibus to meet all trains, except on Sundays. He also supplied 'Time Bills, and every information respecting the line . . . on application'. His namesake Hubert Simmons, who was appointed station master at Thame in May 1864, described Charles Simmons as follows: 'A most important man . . . He was more like the Emperor of Germany than any man I ever saw, gentlemanly in his manners, John Bull in his style, but possessed of a most hasty temper'.

Soon the *Thame Gazette* was carrying large advertisements on its front page placed by various merchants and carriers. Joseph Howard (of Aylesbury) sold coals of first class quality at Thame station. Messrs Howland & Son announced that they had been appointed goods agents to the GWR for Thame and neighbourhood. No extra charge was made for collection or delivery within the town. Coal could be supplied at 17s. per ton, or cheaper if taken by the truckload (5 tons). Mr R. Vernon of High Wycombe advertised 'Coals for the Thame Branch' and also that he had a depot for slates, cement, etc. at Wycombe station. Finally Mr J. Bowen, also of Wycombe, would also supply 'coals per truck load . . . at reduced prices at each of the stations'. He had made arrangements with the Ruabon Coal company for a regular supply of their superior coals 'which he is now selling at very reduced prices'. So the opening of the railway to Thame had already proved of value to the inhabitants, even if they could not afford to travel, coal being an essential commodity, and now available more cheaply than before.

The *Thame Gazette* carried a report that on Thursday 10th August a special train had run from Thame to the International Exhibition in London. Leaving Thame at 6.20 am it had conveyed 201 persons from the neighbourhood (very precise!) at reduced fares of 6s. 6d. 1st class and 4s. second. On arrival at Paddington, having picked up intermediately, it consisted of 27 carriages conveying 1,500 passengers! The band of the Thame Rifle Corps accompanied the throng, playing on the walk to Thame station, at every station at which the train stopped and, on arrival, at Paddington, in front of the GWR Hotel. On the return of the train at 11 pm (presumably its time at Thame) 'an immense crowd of persons awaited its arrival'. The GWR was congratulated on this successful excursion and the paper also praised Mr Crane, the station master, and his staff who were most helpful.

Possibly as a result of the extra advertising, the *Thame Gazette* of 23rd September announced that from 30th September it would double in size to eight pages (or 40 columns) and at the same time reduce its price from 1½d. to 1d. It said that it would be the largest penny paper in the County. The 7th October edition advertised another day excursion to London 'The last of the Season', to take place on Wednesday 15th October, with departure again at 6.20 am and the same fares as before. The train called at all stations to Maidenhead and return from London was at 7.30 pm.

The *Thame Gazette* of 4th November reported on on a court case Hicken v. Wycombe Railway Company. Philip Hicken was given notice by the WRC in October 1857 that they required some three acres of his land in Towersey (compulsory purchase), for the purpose of extending the railway to Thame. In January 1859 Hicken agreed to sell the necessary land to the company for £300 in shares. It was subsequently found that he had only a life interest in the land, it reverting to his children on his death. Furthermore, the land was subject to a mortgage so the consent of other parties was required, but Hicken told the company that he would have their agreement (which he subsequently denied).

The WRC paid him the £300 in January 1860 and took possession of the land the following month. In July Hicken repudiated the agreement to sell. In May 1861 the other parties having an interest in the land filed a Bill of Complaint asking that the WRC be restrained from continuing in possession until its value 'has been properly ascertained'. The company was required to pay £300 into court pending the outcome of the case. The company cross-petitioned Hicken for non-performance of the Agreement. The court ruled that this should 'stand over' until the case brought by the other parties was heard. An appeal against the latter decision by the WRC was considered 'frivolous and vexatious' by the court and dismissed with costs.

The other parties' complaint was heard on 2nd July, 1862 by the Vice Chancellor who had some very undiplomatic things to say about the WRC. The latter knew that Hicken only had a limited interest in the land when they paid him and the Vice Chancellor considered that the railway was in possession of the land 'without any lawful title whatever'. Furthermore, 'this Railway Company in the present state of the cause are behaving unreasonably, oppressively and unjustifiably'. The court ruled that an Injunction would be issued preventing the use of the land until 'its value had been ascertained'. The separate action brought by the WRC to force Hicken to perform the agreement was dismissed with costs.

On 22nd July the WRC appealed against the Vice Chancellor's ruling and, after paying a further £500 into Court, it was agreed that the Injunction could be ignored until the value of the land was established, to enable the railway to open. It was always understood that the railway's compulsory purchase powers would get them the land, it was a question of a fair price being reached.

At last the case was heard before the Under Sheriff at Aylesbury on 24th October. Valuers for the railway came up with figures of £234, £289 and £328, while valuers for its opponents produced values of £534, £607 and £666. The jury decided on an amount of £180 for the land, £250 for severance, plus 3 per cent interest on the land value since February 1860 (£19), total £449.

The Lord Chancellor on 5th November ruled that the Injunction imposed in July was now inoperative and dismissed the railway's appeal against the Vice Chancellor's (July) ruling. The railway was able to get the balance of its money, placed in the custody of the court, returned, after deduction of the £449. However, it had cost them considerably more than this in time, lawyers' fees and the other parties' costs of the various dismissed appeals (not all mentioned here). Further, the opening of the extension had been delayed for a month. This unfortunately rather lengthy description of this case is only the tip of the iceberg; there is sufficient material at the National Archives to form another book on the subject!

Some extracts from the diary of the Revd E. Elton, vicar of Wheatley, who kept an eye on the railway's progress towards his village. On 9th October he notes: 'The railroad is now begun in earnest. Upwards of 100 men near here. Embankment begun near the village . . .' Revd Elton mentions that the men fetched buckets of spirits on yokes from the 'King & Queen' public house. On 15th November he drove through Horspath to Cuddesdon: 'Passed over a new bridge made over the railroad [at Horspath], there are large excavations already made . . .' And on 21st November: 'The railroad rapidly advances near the village . . .'

At 8 am on 29th October, Henry Carey, a 24-year-old labourer working on the Oxford extension was driving a full wagon of earth to a tip at Horspath. The wagon was towed by a horse along (temporary?) rails and Carey was in the habit of walking or running along the rails. He slipped and the wagon ran over him, breaking both legs. He was taken to the Radcliffe Infirmary, Oxford, where both legs were amputated. He survived until 25th November, but died due to 'inflammation of the lungs, secondary to amputation'. The deceased had been in Mr Brotherhood's employ for about nine months and came from Gloucestershire.

In December 1862 Thame lost its midday departure and this was not reinstated until the line opened to Oxford. Also the 9.45 am down departure from High Wycombe was replaced by a 7.10 am departure (Mondays excepted); this was actually the 5 am Taplow goods which became 'mixed' from High Wycombe. Thame had to manage with only three weekday departures until 1st October 1863, when, with the opening of the Aylesbury branch, an earlier departure from Thame (at 6.45 am) was put on. But at the same time they lost their late return service, the 9.35 pm from High Wycombe being replaced by a 6.10 pm departure, the 9.35 pm thereafter becoming an Aylesbury train. However, the Sunday service was doubled with 6.55 am and 6.35 pm departures from Thame and 11.05 am and 9.05 pm departures from High Wycombe. Train services on the Princes Risborough-Oxford branch remained remarkably consistent over the years and will be looked at in Chapter Ten.

As previously mentioned, the 1862 Act permitted the company to negotiate with the holders of the original 6,056 shares, re their first claim on £3,600 rent money on the original line. At the first Finance Committee meeting of 1863, on 22nd January, the solicitor was instructed to draw up an Agreement, applicable from 1st January, 1863, whereby the original shareholders would lose their rights to the £3,600 payment, in return for which they would receive a preferential dividend of 4 per cent, rather than the 3 per cent they had customarily received. The report issued prior to the shareholders' meeting stated that 'this arrangement [would increase] facilities . . . for raising the remainder of the capital required on the Oxford and Aylesbury lines, and for carrying into effect the proposed arrangement for the surrender of Mr Tredwell's shares.' It was authorised at the February AGM.

This report issued in advance of the AGM held on 26th February, 1863, was unusually explicit. Since its opening the Thame line had yielded £1,665 11s. 8d.

(in five months) while the original line had made £4,329 15s. 4d., a total of £6,095 7s. of which the WRC got to keep £4,563 12s. 6d. This was insufficient to pay any dividend on the Thame Extension ordinary shares but would be used for dividends (on the original shares), for which 3½ per cent was recommended, debenture interest and rent charge payments. Some of the new capital raised by issuing shares for the Oxford extension had been used to pay costs arising from the Thame extension (£28,000)* and the Thame account would have to bear the costs incurred in raising that capital. It seemed that the Thame extension would, in the end, cost £170,000 (rather than the £108,000 first anticipated). Of this amount, £30,000 was accounted for by shares issued to Messrs Tredwell in lieu of cash, and the contractor was now looking to sell these shares and would take £15,000 in cash.

The Engineer's report dealt with the Oxford and Aylesbury extensions. Two temporary shafts had been sunk at Horspath tunnel and construction commenced at the Oxford end. It was anticipated that the tunnel would have to be bored through blue clay, and would require lining throughout. All the 'heavier' work on the line had commenced and so far 81,000 cubic yards had been excavated, leaving 560,000 cubic yards to do. Of the brickwork involved with bridges, about one-sixth had been completed. Mr Ward (Engineer) reported that the works were satisfactory; Mr Brotherhood had purchased brick-earth and had rented some stone quarries near Wheatley. He had also brought a locomotive engine 'to the ground'. (The Revd E. Elton, vicar of Wheatley, wrote in his diary that on 23rd February, at 'Littleworth, saw the engine drawing a line of carriages going to & fro, repeatedly up and down from the cutting to the end of the embankment, making an immense saving in labour'.)

The accounts, for the first time, included entries for the Oxford and Aylesbury extensions. Share capital was £61,113 for the original line (out of £100,000 authorised), £76,032 for Thame (£80,000 authorised) and, so far, £108,990 for Oxford & Aylesbury (£240,000 authorised). Not surprisingly, in view of the shortfall, new loans of over £17,000 had had to be taken in the last year, with a corresponding jump in interest and rent charge payments. Construction costs for Oxford, to date, were £3,961 with £21,121 spent on land purchased; Aylesbury, which was further advanced (being shorter and simpler), had involved construction costs of £9,853 and land purchases of £10,165.

Further visits by the Revd E. Elton to see the progress on 'his line' gave rise to the following entries in his diary:

29th March. Walked down the line from Cuddesdon hill east. The line is well and solidly made about a mile.
31st March. Walked to Littleworth, saw steam saw, cutting through timber like cake.
19th April. Walked on line by Littleworth. The digging is now abreast of Brownsell's house in blue Oxford clay.
20th May. Saw the iron materials of great size made for the river by railway maker. Immense girders resting on cylinders.

---

* Might the company have used this Oxford/Aylesbury capital to pay off Tredwells' Lloyds bonds?

Reverting back to the Thame extension, on 8th May Mr Murray wrote that the GWR had fully examined the line and had expressed themselves perfectly satisfied; they were prepared to take over maintenance on 19th May, somewhat less than the customary 12 months for which the owning company was responsible. However, they asked to be paid £200 for the period 19th May - 1st August, which Mr Murray strongly recommended the WRC accept, as the latter's costs, if maintaining the line themselves, would probably be about £250 in this period. There is nothing in the Minute book to show whether this was agreed or not.

The Directors met on 23rd June and a 'Deed of Surrender' of the rights of the original Wycombe shareholders was approved. As compensation these shareholders would receive a 4 per cent dividend while all the other ordinary shares would receive 3½ per cent. The Board agreed to buy the 3,000 shares of *the late* Mr Tredwell for £15,000 (half their nominal value). [No reference has been found in the minutes or elsewhere to the demise of Mr Tredwell.] However, it appears the Board later changed their minds on this purchase. The Board also accepted loans of £11,700 for two years at 5½ per cent interest from Sir C.R. Tempest Bt and £20,000 for six months at 5 per cent from Mr T.D. Anderson; Preference shares would be issued as security for the amount of the loans. Without such help from these wealthy people the whole concern may have collapsed.

On 18th July Mr Murray submitted the final accounts for the two contracts held by Messrs Tredwell - No. 1 the main construction, No. 2 the stations. No. 1 had been completed at £87,008 6s. 11d. (contract price £85,000) and No. 2 at £7,987 9s. (£8,000), a total of £94,995 15s. 11d. The costs of the stations is shown in the accompanying Table.

The Actual Cost of the Thame Extension Stations
Contract No. 2

	£	s.	d.
High Wycombe (alterations)	87	15	0
West Wycombe	922	2	4
Princes Risborough	1,111	5	8
Princes Risborough Goods Shed	656	19	6
Bledlow	1,003	13	6
Level Crossing lodge	130	11	3
Penn Farm Siding	71	11	5
Thame	3,346	1	8
Thame Goods Shed	657	8	8
	7,987	9	0

(From a document dated 15th October, 1862 signed E.F. Murray)

Messrs Tredwell had been paid by £36,709 9s. 4d. in cash, £30,000 in Lloyds bonds and £27,000 in shares (Tredwells' account marked 'not yet received'), leaving a small balance of £1,286 6s. 7d. outstanding. This shows the extent to which Tredwells had supported the railway company; doubtless Lloyds bonds were as good as cash (eventually), but the shares were a different matter. They had paid for these themselves, effectively their investment in the company, and the best offer they had had on those was purchase at half-value, but see below. Many railway contractors who were forced to take shares instead of cash had cause to regret this arrangement, finding the shares of little value or worthless eventually, but at least Tredwells had survived as a company.

At a Board meeting on 23rd July the Board discussed the Contract drawn up on 9th September, 1862 between the company and Mr Rowland Brotherhood, contractor. The Contract entailed regular payments for construction up to an amount of £119,000, but because insufficient Preference shares had been sold to finance construction (and could not be sold except at a discount), on 9th July, the Chairman had reported that he had 'induced' (the legal document's words) the Union Bank of London to pay the contractor on Mr F.R. Ward's guarantee that the Bank would be repaid, with interest, after the opening of the line to Oxford. The arrangement was up to a maximum of £60,000 to be paid in instalments as work proceeded, for which shares worth £72,000 had been deposited with the Bank as security. Now Mr Ward, a solicitor, was rather anxious that, having negotiated this arrangement, he might be personally liable if the WRC failed, and the Board approved a Deed of Indemnity releasing Mr Ward from personal responsibility for the terms of the loan. £60,000 was an enormous sum for 1863, its equivalent value in 2002 being about £3¼ million, hence Mr Ward's anxiety!

At the same meeting correspondence with Messrs C. & H. Bell on behalf of Mr Tredwell was read, but unfortunately not minuted, so once again we do not have the full story. The Board's reply, dated 23rd July, was minuted in full, from which the following is extracted:

Dear Sirs,
   I am sorry to say the Company are not in a position, under existing circumstances, to accede to your proposal. They have to pay several thousand pounds more for land than they anticipated, which is very embarrassing, and upon a recent review of the outlay they have still to provide for the new lines, they are satisfied they would not be justified in undertaking the purchase of Mr Tredwell's shares at any rate for the present. After the Oxford line is completed in May next, the negotiations may possibly, if your clients desire it, be renewed.

The remainder of the letter was to the effect that the company did not feel any responsibility for costs incurred 'by your clients to enable them to sell their shares to advantage'. The final sentence of the letter indicated that the company's original offer to buy included payment in debentures anyway, not in cash! Without the text of Messrs Bell's letter and no reference in the Board's reply to the number of shares involved (nor is there any reference to this matter at the next AGM), it could be assumed that this all relates to the purchase of Tredwell's 3,000 shares at half price, mentioned at the 1863 AGM. As Messrs Tredwell had subsidised the cost of construction by this £30,000 this seems very heartless.

On 7th August the energetic vicar of Wheatley went '. . . to the tunnel, saw the place for brick making, the deep cuttings and the bringing up of earth from the tunnel. Much progress is made'. On 2nd September, 'The scripture reader came and is stationed at Thame . . . I [act as] chaplain to the railwaymen'. But on 6th September, the new contractor, Mr Brotherhood, wrote to Mr Wilson saying that he would have to stop the greater portion of the works for want of funds, and asking for an early meeting. Strangely no written evidence of a meeting to discuss this situation has been found.

The *Thame Gazette* of 29th September reported that a large number of fossilized bones and teeth, etc. of immense size and antediluvian age had been dug up by railway excavations at North Weston in the parish of Thame. The best of the specimens had been passed by Mr Brotherhood's clerk 'to a gentleman, who came from a long distance to inspect them'.

On 1st October, 1863, the Aylesbury branch opened. Thame lost its late train from High Wycombe at 9.35 pm (8.10 from Paddington), the last one now leaving at 6.10 (5.05 from Paddington). It regained its fourth up train, a new one being added at 6.45 am, but a month later lost a down train, the late morning departure (11.25) from High Wycombe being withdrawn. It then had to manage with only three down trains until the opening of the Oxford extension a year later in October 1864. The withdrawal of the late down train meant that, despite the considerably earlier 6.45 am departure from Thame, it was only possible to spend a maximum of 7 hours 40 minutes in London compared with 8 hours 10 minutes when the first up departure left at 9 am or thereabouts. The opportunity had been taken to reduce fares, Thame to London now costing 8s. 3d. (1st), 5s. 9d. (2nd) , and 3s. 5½d. (3rd) single, and 12s. 3d. (1st), and 8s. 6d. (2nd) return. However, 'market pricing' was already in operation causing 'A Lover of Fair Play' to complain to the *Thame Gazette* about the timetable alterations and that a 1st class return to London was 2s. 3d. dearer from Thame than Aylesbury, despite it being a mile closer to London than the latter place! Thame passengers were being 'fleeced'. By careful connections at Princes Risborough it was possible to travel from Thame to Aylesbury, or vice versa, four times a day in about 35 minutes, the 1st class return fares being 4s. 6d. or 3s. second class.

At the first Board meeting after the opening of the Aylesbury branch, 6th October, it was decided amongst other things, that a 176 yds-long loop would be provided at Princes Risborough. Until then trains between Taplow and Thame had only crossed at High Wycombe. With the opening of the Aylesbury branch, the Board had undertaken that 'the engine shall run through between Taplow and Aylesbury' a separate engine shuttling backwards and forwards between Thame and Princes Risborough. However, looking at the plan accompanying the 1878 accident report (*see Chapter Six*), the earliest plan found, the only possible 'loop' is between points A and points 12, the former worked from the ground. The authorities recognised the deficiencies in the layout and, apart from a few early timetables when two passenger trains crossed, subsequent crossing movements were restricted to two goods trains or one passenger train and a goods (this regularly occurred on Sunday mornings). A proper fully signalled crossing loop was installed, it is thought, *circa* 1890.

On 30th November, 1863, Fred Saunders of the GWR wrote to the Secretary of the WRC that 'the Directors are unable to entertain at the present time the suggestion that the narrow gauge be laid over the Wycombe Railway'. There is nothing in the Minutes to hint at what gave rise to this correspondence.

The Revd Elton's last recorded excursion for 1863 notes against 27th December, 'a large steam engine brought here last night stuck in the road going to Littleworth and will not easily be moved . . .' On 8th January, 1864 he notes 'Works on the railway embankment carried on day and night . . .' After a fairly quiet period in the Board minutes, those for 28th January, 1864 note that agreement had been reached with the GWR 'for the latter to move High Wycombe station at a cost to the WRC not exceeding £2,000'. It had obviously been realised that the additional traffic forthcoming once the line was open to Oxford could not be catered for by a dead end station, requiring a reversal for each through train.

The earliest single lines were worked by timetable with help from the telegraph in emergency. In 1858 the Board of Trade announced that, in future, newly opened single lines would only be permitted to be worked by one engine in steam, but after 1860 Train Staff and Ticket working (TST) was permitted. C.L. Mowat writing in the *Railway Magazine* (1933) says that the Wycombe Railway had the distinction of being the first line to use TST on the GWR, 'on the opening of the line to Thame'. But as we have seen from Col Yolland's report, at that time one engine in steam working operated. However, with the extension to Oxford huge amounts of ballast were required from Cookham necessitating the running of three weekday ballast trains, including one in the night hours. On 14th January, 1864 TST regulations were introduced, to operate between Taplow and Aylesbury and Thame from 18th January and on that date a special timetable of ballast trains was published (*see overleaf*).

There were five train staff sections, each with a different shaped and coloured staff, the relevant ticket being the same colour as its staff:

	Colour of Staff and Ticket	Form of Staff	Form of ticket
Between:			
Taplow and Cookham	Green	Round and tapering with brass ends	Diamond shape
Cookham and Wycombe	Red	Round	Round
Wycombe and P. Risboro'	Blue	Triangular	Triangular
P. Risboro' and Aylesbury	White	Square	Square
P. Risboro' and Thame	Brown	Six-sided	Six-sided

No train or engine could leave a staff station without a staff, or if another train(s) was to follow in the same direction, a ticket, the last train in that direction carrying the staff. Once the staff had gone, no train could leave that station until the staff returned. The tickets were consecutively numbered and kept in a locked box in the booking offices, the box being opened by a key on the train staff. The boxes were painted in the same colour as the tickets they contained. In 1864 the guard was in charge of the staff and had to show it (or a ticket) to the driver before departure. Cases of trains leaving without staff or ticket, or carrying them beyond the next staff station, would render the operating staff concerned liable to dismissal. If a ballast train had to *work* on the line, that train must only carry the staff. If a train broke down the staff had to be

Great Western Railway.

ON AND AFTER
MONDAY, the 18th of JANUARY, 1864,

Special Ballast Trains

WILL RUN BETWEEN
THAME
AND
COOKHAM BALLAST PIT
ON WEEK DAYS,
AS PER FOLLOWING TIME TABLE.

UP TRAINS.

			1	2	3
			a.m.	a.m	a.m.
Thame	- - -	dep.	2. 10	5. 55	11.30
Princes Risboro'	-	dep.	2. 30	6. 15	11.50
Wycombe - - -		{ arr.	3. 0	6. 45	12.20
		{ dep.	3. 15	7. 0	12.25
Cookham	- - -	arr.	3. 25	7. 20	12.45

DOWN TRAINS.

			1	2	3
			a.m.	a.m.	p.m.
Cookham	- - -	dep.	3. 35	7. 30	1. 20
Wycombe - - -		{ arr.	3. 55	7. 50	1. 40
		{ dep.	4. 0	10. 0	1. 45
Princes Risboro'	-	dep.	4. 30	10. 30	2. 15
Thame	- - -	arr.	4. 50	10.50	2. 45

On MONDAY, February 1st until Saturday, the 6th February, the Ballast Trains will run to and from Aylesbury instead of Thame.

On the arrival of No. 3 Train at Cookham Ballast Pit the Guard will be required to take the Train Ticket or Train Staff to Cookham Station where he will procure a Train Ticket or the Train Staff for the return journey to Wycombe.

The Engine must on no account leave the Siding at Cookham Ballast Pit until the Guard returns with either the Train Ticket or Train Staff.

N.B.—These Trains must be worked in strict accordance with the Train Staff Regulations, dated 14th January, 1864, and the Station Masters at Cookham, Wycombe, Princes Risborough, Thame, and Aylesbury will be held personally responsible that they are duly observed.

J. KELLEY,

PADDINGTON, *January 14th*, 1864.   *Superintendent.*

Ballast trains timetable, commencing 18th January, 1864.

taken to the staff station from which assistance might be expected, or if a ticket was being carried, to the station where the staff was. (In November 1865 the GWR altered the instructions so that the staff or ticket was held by the driver in future.)

The *Thame Gazette* of 11th February noted that a meeting had been held at the George Inn, Princes Risborough for the purpose of forming a company to supply gas and sell coal and coke. Shares had been sold to the value of £740 and a further meeting next week would choose the Directors and officers.

The report to the shareholders' AGM on 26th February, 1864, held at High Wycombe for a change, said that the Wycombe's portion of the extension line traffic returns (£6,521 2s. 3d.) plus the GWR's rent for the original line would allow a dividend of 2 per cent on the Thame shares. Of the original 6,056 shares, the owners of all but 50 had agreed to forego their rights to the £3,600 rental and these shareholders would receive 4 per cent, the remaining 50 would get 3½ per cent.

Of more interest to the reader will be the accompanying Engineer's report for the Oxford extension. Some 1,311 feet of the Horspath tunnel had been bored, leaving 273 feet to do, the strata had 'turned out to be not unfavourable', blue clay without too much water. Along the line some 527,500 cubic yards had been excavated, leaving 113,500 cubic yards to excavate. All the road bridges, culverts and the river bridge at Wheatley were finished and the large river bridge at Kennington would be ready for a locomotive in a few days. Wheatley station was half finished, about one mile of permanent way had been laid and materials delivered for a further two miles. The biggest other work remaining was the ballasting and it was this that would decide the opening date; there had been a delay waiting for the GWR to give permission to run between the ballast field at Cookham and Thame. [This may well have been while the GWR decided upon and prepared for the TST working.] However, the contractor had purchased a gravel field near Oxford and that would be used to ballast the Oxford end of the line. The Directors commented that they could see no reason, based on this report, why the line should not open on 1st June, but they were to be proved wrong. Finally they announced that they had agreed to pay about £2,500 for a new Wycombe (through) station, for which the GWR would pay an increased annual rental equal to 4½ per cent of the actual cost.

In a report dated 25th March, the *South Bucks Free Press* said that the work of removing chalk to make way for the new station was progressing rapidly. 'We believe it is intended to pull down the old station and use the materials in the erection of the new one. The contract for building it has been obtained by Mr W. Burnham of this town'.

Meanwhile the Revd Elton reported that the navvies had been entertained in the school room at Wheatley on 1st February and had been well behaved. On 11th March he wrote that 'the embankment of the line goes on day and night, nearly carried to Silverford lane'. And on 30th April he reported that Wheatley station was almost finished. On 5th May 'a telegraph station was about to be opened at Wheatley one pole [being] put up in our allotment'. That was his last report on railway progress for several years, even opening to Oxford apparently not being covered by the diarist.

Money must have been getting tight because in April the Finance Committee was authorised to dispose of all unissued Preference shares on best terms and in June they recorded that they would issue these at 20 per cent discount to any parties willing to advance loans taking these shares as security. In July there was correspondence with a William Gray who had undertaken to sell the unissued shares (£100,000 worth!) and would sell £15,000 worth within a month - the Directors approved this action at their 14th July meeting. Time (and money) was obviously running out for the independent company.

Hubert Simmons was promoted to Thame as station master in May 1864. He was 25 and had formerly been in charge at Aynho. After he left the GWR he wrote the two volume *Ernest Struggles or the Life of a Station Master*, Volume One (only) of which was reprinted in 1974 as *Memoirs of a Station Master*. I have written elsewhere of the background to the writing of these volumes and why the author felt it necessary to give the people he described pseudonyms.* Also that because the book was written long after the event, as Professor Jack Simmons said in his introduction to the 1974 volume: 'We cannot take the dialogue in his book literally . . . but much of it carries the stamp of truth and is both consistent and credible'. Hubert Simmons was certainly the only railwayman describing the earliest days at Thame and we are lucky to have his diaries of these times.

> The work at the station was single-handed and hard. I had enough to do. My predecessor, Mr Giant [presumably Mr Crane] was, without exception, the best railwayman I ever met with. He had been promoted to Twyford station. His books were in perfect order, and he had written on one of the fly leaves of his cash book that the chief qualifications for a railway man were 'accuracy and despatch'.

He was expected to supply the company's auditor and his district superintendent† with butter, eggs and poultry each week because it could be bought cheaper locally. This entailed a weekly trip to the market and then the purchases were forwarded, carriage free, by train. The district superintendent 'was a tall good looking man, about 35 years of age. He was the son of the steward of one of the chief shareholders - Sir somebody, and he was what might be termed "a fast man about town"'. Because a visit to Thame entailed a stay of three hours, he was seldom troubled by the superintendent and Simmons was looked upon as a man of some importance in the town.

Simmons writes that on Sunday mornings the 'plough boys' who had saved up their money, had a ride from Thame to Princes Risborough just for the novelty, then walked back to Thame (as there was no return service for four hours). On one occasion he noticed as many as 50 youngsters doing this; the 3rd class single fare was 5½d.

Not long before he arrived there the Staff and Ticket working had started. Simmons used to dream about the Staff as he knew that any error in the arrangements was 'a Board job' and probably meant the sack. One day he forwarded the Staff as usual, only remembering as the train went out of sight, that there was an additional train that day, rarely run, for which he should have kept

---

* See *Windsor to Slough: A Royal Branch Line* (Oakwood Press OL88) pp 59-60.
† In March 1865 Mr H. Besant was district passenger superintendent at Reading and covered the Thame branch.

the Staff. Running into town he called upon a local horse dealer who said he only had an unbroken colt on the premises which 'he wouldn't trust out for a gold watch'. Deciding that this was the lesser of two evils, when the dealer's back was turned, Simmons borrowed the horse and describes the most frightening of uncontrolled rides to Risborough to retrieve the Staff. Fortunately in his younger days he had helped his elder brother break in horses. By the time they reached Risborough he had managed to control the horse. Here, his luck was in - the Staff was hanging up in an empty room. He took it and, the colt now 'behaving admirably', alternatively trotted and cantered back to Thame, arriving just four minutes before the train was due to leave. His porter was almost mad with anxiety, being unable to find either the Staff or the station master, and was sworn to secrecy over the whole affair, which never reached the ears of the Directors. After the train left they cleaned the horse which was a 'mass of white foam' and walked him about to dry him off, before secretly returning him to his owner. Simmons was scarcely able to walk for several days after the experience - such were the perils of getting the Staff working wrong in those days!

> James Sandy, our branch engine driver, was a troublesome man. He was quick, obliging and above the average of engine drivers. But he had some dreadful failings, for he was fond of beer, fond of showing off with his engines, fond of mischief, had a dreadful habit of procrastination, was very hasty, and never saw danger. Smith, the guard who always accompanied him, or 'Mad Sandy' as the men called him, was very often complaining to me about him, and many a lecture I read Sandy.

Simmons writes that there was an old man 'very feeble, who acted as crossing keeper 'two miles distant' (probably the Towersey-Sydenham road) who had once been a prosperous farmer, but was now reduced to living in a miserable hut with his wife and minded the crossing for 10s. a week. His tales of 'Mad Sandy's' conduct would fill a book and he was convinced that one day he would be killed on the crossing. One evening an up train from Thame was awaiting the arrival of a ballast train before it could set off when 'Mad Sandy' decided to leave, without the Staff or the guard! Simmons was unable to stop the train, he only just failed to reach the brake van, 'and sank on the embankment like one who has lost all hope'.

Fortunately the line to the east of Thame was relatively straight and the two trains saw each other and stopped, but not before there was a casualty. The old crossing keeper had taken his signal off for the ballast train when he saw 'Mad Sandy's' train coming as well as the ballast. He shut the gate, thinking they might see it, and moved the signal backwards and forwards whilst his wife waved a red flag.

They both ran in the house when 'Mad Sandy's' train ran through the gates, knocking a large part of one through the house wall, and the trains stopped just 10 yards apart. The old man said 'Thank God!' and fell down dead. 'Mad Sandy' was sent to Oxford to be a shunting driver but the widow of the crossing keeper had her claim against the company ignored. None of this reached the WRC Board room, or if it did no Minute was drawn because no meetings were held between June and November 1864. No official explanation is therefore available as to why the line was not ready for opening beyond Thame by June 1864.

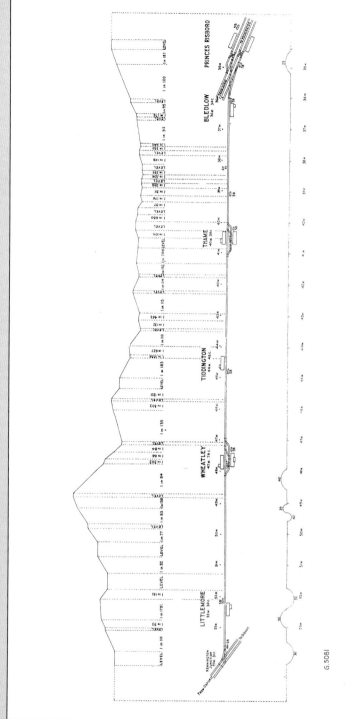

The gradient diagram for the Thame branch issued in 1923. The line at the bottom shows the radius of any significant curves. The milepost mileages shown are those from Paddington via Beaconsfield.

G.5081

One accident that was publicised occurred on 24th May, 1864. A ballast engine was detached from its train at Thame to take water on the engine shed siding. For some reason the engine ran 'with great force into the engine shed, smashing the front of the passenger engine, slivering to pieces large blocks of wood, also forcing completely out the brickwork at the end of the shed. Fortunately no-one was hurt, but the damage done was considerable' [*Thame Gazette* 31st May, 1864]. One wonders if this was another of 'Mad Sandy's' escapades.

On 11th July the company wrote to the Board of Trade (BoT) giving its first Notice of Intention to open. A month later on 17th August, it wrote to the GWR notifying them that the line would open on 1st September. A week later, on 25th August, the company issued its second Notice to the BoT, saying that the line would be 'sufficiently completed by 4th September' and was ready for inspection.

Captain Tyler inspected the line on 2nd September. The steepest gradient was 1 in 70 and the sharpest curve of 15 chains radius. The permanent way was laid with rails of ⌐ section, in lengths of 20 and 24 ft weighing 62 lb./yard. He wanted tie rods on curves of less radius than 30 chains. The ballasting was not quite completed. The fencing needed better supporting posts and should be at least 4 ft in height. Another sign of cheapness, the fence straining posts had been used as gate posts causing the gates to open as the wire expanded, proper gate posts should be provided. A telegraph was required from Wheatley station to a point west of the tunnel 'with proper huts and instruments and signals to avoid risk from trains following another'. The two viaducts over the river had stood up well to testing but the cross girders required strengthening. There were 8 overbridges and 18 underbridges and some settlement required to be watched as did one part of the brickwork in the east end of Wheatley tunnel.

The stations were incomplete; the usual clocks were required (a favourite item for these inspectors) and lamps on the platforms. A second platform was required at the crossing stations (Thame and Wheatley). The signalling at Thame was inadequate: '. . . the signalman has a long distance to go to work points on each side of his cabin, and is without the protection afforded to safety by locking apparatus. A temporary cabin only has as yet been supplied for him, and he requires a clock'.

The inspector had received a complaint at Thame re the need for a footbridge where a footpath crossed the line in a cutting near Thame where 'inconvenient stiles' had been provided. Because of the cutting, pedestrians would be unable to see approaching trains until just before crossing the line, and the inspector recommended that a footbridge be provided. Finally he had not received a certificate as to how the single line would be worked, and it was not surprising that he refused to recommend giving permission for the line to open.

The Board of Trade was kept busy by the Thame-Oxford line during the month of October. First of all, on the 6th, they received a memorial from 21 residents of Thame, Moreton and a few other places, all owners or occupiers of land adjoining or near the railway, complaining of the 'inefficiency and improper character' of the fences. They were constructed of wire and not sufficiently strong. Already many sheep had been killed, and the memorialists feared that passengers would be in great danger. The BoT referred the matter to Captain Tyler who was about to re-inspect the line.

The good Captain's report dated 10th October was another negative one. Although the fences had been strengthened they needed to be 4 ft high; the footbridge he had recommended at Thame had not been built (and he suspected that 'their Lordships had no power to enforce it'). The cross girders of the Kennington viaduct had not yet been straightened [sic]; although a second platform had now been provided at Wheatley it had no shelter, while at Thame the second platform had not been built; furthermore the signal levers there should be centralised on the present platform. A second weak spot in Wheatley tunnel required watching and the Inspector now recommended that duplicate connecting rods be supplied to all the point switches. Finally the certificate stating the method of working the single line had still not been supplied. So he again refused to give permission to open the extension line.

There was a swift response to the BoT from Secretary Wilson in a reply dated 13th October. He pointed out that the fencing was the same height as that on the Aylesbury branch and the Marlborough Railway, both passed recently by the BoT. No 'cover' on Wheatley's new platform had been specified at the first inspection but would be provided within six weeks. Thame was the property of the GWR and 'forms no part of the Railway which is now to be opened'. No point switches on the GWR 'laid on the longitudinal system' had duplicate connecting rods. The company would strengthen the cross girders at Kennington and hoped that, subject to their receiving the single line working certificate, their Lordships would sanction the opening of the line 'which has been ready for some time and is now in excellent condition'.

It seems that the WRC's examples of other similar fencing and their claim that Thame formed no part of this inspection won the day and on 15th October the BoT approved its opening, subject to the cross girders' work, Wheatley platform cover and the undertaking re method of working being received. On the 18th the company supplied this: '. . . shall be worked with a Train Staff in the manner described in BoT Requirements letter C No. 3'.

While all this had been going on the *South Bucks Free Press* in its 7th October edition said that the old station at High Wycombe was now disused and 'the business is carried on at the temporary station. A good deal of dissatisfaction had been expressed at the rigid exclusion of everybody but passengers from the platform'. No overall improvement in train schedules was apparent from the avoidance of the reversal at Wycombe.

In a forthright reply in next week's paper, the Wycombe station master had much to say:

For years it has been notorious that the Wycombe station has been the rendezvous of the idlers and ragtag of the town and to such an extent as to seriously affect the despatch of trains . . . It became a difficult matter to effect an entrance to, or exit from, a train; men, women and children were rudely elbowed and jostled by questionable characters, luggage and parcels trampled upon . . . The public do not fail to complain when trains are unpunctual and fail to meet at the junction, often overlooking the fact that much depends upon their co-operation in the facilitation of traffic. Moreover the company's interests have suffered considerably through the reprehensible practice of passengers travelling without tickets . . . this must be stopped.

The newspaper did not agree with the substance or tone of this reply.

At last on Monday 24th October, 1864 the Thame-Oxford extension was opened, just over 10 years since the line reached Wycombe. For all its previous interest in the line, the *Thame Gazette* carried not a word about this important local happening. Perhaps the paper thought the event was of more importance to the people of Oxford and Wheatley, than to those at Thame. From this date the following passenger service was on offer:

		\multicolumn{4}{c}{Weekdays}				\multicolumn{2}{c}{Sundays}	
		am	*am*	*pm*	*pm*	*am*	*pm*
Oxford	d.	8.35	11.40	2.15	6.15	6.20	5.55
Thame	d.	9.10	12.15	2.55	7.05	6.55	6.30
Risboro'	a.	9.23	12.27	3.10	7.20	7.09	6.45
Taplow	a.	10.10	1.25	4.15	8.30	8.12	8.00
		am	*am*	*pm*	*pm*	*am*	*pm*
Taplow	d.	-	9.10	1.35	5.40	9.32	8.50
Risboro'	d.	7.25	10.09	2.29	6.33	10.35	9.50
Thame	a.	7.38	10.22	2.45	6.45	10.48	10.03
Oxford	a.	8.15	10.55	3.30	7.25	11.25	10.40

This timetable saw the re-introduction of a fourth down train. It would seem that the 8.35 am, 2.15 pm and 6.20 am (Sundays) up were through to London, and the 9. 10 am, 1.35 pm, 5.40 pm and 9.32 am (Sundays) down all started their journeys in London. A new 11.32 am Taplow-Oxford was introduced by May 1865 making five down trains, which service continued in 1866, but the 7.25 am Risborough 'short' working was withdrawn by February 1868, reverting back to four down trains. There was also a 4.20 pm Oxford-High Wycombe in 1865-6, but this was also no longer running by February 1868.

Now that his work was done Rowland Brotherhood, the contractor, advertised an auction sale of his plant to be held at Wheatley station on 21st November. The sale included two 'narrow gauge' locomotives.

In *Wheatley Records 956-1956* the author states: 'After the railway came in 1864 the Oxford road was almost deserted except by tramps, until the internal combustion engine brought to Wheatley residents who work in Oxford and like to drive with the sun behind them'.

At its Board meeting on 22nd November, the WRC discussed possible extensions to Uxbridge and Great Marlow. From the wording of a letter from Francis Ward, Chairman, to the Chairman of the GWR dated 14th December, this does not seem to have been the WRC's idea as Mr Ward expressed great reluctance to become involved with any more extensions.

The company suffered the ultimate indignity when insufficient shareholders turned up to hold the February 1865 AGM. No report or accounts for that non-meeting have been found.

MILEAGE RATES.

To THE GREAT WESTERN RAILWAY COMPANY.

I request that *a* Truck may be ready at the *Wheatley* Station, in which I *may load 2,500 of fire Brick*.

TONS. CWT. QRS.

which I declare to be the true weight and description, to be conveyed from *Wheatley* Station to *Risboro* Station, at the Company's Reduced Mileage Rates, on the Conditions mentioned below,* for—

Mr. *Darvill* of *Risboro*

_____ Truck to be sent, in pursuance with the request contained in this "Mileage Note."

For the Great Western Railway Company.

C. Stanley Sender.

March 22 186*5*

W. Hancock Porter.

67

15-11

* Special Conditions as to "Mileage Goods."

The Company do not undertake the duties of common carriers in respect of articles conveyed under this Agreement. All such articles must be loaded and unloaded by the Owners or their Agents, any assistance voluntarily given by the Company's Servants being at the risk of the Consignor or Consignee, and the Company are not to be responsible for any risk of loading, stowage, or unloading, nor to be answerable for loss or damage, actual or consequential, nor for discrepancy in the delivery, as to either quantity, number, or weight, nor for the condition of articles so carried, nor for any consequences arising from over-carriage, detention, or delay in, or in relation to, the conveying or delivery of them, however caused.

For the General Conditions applicable to the above Goods, see the other side.

Entered by

Truck No. *4931*

The Conditions cannot be altered or dispensed with by any person whomsoever, and are applicable for the whole distance carried over the Great Western, the Bristol and Exeter, the South Devon, the South Wales Railways, and any other Railway or Conveyance in connexion therewith, or with either of them.

A combined 'Truck Order' and Consignment Note for a truckload of 2,500 bricks from Mr Stanley of Wheatley to Mr Darvill of Risborough, dated 22nd March, 1865.

Chapter Five

Financial Difficulties and the
End of Independence

The writing was by now on the wall for the WRC as an independent company. It had simply not sold enough shares to finance its construction and had to rely heavily on loans to make up the difference. The interest it had to pay on the loan debt was draining the blood out of the concern. Over the course of the next 18 months a series of legal documents passed to and fro between the WRC and the GWR, which eventually led to the transfer of the WRC to the GWR. Note 'transfer', not sale - the GWR agreed to take on the company and all its debts.

The first of these legal missives, a draft document from the WRC, dated February 1865, set out 'Proposals for Arrangement with the GWR' (the major parts much abbreviated below):

1. From 1.7.1865 existing financial arrangements to be replaced by the GWR paying a fixed rent sufficient to pay interest on the loans (excluding the debenture debt - see below) and dividends on the shares [the author estimates this rent payment as about £18,000 per annum, the amount was left blank in this draft].
2. The old debt to the GWR for which they held 925 WRC shares as security to be written off, the shares to be returned, but the dividend therefrom to be treated as part of the GWR's rent payment, thus reducing the amount the GWR actually paid.
3. From 1.7.1865 the WRC's considerable Debenture debt (£111,000) to be the responsibility of the GWR (an 1866 document showed that interest on this debt totalled £5,100 pa). The GWR would also undertake the administration of the share register and payment of interest, rent charges and dividends.

Next, in preparing the ground, the GWR (Additional Powers) Act 1865 made provision for the lease or transfer to the GWR of the Wycombe Railway Company.

Not much of railway interest was reported in the local Press in 1865, but on 30th May the *Thame Gazette* mentioned that a Mr John Tomkins, farmer of Horsendon, had been prosecuted by the railway for travelling first class from Princes Risborough to Oxford with a second class ticket. His excuse was the usual one - the second class was full - but as he refused to pay the extra fare the GWR prosecuted. Defendant was fined £2 with 12s. costs.

In June the Directors received a letter from The Hon. Revd I. Bertie (a local landowner) requesting that a station be erected at Tiddington and this matter they referred to their Engineer. The Minutes are silent on the matter after this, but the GWR's Traffic Committee recorded on 23rd May, 1866 that it would be ready for opening on 1st June, 1866.

Some minor expenditure was approved in April 1865 for a cattle pen at Thame (£14) and, in October, additional sidings at Littlemore (£35). In November 1865 rinderpest (a virulent cattle disease) reached Thame and no cattle were brought to the market for almost a year.

Most of the surviving paperwork for 1866 deals with the financial and legal work involved with transferring the company to the GWR, so before getting immersed in that it is worth looking at the daily activities of the railway as portrayed by the March 1866 Working Timetable (which is the first one the author has uncovered). This document is little more helpful than the newspaper, as it does not spell out the through trains to/from London, but it does of course include goods trains. The timetable will be viewed through the eyes of the signalman (probably then 'policeman') at Thame.

At this time the Risborough-Oxford section was not open all night but the first activity of the day at Thame was the arrival at 5.30 am of the 2 am goods from Taplow (which did not run on Mondays). This was allowed just 25 minutes to do its work at Thame, leaving at 5.55 and was due at Oxford at 7 am after calling at Wheatley and Littlemore. Apart from the ensuing activity in the goods shed, there was little to do at Thame until the arrival of the first passenger train, the 7.05 am from High Wycombe which arrived at 7.38 and left two minutes later for Oxford. Arriving in the University City at 8.15 the engine and coaches probably formed the first up train, 8.30 am from Oxford which was back at Thame from 9.06 to 9.08. This was probably a through train to London, and was 'fast' between High Wycombe and Taplow, calling only at Marlow Road.

Nothing stirred at Thame until the arrival at 10.22 of the 9.05 am from Taplow; it left for Oxford 2 minutes later arriving there at 10.55 and probably forming the 11.25 am Oxford to Taplow. This was at Thame 12.02 to 12.05. On reaching Princes Risborough at 12.21 it crossed the 11.27 am Taplow to Oxford, the only crossing movement at Risborough in that particular timetable. The latter service was at Thame from 12.42 to 12.45, when it left for Oxford.

The opportunity was doubtless taken by the station master and staff to go home for lunch as no train now called for a couple of hours. But there was a big burst of activity in the early afternoon when the 1.35 Taplow-Oxford (2.45-2.57), and 2.15 Oxford-Taplow (2.50-2.55) crossed at Thame at the times shown. This would have been a tiring (and time-consuming) business for the signalman for, as Capt. Tyler noted, the signal levers were not concentrated in one position and the signalman would have had to walk to the outlying points to operate them, and then to the signals to work them.

After this rush there was another dead period until the 4.20 pm Oxford to High Wycombe called at Thame from 4.55 to 4.57. All trains between Risborough and Oxford called at all stations (Tiddington was not yet open). Again there was another two-hour break, and time for tea, but then came a repeat of the hectic after-lunch activity with two trains crossing at Thame. The 6.15 pm Oxford to Taplow arrived first (6.49-7.05) and awaited the 5 pm through from London to Oxford (6.51-6.53). These were the last two passenger trains of the day.

Only the signalman and the goods staff would have remained on duty for the last train of the day the 7.45 pm goods from Oxford to Paddington. This was at Thame from 9.00 to 9.30. After leaving Thame it called at Penn Farm Siding, if required, at 9.40, the only weekday train to do so; this siding was at the residence of Edward Griffin, one of the Directors. After calling at all stations except Cookham and Maidenhead (Wycombe branch), the goods arrived at Taplow at 12.45 am and arrived in London at 2.50 am.

Services on Sundays were much more sparse, although spread over a longer day. The 2 am goods Taplow-Oxford, which had called at Penn Farm at 5.20 am, if required, was at Thame from 5.30 to 7 am, where it crossed the 6.20 am Oxford-Taplow (6.53-6.55), the only crossing movement of the day. The goods was probably worked by the locomotive, enginemen and guard of the previous night's 7.45 pm Oxford goods. Next came the 9.45 am Taplow-Oxford, at Thame 10.57-10.59, probably the return working of the 6.20 am from Oxford. The station would then have shut down until the evening with the 5.40 pm Oxford-Taplow at Thame 6.13 to 6.20. The timetable showed that this train conveyed cattle, explaining the extended station time (also at Risborough, 8 minutes). Finally the 8.55 pm Taplow-Oxford called at Thame 10.05-10.07. The station staff would have been booked off (without pay) in the long intervals between trains.

A circular issued by the GWR on 7th April, 1866 headed 'Conveyance of Dead Meat to London' had the following entry re the 'Thame & Wycombe branch':

Vans 2976 or 2850 will travel by the 9 pm train from Thame to Paddington and return by the 2.35 pm via Taplow to Thame; vans 2689 or 2342 will travel by the 8.10 train from Aylesbury to Princes Risborough, and thence by the 8.40 pm train from Princes Risborough to Paddington, and return by the 3 am from London. These vans will convey the meat from Thame, Wycombe and Aylesbury branches.

The 1866 AGM of shareholders was deferred from 27th February to 27th March for no given reason, but possibly to enable negotiations with the GWR to be concluded. The Secretary read the printed Report. Negotiations with the GWR to transfer the WRC to that company were continuing. The transfer would guarantee to the Thame Extension shareholders a 2½ per cent dividend, instead of an uncertain dividend dependent on what was left after paying interest and management expenses. There was no immediate benefit to the original shareholders (apart from protection from the possibility of the company going bust!) but after 1869 certain shares which would be held as security by the GWR in case of liabilities being heavier than expected would be released to these original shareholders. The report also detailed the other financial responsibilities which would be passed to the GWR, in a Heads of Agreement dated 28th March, 1866.

The accompanying accounts showed that the Thame Extension account was in the red to the extent of £31,000. Out of a total capital receipts to date of £173,856, only £77,000 had been funded by share sales, and £31,000 by rent charges and the GWR's rent payments, the remainder coming from loans (£35,000). The £31,000 deficit was presumably met from revenue and/or borrowing from the Oxford account which at present showed an excess of income over expenditure of nearly £25,000. However, this account also presented a disheartening picture: of the nearly £207,000 capital receipts only £90,750 came from sale of Preference shares, all of the remainder except £1,500 rent being loans of some sort.

The Chairman said that since the Report was printed, agreement had been reached with the GWR. The Heads of Agreement were read to the meeting (but not printed in the Minutes) and the meeting passed a resolution that the transfer of the undertaking to the GWR 'be and is hereby approved'. (The Heads of

Agreement showed that expenditure on the Wycombe Railway, up to 31st December, 1864, had been over £½ million: Wycombe branch £89,568; Thame extension £173,262; Oxford extension £173,004; and Aylesbury £70,630.* The Oxford extension had cost over £13,500 per mile, against the £10,000 per mile suggested by Mr Murray back in 1860.)

A fortnight later the Directors met and decided that their remuneration should cease after 1st March (last). The Secretary and Asst Secretary would be paid up to 1st August and the Directors expressed their appreciation of Messrs Wilson's and Theobald's service of 21 years and 7 years respectively.

On 12th June the solicitor submitted an amended Agreement with the GWR, dated 7th June and superseding the one dated 28th March read at the recent shareholders' meeting. In summary, its principal features were:

1 .   Everything belonging to the WRC would become vested in the GWR by a transfer authorised by the GWR (Additional Powers) Act 1865, on and after 31st January, 1867.

2.   The GWR, on and after 31st January, 1867, to adopt the Wycombe's debenture debt of £111,023 on which yearly interest of £5,100 was paid, the rent charges created by the WRC of £1,339 pa and all other debts and liabilities. The GWR would create and issue £334,700 GWR Rent Charge stock on which 5 per cent dividend would be paid.

3.   Subject to these Heads of Agreement being authorised by an Act of Parliament, holders of Wycombe 4½ per cent Preference shares would receive £90 new GWR Rent charge stock for every £100 of WRC stock held; Wycombe 'original' shareholders would receive £80 new for every £100 WRC; and Thame Extension shareholders £50 new for every £100 held. The remainder of the new stock would be issued to clear any other debts and liabilities (other than debenture debt or Rent charges). Any remaining surplus shares would be passed on, first to the original shareholders, then to Thame Extension shareholders in proportion to their holdings.

4.   The 925 Wycombe original shares held by the GWR as security against a debt to be kept by them. All other claims against the WRC to be withdrawn and abandoned.

5.   The GWR would pay £22,000 rent for the year to 31st July, 1866 (out of which the WRC would be expected to pay all dividends arising, interest, rent charges, etc.), and £3,820, plus all dividends arising, for the half-year to 31st January, 1867. The WRC would be expected to pay for all revenue liabilities arising up to 31st January, 1867, but any shortfall would have to be classed as a liability on the Capital Account, on transfer.

Between the 28th March and 7th June agreements, the amount of Rent Charge stock the GWR was to issue to compensate WRC shareholders, creditors, etc., had been reduced by 10 per cent (to the figure of £334,700) but the dividend payable on the stock had been increased from 4½ to 5 per cent (a liability of £16,735 per annum). There is insufficient correspondence available to say why, but there is evidence that the WRC was not happy about this. The Directors, were, of course, substantial shareholders, particularly Mr F.R. Ward, the Chairman, who also held 3,957 shares initially issued to first contractor Mr Peniston.

---

* The 2002 values of these sums are: Wycombe - £4.62 million; Thame - £8.95 million; Oxford - £8.93 million; Aylesbury - £3.65 million, or over £26 million at present day prices for the whole Wycombe Railway.

All this was incorporated in a Bill that the shareholders approved on 12th June, which as the GWR (Wycombe Railway Transfer) Act, received its Royal Assent on 23rd July, 1866; the Wycombe Railway would be transferred from 31st January, 1867. In fact the Wycombe shareholders probably did not realise how lucky they were to obtain this Agreement at all. Bankers Overend & Gurney had collapsed in May 1866, which had a very adverse effect on railway securities, and the GWR was badly affected. It was forced to suspend payment of dividends in cash for two years. A special committee of shareholders was set up to investigate how the GWR's finances could be improved. When the committee reported in August 1867, specific mention was made of the large increase in rent charge debt in the period 1860-1866 when annual payments had risen from £73,797 to £299,138 and would further increase (by obligations already incurred) to £362,656 by 1873. It may well be that a month or two later than March 1866 and the GWR would not have wished to take over the WRC at this time. Maybe this explains why the GWR reduced its compensating Rent Charge stock to WRC shareholders by 10 per cent.

On 28th June F.R. Ward wrote a lengthy letter to the Secretary of the GWR, F.G. Saunders. Once again this is the only part of the correspondence preserved so it is not possible to extract the full facts. It involved the shares initially issued to Mr Peniston, in which both parties had a financial interest, and there would appear to have been disagreement between the two companies as to how the matter should be settled. So much so that the GWR said, as late as 27th June, that it would refuse to sign the Agreement (incorporated in the Bill) between the two companies unless the Wycombe company conceded. The stumbling block appears to have been the imposition of the Supplemental Agreement dated 7th June, which as just mentioned, reduced the compensation payable by the GWR by 10 per cent from that which had been put forward in March and read at the shareholders' meeting. Whether this action was related to the outstanding debt, the GWR's sudden serious financial problems, or a combination of both unfortunately the surviving correspondence does not make clear. In view of what was at stake, the Wycombe company was forced to accept the GWR's conditions and the Agreement was sealed on 6th July.

A further, strongly-worded letter was sent to W. Stevenson, Financial Secretary at Paddington, on 27th July regarding an outstanding £8,730 owed by the GWR to the Wycombe on the Revenue Account. Mr Ward asked for £5,000 (about £239,000) at 2002 values) by 1st August and an early date for payment for the remainder 'or he would be forced to publish this correspondence' to enable shareholders and bondholders 'to see the cause of our insolvency'. So the atmosphere between the top officials at the two companies at this important time was fraught, to say the least. (The post of Financial Secretary on the GWR was abolished at the end of 1866; probably another economy forced upon the company.)

Other, less weighty matters were ongoing during this critical period for the WRC. Tiddington station appeared in the timetable for the first time on 1st June, 1866 and probably opened on that date. On 6th June, a full muster of the members of the Thame Rifle Corps went by train to Oxford for battalion drill. Finally the *Thame Gazette* reported a serious accident on 2nd November when the '7 o'clock down train was coming into the station [due to] the carelessness of [the pointsman]' it was turned into 'the siding, generally used for loading cattle, etc, and had it not been for the engine driver Denham, and the stoker, the two oldest hands on this branch, who at once perceived the mistake, the consequences might have been most serious . . .' The engine smashed into brickwork with considerable force, severely injuring the driver and shocking the passengers. The driver was attended by a local doctor, and the next day sent home to Wycombe. It would be many years before points and signals were interlocked to prevent this sort of thing from happening.

On 31st January, 1867, a final Balance Sheet was drawn up for the WRC, showing estimated Liabilities and Assets at the end of its life as a company. The chief Capital Liabilities were over £81,000 in outstanding loans, including the major one of £58,500 to the Union Bank. These would be discharged by the newly-created Rent Charge Stock.

An Indenture was issued on 1st January, 1868 to release both the GWR and the former WRC Chairman from all future claims and demands in respect of the 3,957 shares issued to Mr Peniston and now assigned to Mr Ward. The GWR had first claim on 3,407 of these, valued at £27,256 in new GWR Rent Charge stock (issued at 80 per cent of the original WRC shares' worth). The GWR claimed £20,774 of this amount and issued new shares valued at £6,482, the balance, to Mr Ward. In addition Mr Ward had 550 of Peniston's former shares entirely in his own right, valued at £4,400 in new GWR Rent Charge stock. All this stock came out of the £334,700 Rent Charge stock.

One of the fine gas lamps that graced Thame.   *J.M. Neville courtesy G.A. Carpenter*

Chapter Six

Swallowed up by the Great Western

With the demise of the company, there are no longer any Directors' minutes or reports to shareholders to help the writer or reader piece together the official side of events, over 136 years ago. As with all small local railway companies swallowed up by a much larger concern, references in future are mainly from newspapers, apart from those more important items that reached one of the Management committees, or even more rarely the Board, of the absorbing company, in this case the GWR.

In December 1866 the Wycombe Railway had drawn up an agreement with the narrow gauge Aylesbury & Buckingham Railway (A&B) that the two companies would each pay half the cost each of a new joint station at Aylesbury to accommodate the new concern. It was to run 12¾ miles through fairly empty countryside to Verney Junction on the Buckinghamshire Railway's Bletchley-Banbury line which was leased and worked by the LNWR.

In late 1867 the GWR began thinking about the problem of mixed gauge at Aylesbury when the Aylesbury & Buckingham opened and, after discussion at the GWR/LNWR Joint Committee, in February 1868 it was reported to the GWR Board that the cost of providing narrow gauge at Aylesbury, and altering the gauge from broad to narrow between Aylesbury and Princes Risborough, would be £3,000, of which the A&B would pay £500. The cost would include provision of a transfer siding and shed at Princes Risborough. The Board approved the £2,500 expenditure on 26th February, 1868.

At the 65th half-yearly meeting of GWR shareholders, held on 5th March, 1868, item 20 of the Report read as follows:

> In contemplation of the alteration of the gauge on the Wycombe Railway, as soon as circumstances will permit, an arrangement has been made with the Aylesbury & Buckingham Company - who under an agreement with the Wycombe Company are joint owners of the Aylesbury Station - to convert the broad gauge line in that station, and between Aylesbury and Princes Risborough, to narrow gauge instead of incurring the expense of temporarily mixing the gauge in Aylesbury Station. The cost to be defrayed by this Company . . . is estimated at £2,500, the Aylesbury Company finding £500.

An Agreement was made, dated 1st April, 1868, between the GWR and the Aylesbury & Buckingham Railway which, *inter alia*, provided for the GWR to work the latter. The GWR would provide a tank engine, five carriages and one break [sic] van 'for service between Princes Risborough and Verney Junction only', as well as engineman, stoker and guard. At least three trains each way would be run daily, except Sundays, and the trains would be 'mixed' (passenger and goods) if possible. The Agreement called upon the GWR to narrow the line by 1st May, 1868 (but this was not done and in any case the Aylesbury company was not ready to open until September). The Agreement was to remain in force for three years but was 'determinable by either Company in the event of the line between Princes Risborough and Maidenhead Junction being altered to narrow gauge in the meantime'. The *Thame Gazette* for 7th April reported that men had been employed 'since last Friday' in removing earth at Princes Risborough in preparations for the alterations there.

An inspecting officer from the Board of Trade went over the line on 18th May on a preliminary visit. His report said that all connection with the broad gauge at Princes Risborough would be abolished, and a new run-round loop would be necessary there with appropriate locking for the Aylesbury branch engine to run-round. A second platform would be required at Aylesbury which would be a crossing place. Turntables would be required at Princes Risborough and Verney Junction.

On 17th August the *Thame Gazette* reported that on the previous Tuesday, in consequence of the engine on the Oxford-bound train breaking down at Princes Risborough, the Aylesbury engine had been used in its place and passengers from Aylesbury had to be conveyed to their destination by omnibus. This would not be possible for much longer, once the two lines were of different track gauge.

On 5th September the *Bucks Advertiser & Aylesbury News* said that some of the carriages for the service to Verney Jn had arrived and that a temporary platform had been built at Aylesbury, for use until the station had been altered to narrow [standard] gauge. The first train on the Aylesbury & Buckingham Railway ran on 23rd September, using the temporary platform at Aylesbury.

The GWR branch from Princes Risborough to Aylesbury was shut from 5 am Wednesday 14th October, 1868 for the purpose of converting the line to standard gauge and the train service replaced by horse omnibuses. On 23rd October Captain Tyler of the Board of Trade inspected the works which he found had been hurriedly performed. He wanted the platform at Princes Risborough lengthened and the signal cabin moved further away from the station building and covered. Further work was also required at Aylesbury in order to accommodate better the intended service of seven trains to and from Princes Risborough and three or four to/from Verney Jn. However, he concluded his report that as the line had been opened for some years, 'it is not competent for me to recommend the Board of Trade to postpone its use for traffic pending completion of the above requirements . . .' and resigned himself to his comments merely being passed forward, hopefully for action. Rail traffic recommenced the following day. The Aylesbury branch was now disconnected from the remainder of the GWR system for almost two years. The GWR continued to work the Aylesbury & Buckingham Railway until 31st March, 1894, when the Metropolitan Railway took over.

The GWR Board discussed the cost of narrowing the Wycombe Railway between Maidenhead and Kennington Junction on 19th November, 1868. The cost of £10,983 was acceptable and would be carried out as soon as possible, subject to the approval of the shareholders. The estimates also included the costs of narrowing the Abingdon branch, a new goods station at Oxford and discontinuing the broad gauge between Didcot and Oxford (total including the Wycombe narrowing £17,581) and if all this work were done, it was only £1,341 more expensive than preserving the broad gauge at Oxford, once the value of recovered materials between Didcot and Oxford etc., and additional works necessary at Oxford for transfer between narrow (the Wycombe line) and broad were taken into account.

Having been very busy with removal of broad gauge rail, or providing mixed gauge, elsewhere on the system, the Wycombe proposition was not put to the shareholders until the 69th AGM held on 11th March, 1870, now at a cost of £12,000. Approval was given. (At a Board meeting on 3rd August, the Directors refined the cost to £10,389.)

On Tuesday 8th March, 1870 the Prince of Wales paid a flying visit to Thame to hunt with the South Oxfordshire Hounds. Arriving at Thame at 11.50 am by special train he retired to the waiting room to don his hunting clothes. After a full day's hunting (no fox was caught) the Prince left Thame, again by special train, at 5 pm. On the 1st June an elderly lady, rather deaf, was knocked down and killed at Mead Lane accommodation crossing near Wheatley by a train coming from the Thame direction at about 10.30 am, the driver being William Denham. The coroner's verdict was 'accidental death', but expressed the opinion that engine drivers ought to sound the whistle at this crossing. Another woman had been killed here in similar circumstances at haymaking time the previous year. The railway promised to give due attention to this recommendation.

The *Oxford Journal* for 3rd September carried a very full report of the narrowing of the gauge of the Wycombe Railway which took place between 22nd and 29th August - less time than the section between Princes Risborough and Aylesbury despite being over four times the distance.The *Oxford Journal* states the line was reopened on Monday 29th August, but MacDermot in his *History of the GWR* says Thursday 1st September. MacDermot may have got this date from the Report to the 70th meeting of shareholders, where, in a report dated 16th August, W.G. Owen, the Chief Engineer, said '(work) is expected to be finished by the 1st September'. However, a circular in RAIL253 228 at Kew agrees with the paper (report follows), it was the 29th August:

Conversion of the Oxford, Thame, and Wycombe Branch into Narrow Gauge

The Great Western Railway Company are gradually introducing the narrow gauge on their line, a step which has been rendered necessary by circumstance, and for some time past the work of conversion has been going on in various localities. These conversions have been carried out with the utmost rapidity consistent with safety and durability, so that the general traffic has been only slightly impeded.

The latest alteration in this respect has been made in our own neighbourhood. This was the alteration of the gauge between Oxford and Taplow - on that portion of the line which runs through the beautiful vale of Buckingham, by way of Thame, Risborough, and Wycombe to Taplow. For this purpose the line was closed, in sections, from Tuesday the 23rd of August until Sunday night last. The work was divided into three parts. Between Oxford and Thame Tuesday the 23rd was set apart for the conversion; Thursday and Friday were devoted to the line between Thame and Wycombe; and from the latter place to the junction with the main line at Taplow the work was finished on Saturday last. Meanwhile the ordinary traffic was as little interfered with as possible, but passengers were not booked through beyond the stations to which the trains ran on the respective days. To meet ordinary requirements, however, coaches plied in the district at moderate fares, the route of the line being adhered to as closely as possible, whilst as each section was completed the line was opened for ordinary traffic. Special arrangements were made for the carriage of goods.

To carry out this vast work as quickly as possible, the resources of the Company were taxed to the utmost, and the whole of the narrow gauge system was completed up to Taplow, and a heavily laden train was over the line, on Saturday afternoon last. This comprises a distance of 40 miles, and the work was completed in five days. The manual labour employed consisted of over 300 of the pick of the Company's platelayers and packers - stout brawny armed fellows, who being promised good pay worked as only an English workman knows how to work. The whole of these men were drafted from various parts of the Oxford division of the Great Western system. Discipline was observed as closely as in an army. The workmen were divided into fourteen gangs of one and twenty each. Over these a ganger had a kind of subordinate rule. A mile of line was then given to each gang; and to every two gangs an inspector was appointed. That no time might be lost none were allowed to leave the line night or day, so that it became necessary for the men to live a kind of gipsy life in the cloughs and sheltered hollows which border the permanent way. By the aid of tarpaulins and a few stakes, with an *ad libitum* supply of straw, a number of sheds or tents were quickly run up at intervals, and in these temporary huts the labourers snatched what few hours were afforded them for sleep. The culinary arrangements of the gangs were as primitive as their housing, but a plentiful supply of food was provided. The first night of the bivouac must have sorely tried the patience of all before commencing operations; the heaviest rain that has been experienced for some time fell continuously and all but drenched every soul to the skin. The black clouds at last, however cleared off, and a few hours' repose was allowed, and at day-break on Tuesday morning fourteen gangs set to work with the same number of miles of line simultaneously. Of course only one line of the rails needed moving, and as each man knew his own department, not the least confusion occurred in relaying the heavy longitudinal sleepers, bolting the holdfasts, screwing up the Transoms, and packing up the line. By ten o'clock on Wednesday morning the line was sufficiently advanced in this, the first section, for a narrow gauge engine to be driven over it, and in three hours later a 'pick-up' train of seven third-class carriages and half a dozen trucks left Oxford for Thame, the 'pick-up' train taking with it the several gangs employed on the work, with their impedimenta, on to the latter town. The men were then transferred to a broad gauge train, and distributed over the second section of the line between Thame and Wycombe, and at day-break on Thursday morning the work began here. This portion was completed on the following day, in an equally satisfactory manner, and a change of quarters followed on the Friday to the section between Wycombe and Maidenhead. It now became apparent that extra-ordinary efforts would have to be put forth to complete the conversion in the allotted time; but as there was no moon, the labourers could not do much during the night. At eleven o'clock on Friday night, before the men began their work, a goods train of broad gauge trucks passed over this section of the line on to Maidenhead, and at half past twelve on Saturday morning, the change of line was commenced. At twelve o'clock at noon the line was converted, so that a special engine ran over it. The return journey was made to Wycombe on the special engine, in order that the workmen might be collected and carried thence to Boyne Hill, to receive their well merited pay. The return journey was accomplished with every satisfaction, and a long train of carriages and trucks being taken on at Wycombe, the gangs along the line, with their tools, were picked up and conveyed to Boyne Hill Station. Here a general halt was made, in order that the men might be paid. This was accomplished in the easiest manner, each inspector having his pay sheet ready, and the cash handy, so that only a quarter of an hour was consumed in paying the whole of the three hundred labourers. No time was lost as the train was again in motion to reach the main line at Taplow, and thence the journey to Oxford was accomplished easily, with only sufficient stoppage to set down the workmen at those stations which were nearest their homes, or on the route thereto.

On Monday morning the line was opened for the ordinary traffic on the narrow gauge system, so that in the short period of five days the whole length of line from Oxford to Taplow had been altered, at no very great expenditure. The Company's officers had been indefatigable in their exertions to carry out the work punctually and with credit, and have succeeded admirably. Mr Owen, the engineer in chief of the Railway, was ably assisted in the execution of the work by the district engineers of the Oxford division, under whose personal supervision the work was carried out, and to whom great credit is due for the excellent arrangements which they had made, as well for the manner in which the line has been so promptly and successfully converted.

A word of praise is due also to the workmen. The success of the work was not marred by a single accident; all behaved very well, and not a single case of misconduct occurred during the whole five days' heavy work.

The line itself - originally, we believe, constructed by an independent company, and afterwards amalgamated with the Great Western system - passes through a most beautiful country, pretty villages and hamlets dotting the scenery here and there, whilst the seats of the country gentry give a charm to the whole which can hardly be surpassed.

Not long after the narrowing the siding accommodation at Thame was extended after expenditure of £189 4s. (approved by the Board on 19th October, 1870). In 1871 the GWR improved the awkward and narrow approach to Wheatley station, where the milk carts had caused a number of accidents, after the Local Board provided the necessary land.

By a circular dated 8th December, 1871, the Secretary of the GWR notified the original shareholders of the Wycombe Railway that it was now possible to pay them the final portion of the settlement made when the GWR acquired the company in 1866. It had been a long process, but the GWR was now satisfied that it had uncovered all the liabilities of the WRC and could pay the original shareholders a further 15s. in GWR Rent charge stock in respect of each £5 of such stock already issued to them. There was no money left for the Thame extension shareholders, however.

The work of removing the broad gauge at Oxford, previously mentioned, was authorised by the Board in January 1872. For the large sum of £17,623 the broad gauge station and rails would be removed, and the narrow gauge station enlarged. As soon as this was completed the broad gauge rails between Didcot and Oxford would also be removed. At the next Board a footpath was authorised along the approach road at Thame (£41) and additional siding accommodation and a cart road would be provided at Tiddington (£189 5s.). This probably enabled Tiddington to deal with goods for the first time as there were only three sidings there and we know the (later) dates of opening of the other two. In April the *Thame Gazette* noted that Messrs Howland & Son were pressing the GWR for more goods accommodation at Thame - 'the place is wretchedly deficient in accommodation' - and the latter had promised improvements 'in a short time'.

The Board minutes of 21st March, 1872 recorded that a draft agreement with the (narrow gauge) Watlington & Princes Risborough Railway (which had received Royal Assent on 26th July, 1869) had been submitted by which the GWR would lay an additional line, alongside the Oxford branch, from the point of convergence to Princes Risborough station, a distance of more than ¾ mile. This would replace the intended junction where the Watlington line converged with the Oxford branch; the cost would be £2,500 of which the Watlington company would pay £1,352. The GWR Board approved the draft agreement. A further £1,061 was authorised on 6th June for the necessary platform and sidings at Princes Risborough. The Watlington company opened for business on 15th August, 1872, worked by the Great Western.

On Sunday 17th November, 1872, the last Sunday train, 8.50 pm from Taplow, due at Oxford at 10.40 pm, was derailed at Kennington Junction. When coming off the single line one portion of the train took the wrong line, throwing the rest of the train off the rails. The Board minutes note that there was no evidence as to the cause of the accident.

The work of removing the broad gauge rails between Didcot and Oxford took place in the autumn and winter of 1872. At the shareholders' meeting held on 28th February, 1873 no less than £41,000 was authorised to be spent on locking signals and points and introducing the block telegraph. Of this amount nearly £800 was approved by the Board (on 30th April) to be spent locking points and signals at the south end of Oxford station - the locking of centre and north ends featured in a separate vote of £2,416 authorised by the Board in January 1874. The Government's Regulation Act of 1873 required railway companies to submit annual returns showing the length of line worked on the block system which encouraged the companies to add this equipment, no doubt faster than would have been the case without the legislation. In 1873 only 48.9 per cent of the total mileage in England and Wales (all companies) was worked on the Absolute Block System - by 1880 the figure was 80.8 per cent. A new goods station and extensive sidings opened at Oxford on 1st November, 1873, a further product of the changeover from broad to narrow gauge. A few days earlier the Board had authorised £125 to be spent on new office accommodation at Princes Risborough.

The *Thame Gazette* for 18th March, 1873 noted that:

> . . . the GWR have decided to raise considerably, and at once, all their rates for general merchandise into our town. A corresponding increase in the mileage traffic, mails, etc. came into operation last month.

The basic facilities initially provided by the WRC were slowly being improved. On 20th May, 1874, £166 was authorised to be spent on increased siding accommodation at Littlemore. Nine months later, on 3rd February, 1875 the Board agreed £184 for a crossover at Thame (no details are given).

The *Thame Gazette* had an interesting report late on in 1874. On 3rd November it reported a presentation to the 'Superintendent of Thame Station for the last seven years' - Mr J. Owen Morris. His friends and colleagues had collected £47 10s. out of which they had purchased a gold watch and chain (made by J. Cheney, watchmaker of Thame) suitably inscribed, the balance of £13 14s. being passed to him in cash together with a scroll listing the subscribers. Although a lengthy report it does not include any remarks from Mr Morris, nor does it actually state that he is leaving Thame. A Mr Nicholl is mentioned as being the station master at Princes Risborough.

The next year, 1875, featured several minor accidents on the line, although it is usually a matter of luck that such reports are preserved (or found) and this year may not be quite typical for the 19th century. On 3rd January a passenger train ran into a landslip in a cutting near Littlemore and the engine was slightly damaged. On 27th January the engine of a passenger train broke down at Wheatley after the spokes in a driving wheel broke, for no apparent reason. Just three days later there was another landslip, this time at Wheatley, following heavy rain; about 30 yards long it was spotted before any train ran into it.

Wheatley again was the location of an accident on 15th November when some empty coaches which were scotched and standing on the main line moved, due to the scotch slipping, ran down the incline and collided with a goods engine which was just running into the station. The driver and fireman were slightly injured, the engine and four coaches were damaged. Finally on 19th November a goods train ran through the level crossing gate at Bledlow, breaking it.

A more serious accident, details of which reached the Board of Directors, occurred on 5th October. The 5 am goods train from Taplow to Oxford left Wycombe for Risborough still carrying the wooden train staff from Bourne End. For this irregularity the superintendent of the line, Mr Tyrrell, dismissed the policeman on duty at Wycombe, Frederick Prior, and the guard of the train (George Gwillim). The driver (Isaac Dicks), however, who fell to be disciplined by the locomotive superintendent, Mr Armstrong, was only fined £2.

On 3rd November, the Directors heard the appeal of guard Gwillim against his dismissal. Having heard the facts, the Directors thought that the driver should have been sacked and Dicks was called before the Board and dismissed. Guard Gwillim's appeal was rejected and his dismissal confirmed. Did driver Dicks get his £2 back?

A report on this incident found its way into the *Thame Gazette* for 12th October. The paper says:

> . . . It was at once seen that no train could be sent on to Wycombe with the wrong staff, and the quickest way in which the emergency could be met was to send on a trolly [*sic*] with a horse to make the exchange. When this was done traffic was resumed, and impatient passengers went safely on their way. Although the failure at Wycombe seems to involve blame somewhere, yet it is satisfactory to find that the first blunder produced a total standstill in the arrangements of the line, instead of being, as is too often the case, followed up by a series of mistakes calamitous in their results.

The onward march of block working and the locking of points and signals continued when the Board, on 1st July, 1875, authorised expenditure of £624 on block telegraph and £608 on locking from Didcot to Oxford, which included 'bell communication through Oxford station yard'.

There seems to have been little to report in 1876. On Saturday 1st April, William Denham, a long-service driver, formerly of Thame (*see Chapter Five*), now working at Oxford, was oiling his engine at Oxford when some trucks were pushed into it. He was struck in the side by a buffer but fortunately his injuries were slight and he recovered at the Radcliffe Infirmary. On Friday 6th October, a Mr Wootton was detraining from a down train at Princes Risborough

(1647)

Great Western Railway LOCOMOTIVE DEPARTMENT.

Engineman's Report 5.0 a.m. 9 Goods Train,

From Taplow Saturday day, the 2nd day of February 1878,

Engineman A Jackson No. 1020 Engine, reports

Delayed at Thame 20 min putting off 12. Wagons.
No water. "This was caused by the Traffic Dept allowing the
Water to run away at the Water Clost, Valve left open."

Foreman's Signature C Houghton

07680

W. Dean Esq
Swindon.

Operating difficulties at Thame caused by water shortage, 2nd February, 1878.

when 'he suddenly staggered over the platform on the Aylesbury side and falling backwards his head came violently upon the rails'. A fortnight later the local paper reported that Mr Wootton was making a slow recovery, although severely injured.

In March 1877 there was quite a lengthy report in the *Thame Gazette* regarding a Cuddington cattle dealer who had loaded 39 sheep at Thame in a vehicle 17 ft long by 7 ft wide, giving each sheep just 3 square feet of space. On arrival at Southall three were dead and most were unable to walk, all being exhausted from trampling on one another. The dealer was prosecuted by the Society for the Prevention of Cruelty to Animals, found guilty and fined £10 with costs. The chairman of the magistrates said that the GWR should be made aware of the circumstances and that proper regulations re carriage of animals should be made.

Following an application from the men who pumped the water at Thame for more money, William Dean at Swindon wrote to the General Manager on Christmas Eve 1877 pointing out that it would be far better if cattle trucks were washed out at Oxford, where water was readily available. He added that if an engine arrived at Thame needing water 'when the supply may be short' because it had been used on the cattle trucks, delays on the single line would be inevitable. The General Manager's office replied on 11th January saying that Mr Allen of the Wagon Office had been instructed to use Oxford 'as far as possible' in future, and the station master at Thame told to use no more water than absolutely necessary on the occasions when he did have to clean out trucks.

Water featured again a few weeks later on 2nd February, 1878, when driver A. Jackson of engine No. 1020, on the 5 am Taplow goods, reported a delay of 20 minutes at Thame -'no water'. Another hand has added to his report: 'This was caused by the Traffic Department allowing the water to run away at the water closet. Valve left open'. Of course such matters had to be fully investigated, and on 15th February the General Manager's office wrote to Mr Dean saying that the water ran away down the Ladies WC, and blaming a passenger by the evening train 'leaving the plug up'. In future staff would be expected to visit the WC regularly to check it was in proper order.

Unlike the preceding two years 1878 was eventful for the Thame branch. On 9th March a John Griffin, labourer of Attington, was summoned for riding in a goods train between Princes Risborough and Thame on the night of 26th January. He was fined 10s. plus 20s. costs, or 14 days in jail if he failed to pay - a bit hard as he had tried to pay the fare at both Risborough and Thame. In May a three-year-old child, one of five young children helping their father grass cutting at Spring Lane level crossing, ¾ mile east of Littlemore, was run down and killed by the 2.57 pm Princes Risborough to Oxford.

An alleged robbery of a stonemason from the West Indies, which occurred on the 11 am Paddington to Oxford on 15th May, occupied much space in the *Thame Gazette* for three consecutive weeks. Joseph Stanley, aged 23, had become an apprentice stonemason at the age of 10 and in the intervening 13 years had worked on government works in Trinidad. Now he had sailed for England, intent on becoming a skilled mason, in order to pursue a three year study of architecture at Oxford University. With him he carried his life savings in cash

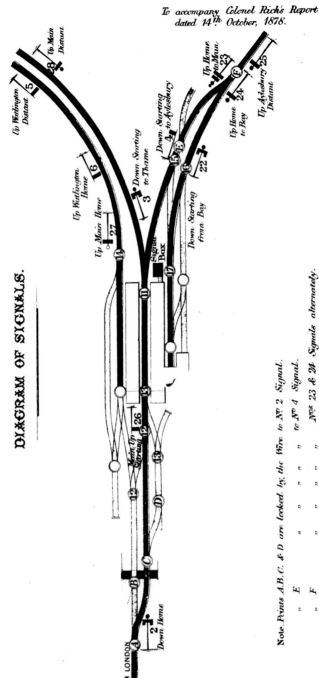

PRINCES RISBOROUGH.

DIAGRAM OF SIGNALS.

To accompany Colonel Rich's Report
dated 14th October, 1878.

Note. Points A.B.C. & D are locked by the Wire to Nº 2 Signal.

" E " " " " to Nº 4 Signal.

" F " " " " Nºˢ 23 & 24 Signals alternately.

The layout at Princes Risborough in 1878. There is a level crossing adjacent to the catch point at 'B' so it would not have been very convenient if the line between points 'A' and 12 was used as a loop.

and notes of various currencies totalling £180, and a gold watch and chain worth £25. The bag containing the money was on the luggage rack, his remaining luggage under the seat.

At Prince Risborough there was only one other passenger in the compartment, and Mr Stanley got out to use the toilet, but on return the train was already on the move. He immediately approached the station master and asked him to telegraph the next station for the money to be secured but 'the telegraph boy failed to send the message'. One can only imagine the agitation of poor Mr Stanley, in a foreign land, with all his life savings disappearing into the distance. He was forced to wait here for two hours for the next train, when, accompanied by an inspector, enquiries were made at stations to Oxford, without success, although his other luggage (not the bag) was found in the train at Oxford. A man had been seen to change carriages at Bledlow from the 11 am Paddington, but had not been challenged as there had been no reason to do so.

The 11th June edition of the paper carried a report of the arrest of a commercial traveller from Birmingham who was charged with the robbery, on the evidence of the wife of a shopkeeper from Thame who said she saw the bag involved, labelled with Mr Stanley's name, in the traveller's possession the following day. However, at the trial a barmaid in Abingdon gave evidence that the traveller was in her hotel in Abingdon at 11.20 on the morning of the robbery and so could not have been on the 11 am Paddington train. With several other people supporting his alibi, the charge was dismissed and poor Mr Stanley was left destitute. A public appeal was made on his behalf by an Oxford charity.

On 15th July there was another of those lengthy (in both senses of the word) excursions, this time from Littlemore to the Crystal Palace in connection with a Band of Hope fete. No departure time was quoted but as arrival at destination was 'comparatively early in the morning' it must have been in the wee small hours. Apparently not many got on at Thame as it was market day, but large numbers got in the 'about 20' carriages at nearly all the stations to Taplow. The programme at the Palace was 'ample varied and interesting, the most prominent features being the two monster concerts, being altogether close upon 10,000 singers'. Not one intoxicated individual was to be seen, although some 60,542 had passed through the turnstiles. Departure time was soon after 9 pm with arrival at Thame at 1.15 am.

On 30th August there was a serious accident at Princes Risborough. Colonel Rich's report produced a useful signalling plan of the layout which is reproduced opposite. The report itself revealed how woefully inadequate the layout was and how long the hours of the staff were, although no comment was made on either of these aspects. The points marked with letters on the plan were worked from the ground, not from the signal cabin.

The night signalman, Winch, came on duty at 8 pm to work until 9 the next morning. He took over the box while the day signalman, Holloway, who had been on since 9 am went outside, basically to work as a ground signalman and shunter. His first job was to put the 5.50 pm Taplow goods on the Chinnor branch, through points 'A' to allow the 6.15 pm Oxford goods to arrive, which it did, on time, at 8.25 pm. The engine of the Oxford goods picked up one truck through points 'C' (which Holloway operated) and then the whole train set back onto the Oxford line, clear of points 11. In the meantime the Aylesbury goods had arrived and that engine was detached and placed in the branch bay siding. Holloway then brought the Oxford engine back onto the Aylesbury line, picked up the goods traffic for London and placed it on the Oxford train. Holloway then returned with the Oxford engine, unlocked points 'E' and placed eight trucks in that siding, after which the Oxford engine returned to its train. Holloway then had to unlock points 'F' to get the Aylesbury engine out, and the latter returned to Aylesbury with its brake van.

After locking points 'F' Holloway returned to the box but forgot to reverse points 'E' and lock them. He returned the keys to their usual place, spoke to Winch and left duty at 9.09 pm. Winch claimed that he asked Holloway if the points had been left set correctly but Holloway could not remember this conversation.

The 7.25 pm from Paddington to Aylesbury arrived at 9.50 pm, five minutes late. Winch pulled off signal 4 and the 5-coach train, hauled by a tank engine, left at 9.55 pm. On reaching points 'E' the train was diverted into the siding, where the engine struck the goods wagons and was thrown off the line and down a low embankment failing on its side in a field, followed by the leading coach. The remainder of the train remained on the line although the second coach was derailed. Driver Collier was trapped under the engine and had to be dug out. Seven passengers and the guard were injured.

Subsequent investigation revealed that the fairly crude interlocking between the signal (No.4) and the points was defective, so that the signal could be lowered even when the points were wrongly set. Col Rich recommended that all points and signals should be locked from raised cabins, interlocked with each other, and that all facing points should be secured with locking bolts and bars. Signalman Holloway, who had only been a signalman for a month, was sacked by the GWR and Winch, who had been there 18 months, decided to leave of his own accord. Doubtless the Directors did not worry over-much that perhaps the layout was as much to blame?

The *Thame Gazette* of 17th September reported that one of the passengers injured, a Mr West, was still confined to his bed complaining of internal injury, and was showing no improvement. Driver Collier also was making slow progress towards recovery.

A week later the *Gazette* was reporting another similar accident at Risborough, which does not seem to have reached the eyes and ears of the BoT. It was again at night, on 18th September, and though no train times are mentioned, they are probably the same two as mentioned above. The down goods being late, the up goods from Oxford arrived first and was shunted onto the Aylesbury branch for the down train to pass. It appears that points 'F' had been left in the wrong position and when the Oxford train attempted to return to the main line, some of the vehicles took the direction of the bay line, causing much damage to the track and the trucks. It took until noon the next day to clear things up. Very observantly, for this was a month before Col Rich's report was published, the paper said:

Behind all this there is of course something wrong for, at a station such as Risborough, where there is much shunting and crossing of the several lines, a proper system of interlocking points and signals should prevent such accidents.

One wonders if this second accident finished signalman Winch or if two entirely new players were involved.

The *Gazette* of 15th October reported that Col Rich's inquiry (into the first accident) had been held at Risborough station on Friday 11th October (his report was dated 14th October) and that Mr Field, another passenger who had been injured, gave evidence to Col Rich that similar occurrences of points wrongly set at Risborough had happened on at least three occasions recently. Guard Lansdowne, the guard on 30th August, could corroborate one of these dates. Mr Field complained that the line was badly managed. None of this appeared in Rich's report.

The outcome to all this was that on 19th March, 1879, the Board agreed to spend £300 on locking the points at Princes Risborough.

Local papers are one of the best sources of information of how railways were regarded at the time and this extract from the *Thame Gazette* of 18th November, 1879, gives a good impression of what the travelling public thought of their train services on the Thame branch:

For some few weeks past a lively correspondence on the insufficient passenger accommodation afforded by the Thame and Wycombe Branch railway has been going on in one of the Oxford papers. It is high time we venture to assert, the matter was taken up; and as regards our own town we should think no other place of equal size and importance within a radius of 30 miles of the Metropolis has such wretched accommodation in this respect. We quite agree with Mr Taunt that 'The Great Western Railway Directors', whom he considers are about the best examples of Dickens' 'circumlocution office' that he knows, 'will require a lot of pushing before they will adopt even a little alteration for the benefit of their travellers, and the only way is to keep agitating till the reform'. Mr Taunt (who is the well-known photographer of Oxford and Wycombe), adds: 'It may be interesting to them (i.e. the Directors) to know that I can, with a dry road, bicycle home from Wycombe and reach it in less time than I can walk to their station and do the journey by train, so slow are the trains on this branch, and if I lived at Littlemore or Wheatley I should rather save time with a tricycle or bicycle than be put to the inconvenience of waiting for their slow trains'. 'Experience', writing in the same journal, clearly demonstrates the disadvantages and inconvenience Thame passengers are subject to. He says: - 'From Princes Risborough to Maidenhead the accommodation can scarcely be complained of, yet a stranger would scarcely credit that passengers from Thame have to wait until 9.13 am before they can proceed to London. But the down train service is still worse. The last train to Thame leaves Paddington at 4.50, and then even third class tickets are not issued'. 'Experience' adds: 'I would suggest that the Company be memorialised to run an early train down and up, and also to continue the train, timed to arrive at Risborough at 9.50 pm on to Oxford. I quite agree with "Expedient" that it would be an immense accommodation if the last up train started a little later. I feel certain that the Company would be not only conferring a boon on the public, but increasing their profits, by revising the train service on the Wycombe Branch.' It may seem almost incredible, but it is nevertheless a fact, that a traveller from Thame obtains but very little more advantage (if any at all) now than he did when the Royal Mail Coach took passengers to Aylesbury Station for London per London and North Western Railway, before the Thame Branch was in existence.

The paper also, on 23rd December, carried an intriguing report which the author is unable to expand upon:

Princes Risborough - we understand that a sum of £6 6s. 0d. has been collected by some gentlemen in the neighbourhood, and presented to John Creech the driver of the engine which recently ran into the station, in recognition of the courage exhibited by him in remaining on his engine at considerable personal risk on the occasion.

On 24th February, 1880 the 6.15 pm up goods from Oxford was very heavy, consisting of 32 wagons laden with coal, timber and cattle apart from miscellaneous goods. It left Risborough hauled by two engines but approaching High Wycombe the train divided and the rear portion struck the front portion with great force causing three trucks conveying large trees to be derailed and overturned, along with two trucks of coal, and substantial track damage occurred. This happened about 9.30 pm, the local staff cleared what they could straightaway, the Paddington and Oxford breakdown gangs arrived at 12.30 am and despite what the paper describes as 'a mangled heap of timber, coal and trucks [under the Amersham Hill bridge], forming a complete barrier to traffic' and the primitive nature of the equipment to clear the line, in fact traffic resumed at 3.15 am, an expeditious clearance which I doubt we could match today!

Eighteen-eighty seems to have been a busy year for the all-day excursions, with adverts for five found in the local paper. On Saturday 10th July there was one to an exhibition of printing machinery in the Agricultural Hall, London; this left Oxford at 6.20 am calling at all stations to Maidenhead (dept 8.40). A few days later on 13th July there was a Temperance Fete at the Crystal Palace which started from Littlemore at 5.25 am and called at all stations to Taplow (dept. 7.35). The Foresters' Fete at the same location on Tuesday 17th August meant leaving Oxford at 5.15 am and again calling at all stations to Taplow (7.35 am). On Monday 13th September, an excursion to Brighton with 8½ hours at the seaside (and the chance to see Sussex playing cricket against the Australians) again meant the customary 5.15 am from Oxford, which called at all stations to Maidenhead. Finally on Thursday 9th December there was an excursion to London for the Smithfield Show, leaving Oxford at 7.25 am, all stations to Taplow then Slough (dept 9.45 am).

The following year, 1881, was the year of 'the great gale' and snowstorm, which struck on 18th January. A Thame postman recalls that the snow was up to his neck. The editor of the *Thame Gazette* waxed quite lyrical in his description of the event, a description of which Charles Dickens would not have been ashamed:

Unquestionably the great gale and snow-storm of Tuesday would have done no discredit to the wildest regions where the Grampians rear their towering heads. It was novelty, a wonder, an almost panic stricken surprise even to the oldest inhabitant to see people half-blinded and rendered breathless on the roads and streets by the furious swirls of snow-laden wind, which raised piles and ridges of drift in many places four and five feet deep. In exposed places, where the circular gale, which seemed to blow from all points of the compass, swept with greatest force, the mounds of snow were still deeper, and looked like solid marble battlements. The snow did not fall in large flakes.

It was pulverised as well as driven about by the hurricane, and it penetrated everywhere. It got into the eyes, ears, mouth, and nostrils of struggling wayfarers. It invaded houses at doors and windows, though all were closed. It found an entrance by every chink and was not to be denied admittance, though an unwelcome guest. Not many hours elapsed from the time the snow first began to whistle through the air and whiten the ground before traffic became almost completely paralysed. In London tramway cars had to leave the rails early; omnibuses in general were also withdrawn, though some struggled bravely with additional teams of horses to help; the steamboats had to cease plying on the river on account of the fierceness of the guest and the danger of coming in collision with ice-flows; while both in the metropolis and the country even railway-trains, though provided with extra steam power, were in many instances brought to a dead halt. The train blocks in the north of Scotland, which they had lately been reading about in the newspapers, came unexpectedly and all too unpleasantly within the personal experience of Southerners, quite close to their own doors. The mishaps, misadventures, and miseries encountered and endured in getting home on the eventful night of the 18th would fill many of the invisible tomes of unwritten romance. Like Napoleon when he ordered a general onset to break the centre of the enemy's line, the January weather made an attack in force and surprised men by the suddenness with which it could paralyse all the mechanical appliances of advanced civilisation. Even telegraphic communication was completely interrupted, and there were no trains that could bring the next morning's London newspapers to the provinces. Surely it was an ill wind that did not blow the newspapers any good. But, after all is said, it affords food for sober reflection that the primeval forces of Nature can still assert their supremacy and paralyse, for one day at least, the traffic moving energies of the most opulent and most powerful nation in the world.

The Oxford branch was blocked by an extensive snow drift between Horspath cutting and Wheatley from Wednesday 19th January until the Saturday morning. A few weeks later the paper reported that the weather had cost the GWR almost £56,000 in loss of receipts. Sixty-four trains had to be dug out and 141 blocks occurred throughout the system.

Until 1881 mail was only dispatched from Thame at night but from 28th February a new daytime dispatch started, leaving Thame by the 11.55 am up train.

At the beginning of December there was a 'dastardly outrage on the railway at Thame' when the up Sunday morning train on 4th December ran into a chopping block and a gate post which had been put on the line at Cuttlebrook. Fortunately the engine's life guard pushed them aside. It was hoped the perpetrator would be speedily brought to justice.

Water, or the lack of it, was again a problem at Thame on 9th December. The driver of the 5 am Taplow goods, J. Cook, with engine No. 951 reported that because of his inability to take water at Thame, he had to refuse wagons at Tiddington, Wheatley and Littlemore and had had to stable the whole train 'excepting the coach' at Wheatley. Here they had to carry about 100 bucketfuls of water to the engine to enable them to get to Oxford. Station master Carter at Thame wired his apologies to the local superintendent's representative at Oxford the next day - the contractor's men had pumped insufficient water the previous evening.

This correspondence caused the Loco Department to claim that, in any case, the water tank at Thame was almost past repair and Mr Dean at Swindon was

(1647) Great Western Railway. LOCOMOTIVE DEPARTMENT.

Engineman's Report 5·0 A͘m. Goods Train.

From Taplow, Fri day, the 9ᵗʰ day of Decᵣ 1881.

Engineman S. Cook No. 951 Engine, reports

No water at Thame, had to refuse wagons at Tiddington
Wheatley & Littlemore. We put off all the steam excepting
the coach at Wheatley, had to carry about 100 bucketfuls of
water to enable us to get home.

S. Cooke

Wᵐ Garlick

Foreman's Signature

Mr. Jno. Armstrong
Swindon.

No water at Thame again! A driver's report, 9th December, 1881.

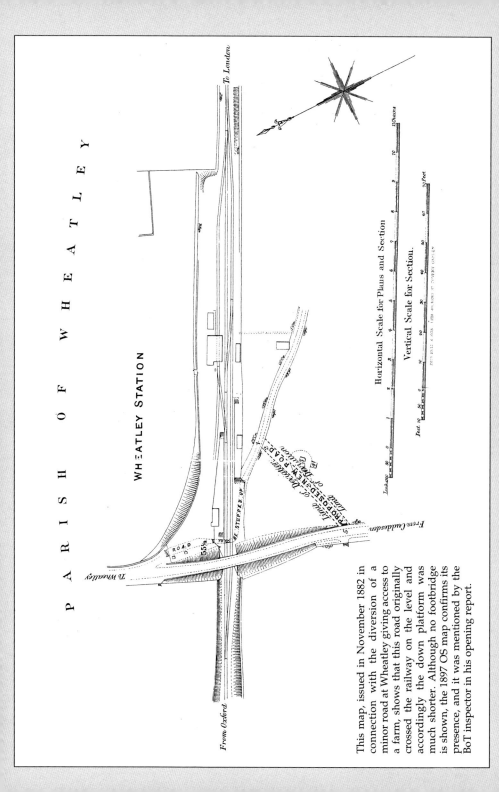

PARISH OF WHEATLEY

WHEATLEY STATION

To London

From Oxford

To Wheatley

From Cuddesdon

ROAD

OF PROPOSED ROAD.

Line of Diversion or Deviation

N. STOPPED UP

Horizontal Scale for Plans and Section

Vertical Scale for Section.

This map, issued in November 1882 in connection with the diversion of a minor road at Wheatley giving access to a farm, shows that this road originally crossed the railway on the level and accordingly the down platform was much shorter. Although no footbridge is shown, the 1897 OS map confirms its presence, and it was mentioned by the BoT inspector in his opening report.

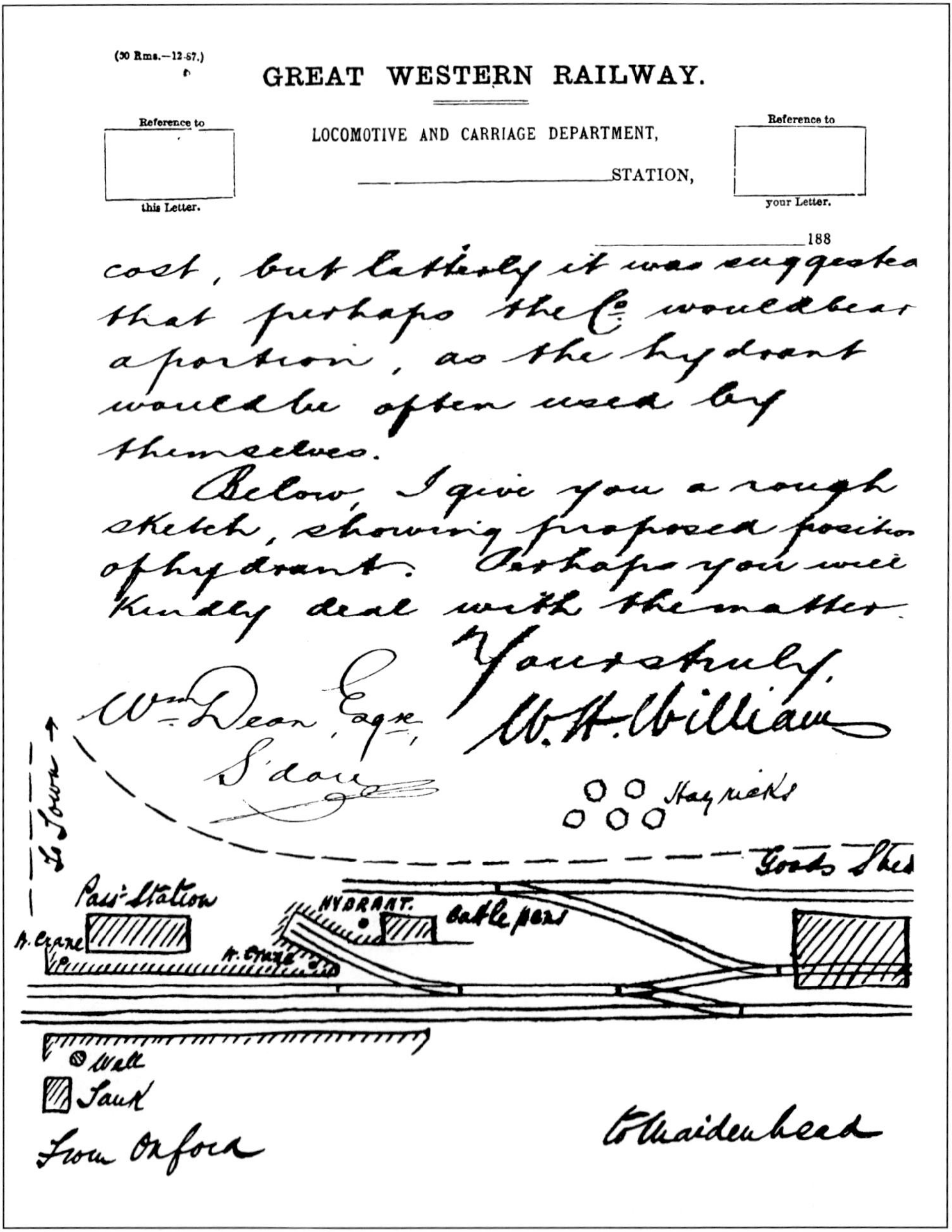

(30 Rms.—12-67.)

GREAT WESTERN RAILWAY.

Reference to this Letter.

LOCOMOTIVE AND CARRIAGE DEPARTMENT,

______ STATION,

Reference to your Letter.

______ 188

cost, but latterly it was suggested that perhaps the Co would bear a portion, as the hydrant would be often used by themselves.

Below, I give you a rough sketch, showing proposed position of hydrant. Perhaps you will kindly deal with the matter.

Yours truly,

W. H. Williams

Wm Dean, Esqre,
S'don

A rough sketch of the layout at Thame in 1888. This shows that there was a down platform and crossing loop, although the water cranes for trains in both directions were on the up platform.

asked to erect a new iron tank in its place. This was approved and in March 1882 Mr Armstrong, locomotive superintendent at Swindon (covering Thame), asked his chief, Mr Dean, to tell Mr Spagnoletti (telegraph superintendent) that the telegraph wires at Thame needed to be raised 18 inches to allow the jib of the new water crane, 'about to be erected', to swing round.

The Great Western ran excursions to the Oxfordshire Agricultural Show at Witney on 24th and 25th May, 1882, from High Wycombe (10.05), Risborough (10.25), Bledlow (10.30), Thame (10.40), Tiddington (10.50), Wheatley (11.00) and Littlemore (11.10). Return from Witney was at 5.30 pm and return fares were single fare and a quarter.

The 20th June edition of the *Thame Gazette* reported the promotion of Mr Yeo, station master at Risborough, to the same post at Thame. He was a 'most able and popular station master' and the paper said that the people of Risborough had expressed regret at this departure, after about a year in the post. In August the Board approved £126 for a cart weighbridge and office at Littlemore.

A small, but brief, improvement to a somewhat sparse train service was the introduction of a train from Princes Risborough to Thame every Tuesday, market day, at 12.18 pm. This began in March 1883 and ran for a month or two and then did not run again until 1897. In July the Board approved the large sum of £2,800 to line Wheatley tunnel (this was the cost of labour only). In January 1884 £770 was authorised to widen and cover the up platform at Princes Risborough.

A station delay sheet for Oxford station on 23rd October, 1885, recording the 13 minute late arrival of the 11 am Paddington (via Thame) baldly states: 'Delay caused by killing a man at Thame by up distant signal and stopping to pick him up and taking him back to Thame'.

Some correspondence between the GWR and the Board of Trade on 31st December, 1886, mainly regarding the working of the Aylesbury branch, gave an undertaking that the line between Maidenhead and Kennington Junction 'shall be worked by Train Staff & Ticket in conjunction with the Block Telegraph'. (As recently as 1880 a Report to the Board of Directors stated that the line was worked by Train Staff & Ticket without Block Telegraph.) On 2nd February, 1887 the General Manager recommended that 'locking and Block Telegraph be introduced during the current year between Maidenhead and Kennington Jn and between Princes Risborough and Aylesbury', but the Directors did not act on this for well over three years.*

An application from the Thame Volunteer Fire Brigade in November 1888 to use the railway's water in the event of a fire at the station end of town led to an investigation by the Swindon loco superintendent. His report included the following information (and sketch) regarding the arrangements at Thame:

> A well supplied by a spring and wrought-iron tank to contain about 11,000 gallons are situated at the west end of the down platform. The water is pumped by three throw-pumps, 5 in. diameter, 10 in. stroke; worked by horse power.
> Two cranes: one at each end of up platform.

---

* The difference between 'Train Staff & Ticket in conjunction with Block Telegraph' and 'locking and Block Telegraph' is thought to be that in the former case the Telegraph was used for information and train regulation purposes and emergencies, whereas in the latter the trains were actually signalled on the Block Telegraph.

The horse power is supplied by Mr Lidington of Thame who is paid 18s. per week. The average time required for pumping per day is 4 hours (slow pace).

Average number of engines taking water - 8 per day. The water has never been known to fail. It flows into the well at the rate of about 600 gallons per hour and can be pumped at the maximum rate of about 1,800 gallons per hour.

The company decided that a hydrant near the cattle pens would also be useful to them, as at present it meant getting water from one of the water cranes to wash out the cattle pens and cattle trucks. However, the correspondence does not indicate whether the work was actually carried out.

Following the Regulation of Railways Act 1889, the GWR had to grasp the nettle and commit some large expenditure to replacing the fairly primitive signalling arrangements that existed on most of its system. Accordingly the Board of Directors, on 9th December, 1890, authorised £25,467 8s. to be spent between Maidenhead and Oxford via Thame on 'Introduction of locking and Block Telegraph . . . and construction of sidings and other works specified'. The *Thame Gazette* in its 25th November, 1890 edition noted:

Princes Risborough. It is stated that some important alterations are about to be effected at the station very shortly. Several new sidings are to be added, a new signal box is to be erected, and a considerable addition made to the levers working signals. These and other alterations when carried out, will tend to greatly facilitate the working of the heavy traffic which has to be dealt with at this station.

It is thought that this work entailed a proper crossing loop at Risborough for the first time.

In November 1892, the modernisation of the signalling arrangements was completed with the authorisation of expenditure of £1,661 to install the Electric Train Staff between Maidenhead and Kennington Jn.

The Board of Trade inspected the new works on the Thame branch and in a report dated 25th January, 1893 the following was noted:

Princes Risborough. There have been considerable alterations to the arrangements of the lines, the points and signals have been interlocked and are now worked from a new signal cabin with 61 working levers and 10 spare and from a subsidiary 5-lever ground frame; down platform widened and lengthened and footbridge erected between two platforms. Some shelter is required upon the down platform. Approved but waiting room arrangements on up platform ought to be improved [substantial improvements were made to the accommodation at Risborough between 1894-6, including the up platform rooms].

Thame. Connection with main line altered. Passing loop and second platform brought into use, new footbridge erected and new signal cabin with 20 working levers and a spare. Approved.*

Wheatley. Passing loop and second platform brought into use. Both platforms lengthened and widened. New footbridge, new signal cabin, 18 working levers and 7 spare. Approved.

* Two passenger trains were booked to cross at Thame before 1893, so it would be interesting to know what 'brought into use' means. The diagram accompanying the 1888 water report shows the down platform *in situ*, although it is significant that both water cranes were on the up platform, one at either end. Similarly, trains were booked to cross at Wheatley before this, but only one goods and one passenger or two goods in the WTTs seen by the author.

Severe flooding struck the line in November 1894. On 12th November a landslip 18 yards long near Thame almost caused the derailment of the 6.15 pm from Oxford, which arrived at Thame with buffers locked. The line was repaired the following day. Kennington Junction was flooded on the night of 15th November and was not cleared until 2 pm on Sunday 18th November.

The Working Timetable for October 1898 is included as an illustration on the following pages. Some notes included therein add further information as to the working of local goods trains at this time:

2 am Paddington-Oxford - Conveys station trucks (ST) Paddington - 64 Watlington, 65 Bledlow, 66 Oxford. Bledlow ST to be put off at Taplow for 1 am from Crimea.
1 am Crimea-Oxford - Conveys ST 82 Windsor-Oxford, 88 Reading-Oxford, 65 from Taplow.
5.55 pm Taplow-Oxford - Conveys ST 83 Taplow-Oxford, ST 84 Taplow-Birmingham. Puts off traffic and takes on cattle and important goods only at Thame.
11.45 am Oxford-Taplow - Conveys ST 133 Oxford-Taplow (plus ST 378 and 537 from further afield).
5.10 pm Oxford-Taplow - To do yard shunting at Thame. A through truck to work from Oxford for Paddington to pick up goods at Tiddington. Truck to be transferred at Thame to 6.20 pm from Oxford.
6.20 pm Oxford (6.05 pm Sundays) to Paddington - To take through goods traffic for Acton and London. To call at Taplow when required only. Conveys ST 134 Oxford-Paddington. On Sundays to put off Paddington goods and cattle traffic at Acton and run to Paddington passenger station with milk.
11.05 pm Oxford to Paddington - Conveys ST 85 Aylesbury-Reading, 137 Oxford-Maidenhead, 128a Oxford-Southall.

Station trucks carried small consignments, not sufficient to justify a truck to themselves, between the various stations serviced by that truck. A separate publication gave details of all the station trucks in each Division, and their calling points and listed the trains by which they were conveyed.

The 1898 timetable showed that the various signal boxes between Risborough and Kennington Jn (Bledlow, Tiddington and Littlemore were not block posts) were open continuously on weekdays and closed on Sunday nights until 6.30/7 am on Monday. Kennington Jn was provided with a block switch for the main line and was only opened on Sundays to pass the few Wycombe line trains.

At 2.25 am on 31st January, 1899, Littlemore station caught fire and the whole of the station buildings were destroyed. The Board approved £1,135 for new buildings, £545 to reconstruct the platform to an altered line requiring slewing of the permanent way and £370 for a 'Standard "C" cottage for the station master'. Work does not seem to have been carried out very speedily, but was completed, with a £162 overspend, by October 1902.

MAIDENHEAD, HIGH WYCOMBE, THAME AND OXFORD.

Single Line, worked by Electric Train Staff between Maidenhead and Kennington Junction. Crossing Stations shewn in Bold Type.

WEEK DAYS.

DOWN TRAINS.

Distance from Maidenhead	STATIONS	1 Passenger	3 Goods	5 Goods (1.0 a.m. Crimea)	7 Passenger	9 Empty Coaches	11 Passenger	13 Passenger	15 Passenger	17 Passenger	19 Goods RR	21 Passenger Tuesdays	23 Passenger	25 Passenger	27 Passenger	29 Passenger	31 Passenger	33 Goods RR	35 Passenger	37 Passenger	39 Passenger	41 Goods	43 Passenger	45 Passenger	47 Passenger	49 Passenger	51	53 Goods	55
M 9	Paddington ...... dep.																												
7	Slough																												
4	Taplow																												
—	Maidenhead ...... arr.																												
0	Maidenhead ...... dep.																												
2	Cookham																												
4	Bourne End { arr. / dep.																												
5	Thomas's Siding																												
6	Wooburn Green																												
7	Loudwater																												
9	High Wycombe { arr. / dep.																												
13	West Wycombe																												
16	Saunderton																												
18	Princes Risboro' { arr. / dep.																												
19	Bledlow																												
23	Thame																												
27	Tiddington { arr. / dep.																												
31	Wheatley																												
35	Littlemore																												
38	Kennington Junc. { arr. / dep.																												
39	Oxford ...... arr.																												

‡ Tiddington arr. 10.13 a.m.   T See note on page 135.   W Stops at Loudwater by signal when required to pick up only and for Staff.

October 1898 Working Timetable. (The T note is that shown on opposite page.)

OXFORD, THAME, HIGH WYCOMBE AND MAIDENHEAD.

WEEK DAYS.

UP TRAINS.

Distance from Oxford (M. C.)	STATIONS		2 Empty Coaches	4 Passenger	6 Passenger	8 Passenger	10 Passenger	12 Passenger	14 Passenger	16 Goods	18 Empty Train	20 Passenger	22 Shunting Engine	24 Passenger	26 Light Engine	28 Goods	30 Passenger	34 Passenger	36 Passenger	38 Goods	40 Passenger	42 Passenger	44 London Goods	45 London Goods	46	48	50	52
			A.M.	A.M.	A.M.	A.M.	A.M.	A.M.	A.M.	D		A.M.		P.M.	P.M.		P.M.	P.M.	P.M.	D	P.M.	P.M.	C	D				
	Oxford	dep.		6 45	6 55	8 20				9 35		11 17				11 45	2 35				5 12			6 20				
	Kennington Junction																											
	Littlemore					8 33						11 27									6 22			6 47				
	Wheatley	arr. dep.			7 4	8 43				10 25		11 37					2 45				6 34			7 10				
	Tiddington	arr. dep.			7 11	8 50						11 44		2 45			2 54				6 47			7 30				
	Thame	arr. dep.			7 18 7 21	9 11 9 18				10 45 11 35		11 52 11 54		2 50		1 0 1 25	3 4 3 16				6 55 7 2			8 10 8 45				
	Penn Farm																											
	Bledlow					9 29											3 30			7 0			8 35				
	Princes Risboro	arr. dep.			7 36 7 39	9 33 9 43				11 45 11 55		12 9 12 14				1 48	3 41	4 54 4 55		7 15 7 28				X				
	Saunderton																											
	West Wycombe				7 51	9 56						12 26				2 13	3 53			7 42				1 50				
	High Wycombe	arr. dep.	1 35	7 56 8 33	10 40 10 45						12 30 12 41		2 57		2 23	3 58	5 0 5 25		7 48	8 0		9 40	2 20				
	Loudwater				8 10	10 10 11 6						12 41					4 8	5 30		8 2	8 13		10 16	2 27				
	Woburn Green				8 15	10 13 11 11						12 45					4 13	5 34		8 7	9 15		10 35	2 50				
	Thomas's Siding																							10 50	3 0				
	Bourne End	arr. dep.		8 19 8 21	8 37 9 1						12 49 12 52		3 33 3 41		3 31	4 17 4 20	5 39 5 41	7 36 7 41	8 11 8 14	9 23 9 27		11 0 11 16	3 20				
	Cookham			8 28	9 13 10 36 11 24						12 58		3 55		4 10	4 26	5 46	7 47	8 20	9 38		11 25	4 27				
	Maidenhead	arr.	2 0	8 34	8 57 9 13 11 30						1 4		3 9		4 18	4 32	6 51	7 53	8 20	9 38		11 33	5 0				
	Maidenhead	dep.	2 5	8 37	9 0	9 16 10 45					1 8		3 12		4 19	4 38	5 55	7 56	8 30	9 41		11 36	5 15				
	Taplow	arr.		8 40	9 3	9 20 10 49					1 12		3 16			4 43	5 59	7 3	8 35	9 45			6 22				
	Slough	arr.	2 15	8 50		9 55 11 25					1 25		3 30			4 57	5 51	7 22	8 50	9 59			6 35				
	Paddington	arr.		9 28	9 37	9 55					2 10		3 55			5 40	6 45	8 10	9 30	10 40			7 0				

R If this Train is ready to leave Princes Risboro' before the 11.45 p.m. ex Taplow is signalled from High Wycombe, the Up Train must be given the preference.

§ Tiddington arrive 8.56 a.m.   ‡ Tiddington arr. 6.40 p.m.   B Bishops Road Station.

T This Train runs to Aylesbury or High Wycombe as circumstances require. Mr. DAVIS, Oxford, to arrange and advise Stations.

October 1898 Working Timetable.

MAIDENHEAD AND OXFORD.

SUNDAYS.

DOWN TRAINS.

STATIONS.		1 D 11.45 p.m. ex Taplow Goods Saturday		3 A Passenger.	5 G Goods.		7 1.0 a.m. Crimea Goods.		9 A Passenger.	11 A Passenger.	13 A	15 A	17 A Passenger.	19 A Passenger.	21	23 A Passenger.
		arr.	dep.	A.M.	arr.	dep.	arr.	dep.	A.M.	A.M.			P.M.	P.M.		P.M.
Paddington	dep.	—	—	12.32	—	—	—	1.0	8.40	8.40	—	—	5.30	—	—	7.55
Slough	"	—	—	12.40	—	—	—	—	9 4	9 4	—	—	5.58	—	—	8.50
Taplow	"	—	—	12.44	3.10	3.30	3 5	3.45	9.41	9.41	—	—	6 8	—	—	8.59
Maidenhead	arr.	—	—	12.50	3.35	3.40	3.45	4.55	9.45	9.45	—	—	—	—	—	9 3
Maidenhead	dep.	12.50	—	—	3.50	—	X5 3	—	9.48	9.48	—	—	6.10	—	—	9.10
Cookham	"	12.56	—	4 0	4.10	5.23	5.13	5.23	9.54	9.54	—	—	6.16	—	—	9.15
Bourne End	arr.	1 1	—	X4 17	—	5.28	5.28	—	9.58	9.58	—	—	6.20	—	—	9.17
	dep.	1 8	—	—	—	—	5.35	—	10 1	10 1	—	—	6.23	—	—	9X23
Thomas's Siding	"	—	—	—	—	5.45	5.39	—	—	—	—	—	—	—	—	—
Wooburn Green	"	1 7	—	4.55	5 5	5.49	5.49	—	10 6	10 6	—	—	6.29	—	—	9.27
Loudwater	"	1.12	—	5.13	5.35	6 10	6 10	—	10.11	10.11	—	—	6.33	—	—	9.33
High Wycombe	arr.	1.18	—	5.43	—	6.52	6.52	—	10.17	10.17	—	—	6.40	—	—	9.37
	dep.	—	1 0	6.20	—	6.40	6.40	—	11.0	11.0	—	—	6.40	—	—	9.40
West Wycombe	"	—	—	—	—	—	—	—	—	—	—	—	—	—	—	9.46
Saunderton	"	—	—	—	—	6 47	6.55	—	10.20	10.20	—	—	—	—	—	9.50
Princes Risboro	arr.	1.34	—	—	6.45	7 15	—	—	10.35	10.35	—	—	—	—	—	9.59
	dep.	X	1.48	7 0	—	8 2	8.15	—	10.42	10.42	—	—	—	—	—	10 3
Bledlow	"	2 5	—	7.15	7.15	8 15	—	—	10.47	10.47	—	—	—	—	—	10.17
Thame	arr.	—	2.15	7.43	7.43	8.40	—	—	10.55	10.55	—	—	—	—	—	10.29
	dep.	2.35	—	7.55	8.10	9.49	8.55	—	11 9	11 9	—	—	—	—	—	10.30
Tiddington	"	—	2.45	8.10	—	9.11	9 0	—	11.17	11.17	—	—	—	—	—	10.40
Wheatley	arr.	—	—	8 18	8 18	9.26	9.8	—	11.22	11.22	—	—	—	—	—	10.45
	dep.	—	—	—	—	—	9.40	—	11.27	11.27	—	—	—	—	—	10.50
Littlemore	"	—	CS	OR OS	—	—	9.58	—	C8	C8	—	—	—	—	—	C8
Kennington Junc.	"	—	—	—	—	—	50	—	—	—	—	—	—	—	—	—
Oxford	arr.	3.10	—	8.40	—	10.15	10.20	—	11.35	11.35	—	—	—	—	—	10.52

OXFORD AND MAIDENHEAD.

SUNDAYS.

UP TRAINS.

STATIONS.		2 A Empty Coaches.	4 D 11.5 p.m. ex Oxford Goods Saturday		6 A Passenger.	8 A Passenger.	10	12	14 A Passenger.	16 A Passenger.	18	20 G Goods and Milk Train. R		22	24
		A.M.	arr.	dep.	A.M.	A.M.			P.M.	P.M.		arr.	dep.		
Oxford	dep.	—	—	—	6.40	—	—	—	5.50	—	—	—	6 5	—	—
Kennington Junc.	"	—	—	CS	C8	—	—	—	CS	—	—	—	CS	—	—
Littlemore	"	—	—	—	6.50	—	—	—	6 0	—	—	—	OR	—	—
Wheatley	arr.	—	11.30	—	6.59	—	—	—	6 9	—	—	—	6.33	6.43	—
Tiddington	"	—	—	12 5	7 3	—	—	—	6.12	—	—	—	6.53	6.56	—
	dep.	—	12.23	—	7.17	—	—	—	6.24	—	—	—	7.10	—	—
Thame	arr.	—	12.23	—	7.26	—	—	—	6.32	—	—	—	7.33	—	—
	dep.	—	—	7X35	7X35	—	—	—	6.34	—	—	—	—	—	—
Penn Farm	"	—	—	—	—	—	—	—	—	—	—	—	—	—	—
Bledlow	"	—	—	—	7 45	—	—	—	6.44	—	—	—	OR	—	—
Princes Risboro	arr.	—	12.35	—	7.50	—	—	—	6.49	—	—	—	7.46	—	—
	dep.	—	—	X1.26	7X54	—	—	—	6.54	—	—	—	—	8 0	—
Saunderton	arr.	—	—	—	—	—	—	—	—	—	—	—	—	—	—
West Wycombe	"	—	—	—	—	—	—	—	7 7	—	—	—	—	—	—
High Wycombe	arr.	1.30	1.50	—	8 6	—	—	—	7.13	—	—	—	8.25	—	—
	dep.	C8	2.27	—	8.11	11.35	—	—	7.18	7.30	—	—	8 47	8.50	—
Loudwater	"	CS	3 0	—	8.14	11.31	—	—	7.23	7.37	—	—	8 57	9 0	—
Wooburn Green	"	—	—	3.15	8.23	11.35	—	—	7.29	7.42	—	—	9 7	9.16	—
Thomas's Siding	"	—	—	—	—	—	—	—	—	—	—	—	—	—	—
Bourne End	arr.	C8	3.20	—	8.29	11.40	—	—	7.37	7X45	—	—	9.30	—	—
	dep.	CS	4.52	—	8.32	11.43	—	—	7.42	7.50	—	—	X	—	—
Cookham	"	CS	—	4.58	8.36	11.49	—	—	7.50	8.56	—	—	9.43	9.50	—
Maidenhead	arr.	2 0	—	5X23	8.44	11.55	—	—	7.57	9 2	—	—	9.59	—	—
	dep.	2 5	—	5.15	8.49	11.57	—	—	8 9	9 5	—	—	10 0	10 7	—
Taplow	"	—	—	5.22	8.53	—	—	—	8 7	9 6	—	—	10.46	10.30	—
Slough	"	2.15	—	5.35	9 0	—	—	—	8.20	9 7	—	—	11.25	10.46	—
Paddington	arr.	—	—	9 5	10 0	—	—	—	9 0	10 0	—	—	12.40	—	—

Single Line, worked by Electric Train Staff.

R Returns from Paddington to Oxford via Didcot at 11.40 a.m. on Mondays.

October 1898 Working Timetable.

Chapter Seven

A New Century brings improvement

One of three new railways promoted in the 1897 Parliamentary Session was one from Acton to High Wycombe, which had been prompted by a competing Harrow, Uxbridge and High Wycombe Railway promoted by the Metropolitan District Railway. As well as securing the district for the GWR this would be a first step to providing a shorter route to Birmingham than that via Oxford, and to Oxford itself. At one stage the GWR considered doubling the line from High Wycombe to Oxford via Thame, but this was dropped in favour of a new direct line from Princes Risborough towards Banbury.

In 1899 the Great Central Railway (GCR) opened its London extension to Marylebone, some 40 miles of which used the Metropolitan Railway from Quainton Road, north of Aylesbury, to Neasden, which involved some steep gradients. The Great Central entered discussions with the GWR to see if the Acton-Wycombe line could form part of a new route for its trains. The two companies agreed to form a Great Western & Great Central Railways Joint Committee, which could:

1. Take over construction of the Acton and Wycombe between Northolt and Wycombe.
2. Purchase the Wycombe-Risborough section from the GWR, double and improve it.
3. Construct a new railway from Risborough to Grendon Underwood (near Calvert) on the GCR, about 15 miles long.

The first nine miles of 3, *above*, to what, later, became Ashendon Junction, would eventually form part of the GWR's new direct route to Birmingham, but this final stage, beyond Ashendon Junction, was not authorised until 1905 and opened in 1910.

The doubling work between Wycombe and Risborough began in June 1902 [*GWR Magazine*, October 1904]. The cheaply-built Wycombe Railway had a ruling gradient of 1 in 88 between these places, but on the new line it would be a much more comfortable 1 in 164. Additionally the somewhat sharp curves would be improved. An entirely new Princes Risborough station would be built, some 100 yards south of the existing one. It would have two through lines between the two platform roads and a much more spacious goods yard than before. As the *GWR Magazine* for October 1904 described it, 'Princes Risborough now becomes a rather important junction . . .'

The contractor's locomotive *Lizzie* was authorised to work over the GWR lines at Princes Risborough between the contractor's siding (which was on the Wycombe side of the station) and the station sidings 'for the purpose of fetching and taking trucks from or to these points'.

The *Thame Gazette* reported that the new down platform at Princes Risborough was brought into use for the first time on 20th March, 1905, 'all three platforms are therefore now completed'. The large footbridge spanning the whole layout was nearing completion.

A photograph of the upside station buildings at Oxford on 18th June, 1911.

Lens of Sutton Collection

Looking across from the upside to the downside at Oxford at an early date.

Lens of Sutton Collection

There was a fatal accident at the railway's Littlemore sand quarry on 6th December, 1905. Mr W. Edney, a 38-year-old labourer, stepped back to avoid a stone which had been excavated when the ground beneath him gave way and he fell a distance of 10 feet. The stone rolled onto his leg and fractured his right thigh. At the subsequent Coroner's inquest the verdict was that he 'died from pulmonary thrombosis following an accident'.

Just before the opening of the Great Western and Great Central Joint Railway, the 23rd March, 1906 edition of *The Railway Gazette* reported that five through trains would run each way daily to and from Oxford over this route, connecting at High Wycombe with the 'already existing trains running via Maidenhead'. The new route would save half-an-hour over the former timings. There would be two through trains each way on Sundays. The new trains would convey 1st and 3rd class passengers only.

The opening of the new line on 2nd April, 1906 (although goods traffic had used it since November 1905), was celebrated in great style. Special trains were run from Paddington and Marylebone to High Wycombe, where the Directors and officials of both companies were entertained to luncheon at the Town Hall by the High Wycombe and District Chamber of Commerce. After-lunch speeches were made by Alfred Baldwin MP (Chairman of the GWR) and Sir Alexander Hudson (Chairman of the Great Central). In his speech Sir Alexander mentioned that a railway with two lines of way and not very elaborate stations had cost £40,000 per mile; he knew (from the GWR Chairman) of the inexpensiveness of the old line that had previously served Wycombe, but the new line had easy gradients and good curves. The new through express trains would not start for three or four months.

After the speeches, the two special trains were joined and run to Calvert, returning thence to Wycombe where they were again separated and each run to their respective terminus.

Returning to more mundane matters, in December 1904 the chief goods manager was concerned at the cost of pumping water at Thame: £78 was being paid annually to a local man for the use of a horse and he asked G.J. Churchward, who had now succeeded William Dean as locomotive and carriage superintendent, whether it could not be done by themselves more cheaply. The latter's reply has not been traced but in September 1905 a New Works order was issued in the sum of £239 to convert the horse-driven pump to oil driven.

However, this led to the Secretary of the local gas company in January 1906 writing to the divisional superintendent at Paddington, Mr W.A. Hart, suggesting that purchase of their gas to power the pump would be no more expensive and it would require less cleaning and obviate any smell. Referred, as all technical matters were, to Mr Churchward, the latter responded that the gas at Thame at 4s. 2d. for 1,000 cubic feet was too expensive. Still the matter rumbled on when Mr Hart, the following June, sent Mr Churchward a copy of a court case reported in the *Thame Gazette* (12th June edition) where a local householder summonsed the manager of a hook and eye factory at Thame over the offensive smells given off by his oil engine. The judge largely upheld the complaint and required extensive modification to the exhaust system of the pump. Mr Churchward confidently replied on 21st June '. . . do not anticipate that we shall have any trouble with our oil engine'. The engine was installed in

A close-up of the bookstall area of the up platform at Oxford.   *Lens of Sutton Collection*

The GWR First Aid (or 'Ambulance') team from Wheatley, photographed at the station *c.*1920.
Courtesy Pamela Marchbanks

August. At Wheatley, the Board authorised expenditure of £140 in February 1906 to install a cattle pen.

In a bid to stimulate Oxford suburban traffic, the GWR opened several 'motor car halts' south of the city, including three on the Thame branch. They were all only 150 ft long with a 20 ft by 7 ft corrugated iron shelter (on each platform for the halts on the main line). Halts at Horsepath (at 57¼ mp), Garsington Bridge (at 58½ mp, 1 m. 39½ ch. from Littlemore and 2 m. 74½ ch. from Wheatley), Abingdon Road (near 61¾ mp) and Hinksey (near 62¼ mp) were all approved by the Board of Trade on 6th December, 1907. Another, at Iffley (near 60¾ mp, 2 m. 43½ ch. from Oxford, 63½ ch. from Littlemore, between Kennington viaduct and Kennington Jn) was applied for later and approved on 23rd January, 1908. All were inspected by Col Yorke on 2nd March, 1908, having opened to traffic on the 1st February. They had a short life, closing because of war conditions on 22nd March, 1915, although two of them had fresh lives in the 1930s.

In 1907 the branch saw what was possibly its most intensive use ever over a short period. The Army carried out manoeuvres at Aylesbury and Thame requiring 14 trains from Windsor to Aylesbury and 14 from Twyford to Thame during the night of Saturday 14th and the day of Sunday 15th September, 1907. The superintendent of the line issued a 16 page notice detailing arrangements, its cover marked 'Information must not, under any circumstances, be given to ANYONE who will not have to take part in carrying out the arrangements'.

So far as the Thame movement was concerned, the 14 trains were needed to move 210 officers, 4,800 other ranks, 55 officers' horses, 120 other horses and 60 pairs of wheels. The formation of the trains is included as an illustration; note that 240 other ranks per train had to travel in open goods wagons, 24 to a wagon. Each train came empty from Reading, loaded up in Twyford up relief platform and ran to Thame via Didcot and Kennington Jn (reverse); here two fresh engines were attached for the journey up Wheatley Bank to Thame. Six sets of stock were required (sets U-Z), each of these making further journeys after discharging their load and returning empty to Twyford. The working timetable for the loaded and empty movements is included as an illustration as are the arrangements at Kennington and Thame. The movements from Windsor ran via Maidenhead and Princes Risborough to Aylesbury. No mention is made of how the troops got home after the exercise.

The notice indicated that not all the trains might be necessary and the *GWR Magazine* for October 1907 gave a useful report on what actually happened:

> . . . Eleven [specials] were run from Windsor to Aylesbury and ten from Twyford to Thame between the hours of 10 pm and 8 am, carrying about 10,000 officers, NCOs and men, and a large number of horses, guns, general service wagons (loaded with baggage, equipment, etc.), carts and cycles. By desire of the military authorities each train was partly composed of vacuum-fitted open goods wagons for the conveyance of soldiers, and the men who travelled in this manner seemed to enjoy the experience. The railway officials and the military staff officers worked throughout in perfect harmony, and the arrangements were carried out without a hitch, to the entire satisfaction of the headquarters staff.

After this excitement, the remaining years of the Edwardian era and the first few of King George V's reign, up to the start of World War I, in August 1914,

About 210 Officers, 4,800 other ranks, 55 Officers' chargers, 120 other Horses, and 60 pairs of wheels.

MOVEMENT OF 2ND DIVISION, TWYFORD TO THAME.

SATURDAY NIGHT and SUNDAY, SEPTEMBER 14th and 15th.

Train Set	Special Train No.	READING Empty Trains dep.	TWYFORD Empty Trains arr.	TWYFORD {Up Relief Line Platform} dep.	Reading pass	Didcot East Junction pass	Kennington Junction (CS) arr.	Kennington Junction (CS) dep.	Wheatley (CS) arr.	Wheatley (CS) dep.	THAME (CS) arr.
*		P.M. 8 40 RL	8 53								
U	1	P.M. 9 15 RL	9 28	P.M. 10 5 RL	10 15	10 41	10 55	11 11	11 16	11 17	11 32
V	2	P.M. 9 55 RL	10 11	11 5 RL	11 10	11 36	11 50	11 56	12 13	12x20	12 35
W	3	P.M. 10 50 RL	11 5	NIGHT 12 0 RL	12 10	12 36	12 50	12 56	1 13	1x15	1 30
X	4	P.M. 11 50 RL	12 5	A.M. 1 0 RL	1 10	1 36	1 50	1 56	2 13	2x15	2 30
Y	5	A.M. 12 50 RL	1 5	2 0 RL	2 10	2 36	2 50	2 56	3 13	3x15	3 30
Z	6	A.M. 1 50 RL	2 5	3 0 RL	3 10	3 36	3 50	3 56	4 13	4x15	4 30
U	7	A.M. 2 50 RL	3 5	4 0 RL	4 10	4 36	4 50	4 56	5 13	5x15	5 30
V	8	A.M. 3 50 RL	4 5	5 0 RL	5 10	5 36	5 50	5 56	6 13	6x15	6 30
W	9	A.M. 4 50 RL	5 5	6 15 RL	6 25	6 51	7 5	7 11	7 28	8x15	7 45
X	10	A.M. 6 0 RL	6 20	7 0 RL	7 10	7 36	7 50	7 56	8 13	8x15	8 30
Y	11	A.M. 6 50 RL	7 5	8 0 RL	8 10	8 36	8 50	8 56	9 13	9x15	9 30
Z	12	A.M. 7 50 RL	8 5	9 0 RL	9 10	9 36	9 50	9 56	10 13	10x15	10 30
U	13	A.M. 8 50 RL	9 5	10 0 RL	10 10	10 36	10 50	10 56	11 13	11x20	11 35
V	14	A.M. 9 50 RL	10 5	11 0 RL	11 10	11 36	11 50	11 56	12 13	12x15	12 30

Timings of the military specials to Thame for the big exercise in 1907.

EMPTY TRAINS :—

TRAIN SET.	U	V	W	X	Y	Z	U	V	W	X	Y	Z	U	V
	A.M.	A.M.	A.M.	A.M.	A.M.	A.M.	A.M.	A.M.	A.M.	A.M.	A.M.	A.M.	P.M.	P.M.
THAME ... (CS) dep.	12 5	12 57	1 57	2 57	3 57	4 57	5 57	7x47	8x32	9x32	10 0	11x37	12x32	1 4
Bledlow / Princes Risborough (CS) dep.											10 25			
Wheatly ... (CS) { arr.	12 19	1 12	2 12	3 12	4 12	5 12	6 12	8 2	8 41	9 41		11 57	12 42	1 19
Wheatly dep.	12x20	1x20	2x20	3x20	4x20	5x20	6x20	8x15	9x15	10x15		12x15	12 48	1 20
Kennington Junction (CS) { arr.	12 35	1 35	2 35	3 35	4 35	5 35	6 35	8 30	9 30	10 30		12 30	1 3	1 35
Kennington Junction dep.	12 41	1 41	2 41	3 41	4 41	5 41	6 41	8 36	9 36	10 36		12 36	1 9	1 41
Dilcot East Junction ... pass.	12 53	1 55	2 55	3 55	4 55	5 55	6 55	8 50	9 50	10 50		12 50	1 23	1 55
Reading (RL Platform) { arr.	RL	RL	RL	RL	RL	RL	RL	RL	RL	RL		RL	RL	RL
Reading dep.	1 21	2 21	3 21	4 21	5 21	6 21	7 21	9 16	10 16	11 16		1 16	1 49	2 21
TWYFORD ... arr.	3 5	4 5	5 5	6 20	7 5	8 5	9 5	9 50						
To form Trains leaving Thame at [RL] ...	4 0	5 0	6 15	7 0	8 0	9 0	10 0	11 0						

(Y column note: *To Old Oak Common Via Northolt Junction. See Page 5.*)

C *These Empty Trains (including the Horse Boxes and Cattle Wagons) must be cleaned and the old straw taken out of the Open Goods Wagons AT READING.*

The 10.28 p.m. Henley to Reading must run into the Bay at Twyford instead of to up Relief Line platform, and passengers for Reading must change into a local special from Twyford at 10.20 p.m., and run via Main Line. The Empty Train to form this Special to leave Slough for Twyford at 10.20 p.m., and run via Main Line.

The Engine of the 10.28 p.m. ex Henley must run round its train at Twyford immediately the loaded Carriage Trucks for the 11.0 p.m. Special have been taken out of No. 2 Bay Line.

The Engine of the 11.40 p.m. ex Henley must run round its Train immediately it arrives at Twyford (if Carriage Trucks are clear), and the Engine and Train must then be shunted to the Sidings until required to form the 1.8 a.m. Twyford to Henley.

The 11.2 p.m. Saturday passenger Train Reading to Twyford to run via Main Line, and passengers for Henley must change into the Branch Train, which will start from the Bay. The Empty Train will afterwards proceed from Twyford to Slough.

The 12.17 a.m. ex Paddington must run via Main Line on Sunday morning, September 15th. The usual Henley Coach will be provided, but must work through to Reading ; Henley passengers to change at Twyford.

※ This Train to take the four ordinary flap-sided carriage trucks and the one eight wheeled brake third to form the 10.5 p.m. Special from Twyford. The remainder of the Train to leave Reading at 9.15 p.m. as shewn. Immediately the four carriage trucks and brake third arrive at Twyford, they must be placed in position for loading in the Outer Bay Line (trucks next shoot, and brake third at Bristol end).

¶ *When these Loaded Trains arrive at Thame they must run sufficiently far ahead to be well clear of the Loop points at the Oxford end of the Station. The object of this is to enable the Return Empty Trains booked to leave Thame at 7.47 a.m., 8.32 a.m., 9.32 a.m., 11.37 a.m., and 12.32 p.m. to leave as soon as the Loaded Trains have arrived.*

Timings of the empty military specials from Thame for the big exercise in 1907.

FORMATION OF TWYFORD TO THAME SPECIALS.

Each of the 6 sets of Specials from Twyford to Thame will be formed at Reading and the vehicles must be so marshalled as to be in the following order when running in the Empty and Loaded Trains:

EMPTY TRAINS FROM READING TO TWYFORD. ✦✦

Description.	Each Vehicle to accommodate	Total Carrying Capacity	Approx. Buffer to Buffer length	Number of Wheels.	Reference to Notes.
			feet		A
Engine	—	—	—	—	
1 Six-compart. 8-wheel Brake Third...	48 men	48 men	54	8	—
1 Six-compart. 8-wheel First... ...	36 officers	36 officers	54	8	—
4 Eight-compart. 8-wheel Thirds ...	64 men	256 men	200	32	—
1 Seven-compart. 8-wheel Brake Third	56 men	56 men	54	8	D
10 Vacuum-fitted Open Goods Wagons	24 men	240 men	180	40	
3 Horse Boxes	3 chargers	9 chargers	60	12	—
3 oil-lubricated Vacuum-fitted Cattle Wagons ...	8 horses	24 horses	66	12	
1 Eight-wheel Passenger Brake Van ...	All baggage	All baggage	54	8	—
4 Flap-sided Open Passenger Carriage Trucks	2 pairs wheels	8 pairs wheels	80	16	
TOTAL ☞		36 officers 600 men 9 chargers 24 horses 8 pairs wheels Baggage	802 feet without Engine.	144 wheels	—

LOADED TRAINS FROM TWYFORD TO THAME.

Description.	Each Vehicle to accommodate	Total Carrying Capacity.	Approx. Buffer to Buffer length	Number of Wheels.	Reference to Notes.
			feet.		A
Engine	—	—	—	—	
1 Eight-wheel Passenger Brake Van ...	All baggage	All baggage	54	8	—
3 oil-lubricated Vacuum-fitted Cattle Wagons	8 horses	24 horses	66	12	
3 Horse Boxes	3 chargers	9 chargers	60	12	—
10 Vacuum-fitted Open Goods Wagons	24 men	240 men	180	40	D
1 Seven-compart. 8-wheel Brake Third	56 men	56 men	54	8	C
4 Eight-compartment 8-wheel Thirds	64 men	256 men	200	32	—
1 Six-compartment 8-wheel First ...	36 officers	36 officers	54	8	
1 Six-compart. 8-wheel Brake Third...	48 men	48 men	54	8	C
4 Flap-sided Open Passenger Carriage Trucks	2 pairs wheels	8 pairs wheels	80	16	B
TOTAL ☞		36 officers 600 men 9 chargers 24 horses 8 pairs wheels Baggage	802 feet without Engine.	144 wheels.	—

✦✦ The Empty Stock for the 10.5 p.m. Special from Twyford to Thame will be run from Reading to Twyford in two parts, as shown on page 6.

A Two Engines from Kennington Junction to Thame and vice versa.

B The position of these Carriage Trucks is specially authorised as an exception to the rule that such vehicles must not be formed in front of eight-wheel bogie-stock.

C No Baggage must be loaded in these Brake Thirds.

D High-sided (*i e*, 4 feet 3 inches deep) and coupled together with screw couplings. See note on page 2.

Each Train must be distinctly labelled both ends with its proper letter as allotted in this Notice thus :—

The 10.5 p.m., 4.0 a.m. and 10.0 a.m. from Twyford to Thame will be :—

☞ The Special Trains must be formed complete in all respects by 3.0 p.m. at the latest, on Saturday, September 14th. Inspector Taylor will be responsible for the formation of the Empty Trains and District Inspector Ackland for seeing to their punctual dispatch from Reading.

Formations of the military specials to Thame for the big exercise in 1907.

SPECIAL INSTRUCTIONS AFFECTING KENNINGTON JUNCTION

District Inspector Hooper will be in charge of the work at Kennington Junction.

The trains must be dealt with at this place in the following way :—

Loaded Trains.—These trains must run beyond the points No. 14 leading from the refuge siding to the down main line at the Oxford end of the loop sufficiently far to admit of two engines already standing in the down loop line to be backed on to them. The front engine must then be detached, the two engines from the loop attached, and the train made ready to leave for Thame via the crossover road between the up and down main lines.

Empty Trains.—These trains upon arrival must run well over the points No. 14, leading from the loop to the down main line at the Oxford end of the loop. The train engine to take the train from Kennington Jct. to Twyford must then back on to it from the loop. The two engines which brought the train from Thame must be detached, and the train will then be ready to leave via the crossover road and the up main line for Twyford.

It is important that the work at Kennington Junction shall be done smartly, and Inspector Hooper will be held responsible for seeing that this is accomplished.

A Telegraph Operator must be on duty at Kennington Junction Signal Box during the whole time that the special trains are passing.

A Locomotive Inspector or Foreman will also be on duty at Kennington Junction.

Engines.—Three sets of two engines each will be provided for the working between Kennington Junction and Thame.

The first set of two engines must be at Kennington Junction not later than 10.0 p.m., the second set not later than 11.0 p.m., and the third set not later than 12.0 midnight.

SPECIAL INSTRUCTIONS RE WORKING AT THAME.

Military Office.—The Waiting Room on the Up Side (with fire lit, and chairs, pens, ink and plain stationery) must be reserved for the use of the Military Staff Officer. **Mr. F. R. Potter will represent the Company at Thame, and will keep in touch with the Military Staff Officer there.**

Spare Engines.—Two spare engines must be in readiness in the siding at the Oxford end not later than 11.0 p.m., on the Saturday night, and these engines will be the train engines of the 12.5 a.m. empty train from Thame, the train engines of the 10.5 p.m. Special from Twyford, returning with the 12.57 a.m. empty train from Thame, and so on.

Unloading of Traffic.—All the traffic will be unloaded on the up side at Thame, and the four carriage trucks of each train must be placed in the Carriage Dock there, so that the vehicles may be unloaded whilst the platform work is being done with the other portion of the train. The carriage trucks must be formed in front of the return empty trains on leaving Thame for Twyford.

☞ A good layer of sand must be sprinkled over the platform where the Horses will be unloaded, and it must be renewed as often as may be necessary.

NOTE.—Special efforts must be made by all concerned (in conjunction with the Military Authorities) to finish the unloading of each train in sufficient time to allow the empty trains to be afterwards made ready to start punctually.

Goods Shed Siding.—The goods shed siding must be kept clear of ordinary traffic from end to end the whole of the time the special trains are being dealt with. Mr. FRANKLIN to see specially to this.

Protection of Trains standing at Up Platform.—"The Blocking Back Inside Home Signal" (2-4) must be sent to Wheatley, and must not be released until the Up Platform Line is clear.

Staff.—The following Staff must be on duty to deal with the Special Trains and Traffic :—

Mr. FRANKLIN.
1 Telegraph Operator.
1 Telegraph Messenger.
Inspector ADAMS.
1 Foreman.
3 Shunters.
4 Porters.
1 Lavatory Attendant.
2 Permanent Way Men to see to sand on platform.
1 Loco. Inspector or Foreman. } Locomotive and Carriage Department
1 Carriage Department Examiner. } will provide.
4 County Police Constables.

NOTE.—The Staff must be relieved after 12 hours' duty, but the Relief Men must come on duty at least one hour before the first set of men leave duty in order that they may see what is required to be done. Each department concerned will provide its own Relief Staff, but Chief Inspector Clarke will be responsible for providing the Relief Staff for the Traffic Department.

Flare Lights.—The Locomotive Department will supply three flare-lights (with attendants) which will be placed in the best positions for giving a good light where most needed.

Open Goods Wagons.—There will be 10 high-sided "vacuum" open goods wagons on each train and about 24 men will ride in each of these vehicles. The Military Authorities have undertaken that the men themselves shall open the doors of the goods wagons to enable them to alight at the platform, and also to close the doors after them, but the Head Guard on each Train will be responsible for seeing that all doors, flaps, and fastenings are properly closed, secured and pinned before his train is moved.

Refreshments.—Mr. Buott will arrange for Coffee and Food for Company's Servants to be available at a convenient place on the Down Platform.

The special arrangements for working at Kennington Jn and Thame during the military exercise in 1907.

GREAT WESTERN RAILWAY

DAY TRIP TO THE SEASIDE.

On Saturday, August 17th, 1907,

A DAY EXCURSION TRAIN

WILL BE RUN TO

WEYMOUTH

AS SHEWN HEREUNDER:

FROM	AT	Return Fare (3rd Class).	FROM	AT	Return Fare (3rd Class).
	A.M.	S. D.		A.M.	S. D.
Greenford ...	5 10		Chinnor ...	5 50	
Ruislip and Ickenham	5 15		Bledlow Bridge Halt*	5 55	
Denham ...	5 20	6 0	Bledlow ...	6 10	
Gerrard's Cross	5 25		Thame ...	6 20	5 6
Beaconsfield	5 35		Tiddington ...	6 30	
High Wycombe	5 45		Wheatley ...	6 35	
West Wycombe	5 50		Littlemore ...	6 45	
Saunderton ...	5 55		Oxford ...	7 0	
Princes Risborough	6 5		Steventon ... A	6 50	
Aylesbury ...	5 35		Wantage Road ... A	7 0	
Little Kimble	5 45	5 6	Challow ... A	7 10	4 9
Watlington	5 30		Uffington ... A	7 15	
Lewknor Bridge Halt*	5 35		Faringdon ... A	6 45	
Aston Rowant ...	5 40		Shrivenham ... A	7 25	
Kingston Crossing Halt*	5 45		Swindon ... A	7 55	4 3

* Passengers who desire to join the Train at the Halts are requested to obtain Tickets on the previous day from one of the Stations.

A On the forward journey passengers from these Stations will change at Swindon and proceed at 7.55 a.m. and on the return journey change at Swindon and proceed at 10.30 p.m.

RETURN ARRANGEMENTS.—Passengers will return the same day from Weymouth at 7.45 p.m.

Tickets and Bills can be had at the Stations. Tickets from Aylesbury can also be obtained from **Mr. F. Samuels**, Kingsbury Printing Works, Aylesbury ; and tickets from High Wycombe can also be obtained from the **Great Western Coy.'s Receiving Office, 20A, High Street, High Wycombe.**

The Tickets are not transferable. Should an Excursion or Cheap Ticket be used for any other Station than those named upon it, or by any other Train than specified in this Bill, it will be rendered void, and therefore the Fare paid will be liable to forfeiture, and the full Ordinary Fare will become chargeable.

One package of Personal Luggage allowed each Passenger, at his or her own risk.

Any further information may be obtained at the Company's Stations, Offices, of **Mr. W. A. Hart**, Divisional Superintendent, Paddington Station, W., of Mr. J. Morris, Superintendent of the Line, Paddington Station, W.

PADDINGTON, July, 1907.   **JAMES C. INGLIS**, General Manager.

Excursion to Weymouth 1907.   *Courtesy David Castle*

appear to have been quiet for the Thame branch. Although the February 1908 *GWR Magazine* reported that Bledlow was dispatching 2-3 tons of ducks to the London markets on three days a week in season, the total for the year weighing nearly 100 tons, and was probably the most used station for this traffic in the district. The July 1911 *Magazine* reported that a man had been sentenced to three months' hard labour after breaking into Thame goods warehouse. An alert signalman Southam had heard a suspicious noise at 10.45 pm and called the police; the thief was suspected of an earlier robbery at Thame station. Minor works took place at Littlemore (a horse loading and carriage dock in 1911 for £190); at Thame (more siding accommodation in 1911 for £830); and at Tiddington where more siding accommodation was provided in 1913 at a cost of £526.

A rather larger scheme took place at Littlemore with provision of access to the sand quarry there. This was authorised by the Locomotive Committee in August 1912 (at a cost of £1,087) as the sand was for use by the Chief Mechanical Engineer's Department. A new connection, facing to down trains, admitted trains to the siding on the upside of the line. The lever in the box which worked this connection was locked by a key attached to the electric train staff. The works were ready for inspection on 3rd April, 1913 and were inspected by Sir Arthur Yorke on the following 10th May:

> . . . connection worked from the old signal box, which is now practically a ground frame (the place no longer being a passing place or staff station), the levers being locked by keys on the electric train staff . . . interlocking correct and arrangements satisfactory I can recommend BoT to sanction the use of this new connection.

The siding was extended in 1916/7 at a cost of £316.

The March 1913 *GWR Magazine* reported a presentation to Mr Walter Cripps, station master at Littlemore for the last 15 years, on his promotion to a relief station master attached to the Paddington district superintendent's office. At this time the Littlemore station master's pay was 45 shillings a week (a class 2 station).*

In 1914 the GWR extended the Platform Ticket system which had been 'revived' in 1912 to a further 24 stations, including Thame. Its principal aim was to prevent people entering platforms without tickets so as to avoid the delays occasioned by having to 'excess' passengers without tickets while their train stood at the station. Station platforms were also kept clear as it cost a 1*d.* to enter the platform if not travelling.

The *History of Thame* (published in 1935) states that Thame and Tiddington platforms were always crowded with milk churns, but a survey in 1914 revealed that the onset of the internal combustion engine had led to the diversion of a lot of that traffic to Aylesbury.

There was a very interesting wartime short term development close to the former Garsington Bridge Halt (which had closed in March 1915) in May-June 1917. To service a munitions factory there was a meeting 'on the ground' to decide what rail facilities were required. Two loop sidings on the upside of the line, controlled by ground frames at 15 m. 64 ch. and 16 m. 4 ch. with facing points and locks locked by keys on the electric train staff, were sufficiently advanced for traffic to start by 30th May. The BoT provisionally authorised the

---

* The gradings and rates of pay for Littlemore, Tiddington and Bledlow in 1914 are taken from a *Staff Regulation Passenger Department* book (details kindly supplied by Larry Crosier). The gradings must have altered by 1925 (*see Appendix Two*).

works on 8th June and were advised they were ready for inspection on 19th July. However, the Board's file is marked (on 14th September): 'These works have now been removed and inspection is not therefore necessary'. The cost of £5,726 was met by the Government. Could today's railway provide such a speedy reaction to an urgent requirement?

Other wartime work entailed the provision of a siding for timber traffic at Tiddington, authorised in October 1918 at a cost of £460. In June 1919 Mr J.O. Lawrence retired from the post of station master at Tiddington where he had been for nearly 12 years. In his career he had spent 37 years on the Wycombe-Oxford line. In 1914 the Tiddington station master's pay was 37s. 6d. a week (a class 2 station).

From a notice issued on 8th June, 1920, by the divisional superintendent, Worcester, we are informed that on that day 'Change of Gradient Boards' are to be brought into use at 6 m. 8 ch., 6 m. 40 ch. and 7 m. 10 ch. all between Thame and Tiddington. The boards, illuminated at night, were to tell drivers and guards that their trains were about to enter a descending gradient to help them in the control of unfitted freight trains. The long-burning lamps were attended by a porter from Thame.

In 1922 the City of Oxford District Motor Bus services started running to Thame, at first on Tuesdays, Wednesdays, Saturdays and Sundays only. The journey took an hour and cost 2s. Thus began road competition with the Thame branch that continued for the rest of its life. In 1922 also, Mr W. Knight, gateman at Bledlow, retired after 48 years continuous night duty! His colleagues presented him with an adjustable oak armchair. One wonders whether he was able to sleep at night in his retirement.

An important work took place at the Oxford end of the branch, near Kennington Junction, in 1923. This was the reconstruction of the Kennington viaduct over the River Thames. The original viaduct was built in 1863 and was an iron structure of five spans resting on brick abutments at either end, and intermediately on cast-iron screw piles filled with concrete sunk in the river bed. Early in 1914 slight settlement of some piles was noticed, possibly because of heavier locomotives crossing the structure, but more probably because of deterioration of the beds of the screw piles. Because of war conditions it was impossible to consider reconstruction at that time, and each of the screw piles was supported by wooden trestles resting in concrete laid in bags on the river bed.

Because the viaduct was on a sharp (12 chain) curve, reconstruction of the original structure would have been costly because the new foundations would have had to be placed outside the earlier ones, increasing the width of the viaduct. So it was decided to build an entirely new structure alongside the old one, involving about 10 chains of deviated track on its approaches. Authorised in July 1921 at a cost of £22,065, the new viaduct consisted of three equal spans of 83 ft, carried on steel cylinder piers in the river. The superstructure consisted of open web main girders of the bowstring type, 11 ft deep at the centre, and with cross girders hung at 9 ft intervals.

The cylinder piers were sunk at depths varying between 15 ft and 22 ft and filled with concrete. The sinking of the piers took three months to complete, during which time the new abutments and wing walls were built at either end.

The 83 ft-long girders, each weighing 23 tons, were brought to the site by rail, two at a time, by special train. Before the 'Pollen C' trucks conveying the girders could be brought onto the old viaduct, all the cant had to be removed from the permanent way, for fear of the trucks overturning.

The unloading and placing of the outside girders was particularly difficult, partly because of the skew of the viaduct, and partly because the old viaduct was too narrow to allow the extension girders, which are pulled out when a crane is operating (to prevent it from toppling over), to be fully extended. Each outside girder, with the help of a crane at each end, had first to be placed on an inner pier, then the cranes moved closer together and, with their extending girders placed as far out as possible, the bridge girders were again picked up and placed on the outside pier. The first outside girder took two hours to be placed in its final position, but by the end of the operation this had been reduced to half an hour.

The new viaduct came into operation on Sunday 29th July, 1923, some 15 months after work started. Following this the temporary supporting trestles of the old viaduct were removed and then the original viaduct and its cast-iron screw piles were taken down.

The Branch Stations described

The layout descriptions are based on the accompanying diagrams issued by the GWR in 1923 but updated as necessary.

Bledlow

The 1½ miles from Risborough to Bledlow was on a falling gradient, the station itself being located on a 1 in 95 slope. Bledlow was about as basic as a station could be. A single 340 ft-long platform housed a ticket office and waiting room and the station master's house. Later a corrugated iron store was erected. Just off the platform was 'Bledlow Signal Box' which was 15 ft by 12 ft with a 16 lever frame, but had lost its capacity to signal trains by 1902 (and possibly much earlier as it was not a Staff station. It was there solely to operate the adjacent level crossing gates on a minor road which led from the Lower Icknield Way (later B4009) to Bledlow Mill and North Mill, and the associated distant signals, and the siding connection. The railway line here was practically straight in both directions.

In November 1902 the instructions to the staff here were revised as follows:

> Road vehicles etc. may be allowed to cross the line at this level crossing whilst trains are approaching as under:
> *Up Passenger Trains* - Up to 3 minutes after 'Train Entering Section' (TES) signal is sent from Thame to Princes Risborough.
> *Up Goods Trains* - Up to 5 minutes after 'TES' signal is sent from Thame to Princes Risborough. The signalmen at Thame must ascertain and advise Bledlow when an up goods train is stopping at Penn Farm so that the staff at the latter station may use their discretion as to opening and closing the gates.
> *Down Trains* - Until 'Train on Line' has been pegged for a Down train (Passenger or Goods).

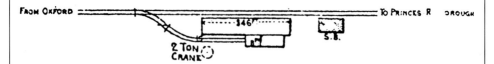

Bledlow station diagram the first of a series for the branch stations issued by the GWR in 1923. These show mileages from Paddington, whereas the accompanying diagrams by John Gillham (traced from OS maps) show the mileages from Princes Risborough. The mileage of Princes Risborough (24 m. 39 ch.) is measured from Northolt Junction.

A rather indistinct view, said to be *c.*1912, with a down train arriving at Bledlow. There seems to be a massive amount of what looks like hay in the goods yard.   *Lens of Sutton Collection*

An old postcard from the 1930s showing the full range of passenger facilities at this small station. *Lens of Sutton Collection*

The 4.02 pm Princes Risborough to Oxford arrives at Bledlow on 18th May, 1959.
Michael Hale

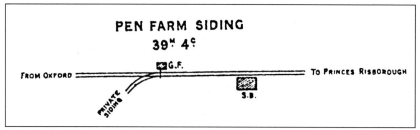

Previously gates had to be closed, and signals lowered, immediately 'Train on Line' had been pegged.

There was a single siding, to accommodate 15 wagons, alongside which, at the Oxford end, was a fixed 2 ton yard crane (worked by hand). Despite its limited facilities it was a busy enough place, the duck traffic has been mentioned earlier, and in July 1931 the *GWR Magazine* carried an article about trawl boles shipped from Bledlow. These were manufactured by J. Walker & Sons of Longwick, a village about 1 mile north of Bledlow station; trawl boles were an elm bobbin attached to the bottom of the trawl net to facilitate its passage over the sea bed and prevent it being caught in crevices etc. The magazine article showed several open truckloads of these boles awaiting dispatch. Another traffic at this station was watercress in the season.

Just a mile down the line was Hinton Crossing where a very minor road crossed the railway. It employed a resident crossing keeper, but in 1959 the crossing was converted to accommodation status, the signalling removed and the crossing keeper made redundant. Just over ½ mile west was Penn Farm siding, sited here for the convenience of Edward Griffin one of the early Directors. Scarcely used by 1933, it was removed in 1939. The 1923 diagram produced by the GWR is intriguing; why should there be any need for a signal box near here, the siding being controlled by the ground frame? The line diagram showing gradients, loops, etc. (*page 60*) also shows this 'signal box' so it is not accidental [but, it is thought, is probably a clerical error]. Another 1⅛ miles west, and on track that had been practically straight all the way from Bledlow, was Towersey Halt, opened in 1933. Just 100 ft long, it was supervised by the station master at Thame.

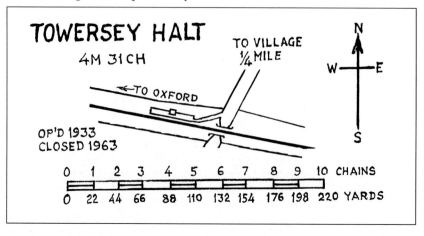

Thame

This was the biggest station on the line until the opening of Morris Cowley and the rapid development of its goods yard. The GWR diagram shows three yard sidings on the upside holding 24, 14 and 14 wagons respectively, the middle one having been built in 1911 or 1912. There was a 30 ton weighbridge in the yard. Behind the up platform stood cattle pens and an end dock for loading carriages, etc. this fourth up siding holding eight wagons. In 1931 new replacement cattle pens were provided alongside the siding which ran behind the down platform, the siding held 21 wagons. At the Oxford end of the layout was a further downside siding, holding 12 wagons, access to which was controlled by ground frame, which also controlled the facing points at this end of the crossing loop.

The 1923 diagram shows the (brick-built) goods shed as 44 ft long. There was a 6 ton fixed hand crane in the yard, presumably provided after the 1923 diagram was drawn, which just shows a 3 ton crane inside the shed.

The crossing loop here was 1,253 ft long and the passenger platforms about 350 ft long and partly covered by a timber all-over roof some 90 ft long and 46 ft wide. The station offices, etc. (51 ft by 20 ft) were contained in a brick building behind the wooden train shed on the upside. There was a footbridge between the two platforms hemmed in between the train shed and the road bridge just beyond the platform ramps at the Oxford end of the station.

Thame signal box dated from 1891/2, the second signal box here, replacing one opened at an earlier date, the earliest mention of a signal cabin being 1864, and was 20 ft long and 12 ft wide containing a 29-lever frame. In 1959, less than a decade before closure, a new frame of 36 levers was installed enabling the box to work both ends of the loop for the first time, and the abolition of the ground frame.

The large water tank on the downside was another feature of Thame. This was 16 ft x 16 ft x 7 ft and carried 10,400 gallons. It fed water columns on each platform. Adjacent was the well and pump house in corrugated iron (20 ft by 8 ft); this had been electrified in 1936 superseding the oil-driven engine and previous horse pumping arrangements mentioned earlier.

In 1958 an oil storage depot was opened at Thame on the downside of the line about ¼ mile on the Oxford side of the station. At this time the short downside siding controlled by ground frame was stop-blocked at the station end but extended westwards to the oil depot to form a reception or stabling siding holding 22 tanks. Two further sidings inside the depot gate, each holding 13 railcars, were used for the discharge of the oil into storage tanks.

Tiddington

Between Bledlow and Thame the line was relatively level although full of short changes of gradient, but between Thame and Tiddington there were frequent strong changes of gradient, necessitating the 'Change of Gradient' boards already mentioned. Tiddington was another small station like Bledlow, although it had a bigger goods yard, and, surprisingly, its single platform was slightly longer than those at Thame (at 359 ft). Access to the sidings was

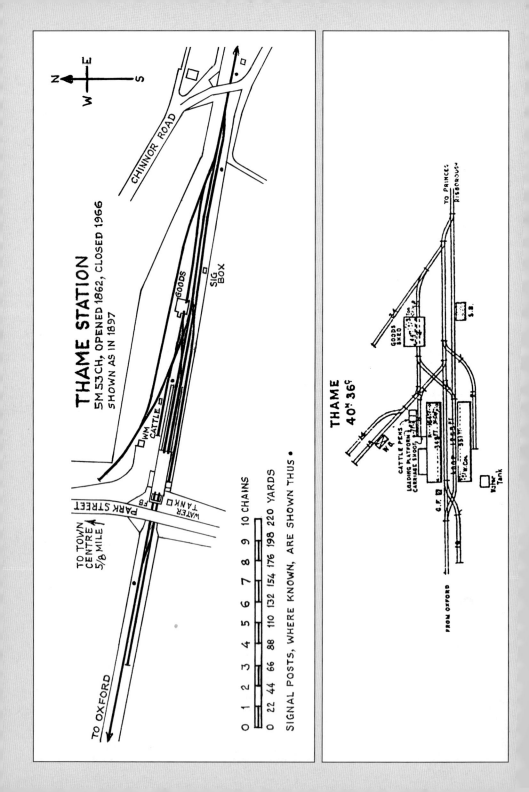

THAME STATION

5M 53CH, OPENED 1862, CLOSED 1966
SHOWN AS IN 1897

CHINNOR ROAD

GOODS

SIG BOX

WM CATTLE

WATER TANK

PARK STREET

FB

TO TOWN CENTRE 5/8 MILE

TO OXFORD

N E S W

0 1 2 3 4 5 6 7 8 9 10 CHAINS
0 22 44 66 88 110 132 154 176 198 220 YARDS

SIGNAL POSTS, WHERE KNOWN, ARE SHOWN THUS •

THAME
40M 36C

TO PRINCES RISBOROUGH

GOODS SHED

S.B.

CATTLE PENS
LOADING PLATFORM
CARRIAGE SHOOT

G.F.

W.Cm.

Water Tank

FROM OXFORD

A nice period view (1930s) of Thame looking towards Oxford. The train in the up platform, which is hauled by what appears to be a 'Metro' tank, has a couple of cattle wagons behind the locomotive and there are several others in the sidings. Note also the 'old' and 'new' style milk churns.   *Brunel University: Mowat Collection*

A view in the opposite direction, taken at the same time. The goods shed office is half its size shown in the later photographs. The yard is well filled, at this period practically all freight went by rail.   *Brunel University: Mowat Collection*

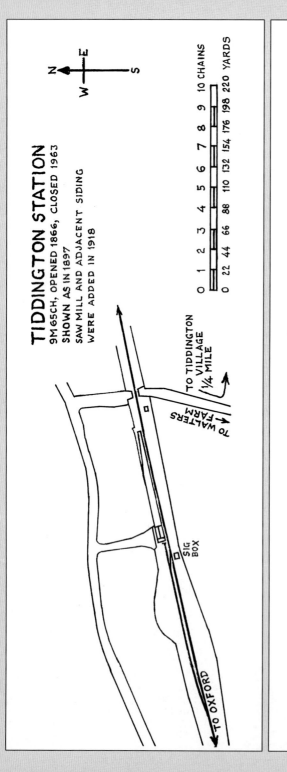

TIDDINGTON STATION

9M 65CH, OPENED 1866, CLOSED 1963
SHOWN AS IN 1897
SAW MILL AND ADJACENT SIDING
WERE ADDED IN 1918

TO TIDDINGTON
VILLAGE
¼ MILE

TO WALTERS
FARM

SIG
BOX

TO OXFORD

0	1	2	3	4	5	6	7	8	9	10 CHAINS
0	22	44	66	88	110	132	154	176	198	220 YARDS

TIDDINGTON
44ᴹ 48ᶜ

W.B (Private)

W.F JOHNSON
PRIVATE SIDING

LOADING
PLATFORM
37FT.

25 cwt. Crane

359'

S.B.

TO PRINCES
RISBOROUGH

FROM OXFORD

controlled by Tiddington 'signal box' although this had been no more than a ground frame since at least 1902. The box was 16 ft 1 in. x 11 ft and at ground level with a 15-lever frame. Nearest the main line was a long siding (probably dating from 1872) which held 12 wagons and connected with the single line at either end, there was a short stub at the Risborough end of the loop siding which served a loading platform and held a further two wagons.

Another dead-end siding, added in 1913, held a further 12 wagons and between these two sidings was a 25 cwt yard crane, later increased in capacity to 3 tons. Finally in 1918 a siding was installed for the Board of Trade timber supply department; in 1922 this became a private siding for W.F. Johnson & Co. Ltd but their use finished at the end of 1925. In 1933 the GWR purchased the siding for additional space for its own traffic at a cost of £140.

Apart from a considerable traffic in milk, another prominent traffic handled was agricultural machinery from Messrs Jarmain's works at Haseley, a mile or two south of the station. Passengers were catered for by a basic wooden station building with a small canopy with ticket office and parcels/goods store; there was a small corrugated iron hut adjacent.

The 3 miles 30 chains between here and Wheatley was more or less evenly divided between rising and falling gradients, but the actual entry to Wheatley station was on a steep 1 in 84 rising.

Mr Mowat framed this classic picture of Tiddington c.1930; it's a pity the date of the Fete advertised on the poster on the railings cannot be read. In this view, looking towards Oxford, the importance of the milk traffic can be seen, and admire the beautiful gardens opposite the platform.   *Brunel University: Mowat Collection*

A fine portrait of Wheatley, looking towards Risborough, *c.* 1930. Avery's Sawmill can be seen right complete with steam crane running on rail tracks. There is a subsidiary shunting signal with an 'S' on the arm below the down starting signal (foreground). The hut on the down platform, just this side of the waiting shelter, is the former ground frame, out of use if the date of this photograph is correct. The GWR publication *Holiday Haunts* is well advertised by poster, but unfortunately the date cannot be read. *Brunel University: Mowat Collection*

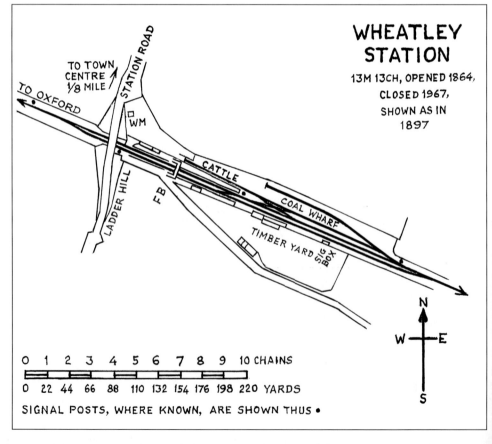

WHEATLEY STATION

13M 13CH, OPENED 1864, CLOSED 1967, SHOWN AS IN 1897

TO TOWN CENTRE 1/8 MILE

STATION ROAD

TO OXFORD

WM

LADDER HILL

FB

CATTLE

COAL WHARF

TIMBER YARD

SIG BOX

N
W E
S

0 1 2 3 4 5 6 7 8 9 10 CHAINS

0 22 44 66 88 110 132 154 176 198 220 YARDS

SIGNAL POSTS, WHERE KNOWN, ARE SHOWN THUS •

Wheatley

The crossing loop was shorter than that at Thame, at 931 ft (according to the station diagram but 959 ft in the 1922 Appendix), and the two platforms were about 310 ft long.

Both sidings here were on the upside of the line, the diagram unfortunately omitting the holding capacity of the northernmost one. Its neighbouring siding held 20 wagons and gave access to a cattle pen (authorised in 1906) and finished with a loading platform and a carriage shoot. As it ran along the back of the up passenger platform, access to wagons could also be had from here. (In 1957 the yard's wagon capacity was given as 30.) There was a weighbridge but no yard crane shown in the diagram, but as can be seen from the photographs one must have been provided later.

The limited passenger facilities consisted of a brick-built ticket office/waiting shelter and toilet facilities on the up platform. Alongside was a brick-built parcels/goods store. On the down platform there was simply a brick-built waiting shelter. There was no footbridge here,* steep steps leading to the adjacent road bridge which was used for the purpose, but doubtless some unofficial crossing of the line by the barrow crossing took place.

Wheatley signal box, like Thame, dated from 1891 or 1892 and replaced an earlier structure probably dating from the opening of the extension to Oxford. The building was 18½ ft x 12 ft and contained a 25-lever frame. Until 1929 there was a ground frame in the centre of the down platform which operated the facing points at the Oxford end of the layout but in 1929 these points were put on the box and the ground frame abolished.

Just over ¼ mile west of Wheatley was Cooper's Crossing, the arrangements for which are described in Chapter Ten. Nearly ¾ mile beyond was the eastern portal of Horspath tunnel 524 yards long, ⅜ of a mile beyond which was Horspath Halt, like Towersey just 100 ft long and also opened in 1933. Interestingly the plan for both halts shows 150 ft platforms but in the event they were built at just 100 ft. Horspath came under the Morris Cowley station master.

The gradient for the first mile or so from Wheatley, including the tunnel, was a steep 1 in 84 rising, after which it fell at (generally) 1 in 83 and 1 in 82 for the two miles to Morris Cowley.

Morris Cowley

The birth of this station in 1928 is dealt with in the next Chapter. As the more or less continuous expansion of its facilities is described in this and subsequent chapters, we will not consider the station here.

---

* But there had been earlier, it is mentioned in the opening inspection Report and shown on the 1897 OS map.

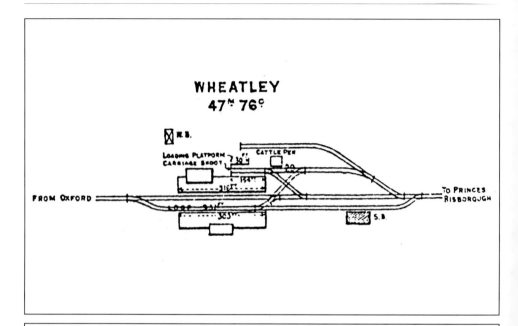

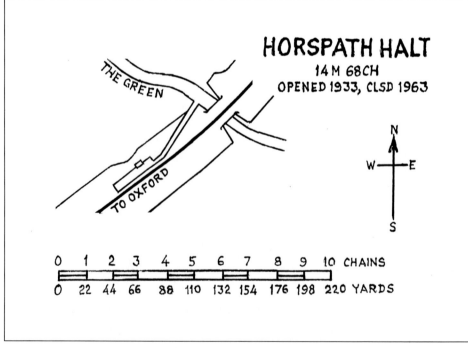

Littlemore

Starting from Morris Cowley on the 1 in 82 failing gradient, the line soon became level and continued so the 1½ miles to Littlemore apart from a short section at 1 in 161 rising approaching the station with its 295 ft-long single platform.

Initially a single traffic siding was provided on the downside, its points just east, or Princes Risborough side, of the platform. However, in 1870 a wagon turntable was put in at the stop blocks end of the siding and another siding led off this at 90 degrees to the Littlemore Asylum. This second siding (see 1897 map, the Asylum siding is not shown on the 1923 diagram) was private to them and used for the reception of coal for heating. Between 1870-1880 (possibly the 1874 work) the first (traffic) siding was made into a loop with points at the east end replacing the stop block; it held 16 wagons. By 1897 a second traffic siding had been installed connected with the first, that shown on the 1923 diagram to hold 24 wagons. The horse loading and carriage dock in 1911 and the sand siding (which ran parallel with the running line for about 500 yards) in 1912 have been mentioned earlier in this chapter. On the 1923 diagram the latter is the siding on the signal box side of the running line which splits into two at its Oxford end. There were two fixed cranes at Littlemore, the 6 ton model being authorised in 1907; it is not known when the 2 ton model was put in. The weighbridge shown was only suitable for horse-drawn vehicles and was replaced (as late as 1937) with a 20 ton model suitable for motor vehicles.

In 1929 a connection to a private siding for the National Benzole Co. was put in partway down the sand siding. This siding was later superseded by a new siding for Shell Mex & BP Ltd installed in 1964 (*see Chapter Eleven*).

In 1899 the station buildings burnt down as recounted earlier and were replaced by those shown in the photographs. Basic booking, waiting and toilet facilities were provided.

The signal box here, like the others, dated from 1891-2. It was 16 ft 1 in. x 11 ft and had a 15-lever frame. It had become a ground frame by 1902 (by 1913 only 7 of the 15 levers were in use), and was closed in 1951, as described in Chapter Nine.

As late as January 1963, coinciding with the withdrawal of passenger trains, an instruction was issued as follows:

> Before the Leading Porter commences to operate the turntable to divert wagons to the Littlemore Mental Hospital he must advise the signalmen at Kennington Jn and Morris Cowley signal boxes and no trains will be allowed to pass over the Single Line while the work is in progress. These signalmen must also be advised immediately the work is completed.

As this wagon turntable, adjacent to the running line, had been in use since 1870 one wonders why it took nearly 100 years to decide to stop trains whilst it was in use. Had there been an accident?

The remaining mile of the branch to Kennington Jn was on a falling gradient, the steepest portion of which was 1 in 93.

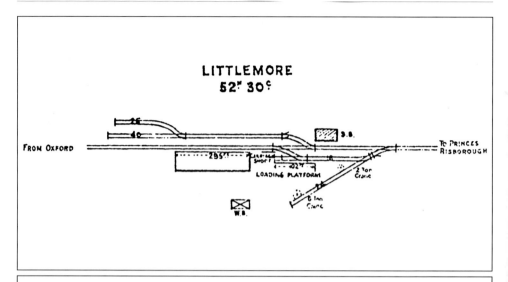

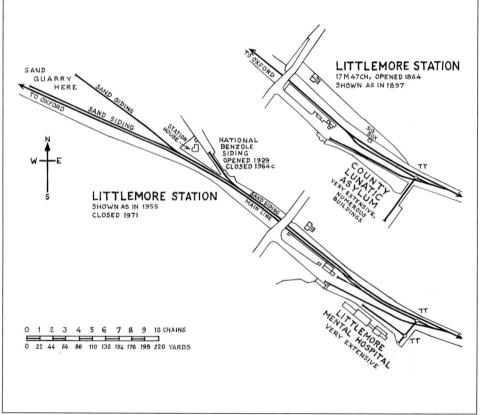

Littlemore, looking towards Princes Risborough *c*.1930. The signal box, by then a ground frame, can be seen in the middle distance, *left*. A train is standing in the sand siding, or possibly these are wagons waiting to be berthed as the yard seems very full. The yard weighbridge can be seen to the right of the station building. Behind the railway boundary looms the bulky presence of the Mental Hospital. *Brunel University: Mowat Collection*

A similar view, but note that the horse loading and carriage dock siding has not yet been built, dating this picture pre-1911. *Lens of Sutton Collection*

The beginning at Cowley - the first train from Oxford arrives at the single siding serving the new Garsington Road site of Pressed Steel in 1926. The prairie tank-hauled goods train has just entered the ¼ mile-long loop siding which ran between two ground frames at 16 m. 4 ch. and 15 m. 62 ch. (the 16 milepost can just be made out against the fence). The private siding for Pressed Steel left the loop at 15 m. 74 ch.; this train will reverse into it. It would be another 2½ years before Morris Cowley had a signal box. The scaffolding for the building that became Pressed Steel 'A' block can be seen, *right*.   *British Motor Industry Heritage Trust*

By mid-1928 the layout at Cowley had expanded to this, photographed from approximately 15 m. 63 ch. looking towards Oxford. In the foreground is the single line, then the loop siding seen above, then three GWR double-ended reception/forming-up sidings, and behind the fence three private sidings for Morris Exports Ltd opened in July 1928. One of the wagons therein is marked 'LNWR'. There are as yet no downside sidings (behind the photographer) but the piles of rails and sleepers signify that they are presently being constructed, the signal box opening on 24th October, 1928 and the goods facilities the following 10th December. The connection for the original Pressed Steel building, seen in the distance, now comes off one of the new reception sidings rather than the loop.   *British Motor Industry Heritage Trust*

Chapter Eight

Into the Motor Age

William Richard Morris (1877-1963) produced his first car at Cowley in 1913, on the site of a former military training college. The Morris Oxford was built from parts made by other manufacturers; bodies, for example, were made in Coventry and brought by rail to Oxford, from where they came to Cowley by horse and cart. By the end of 1914 Morris had sold 1,300 cars at £175 a time.

During World War I WRM Motors produced munitions (hand grenades, parts for mines and shell cases) but still managed to assemble over 1,300 cars by the end of the war. However, in the following period of high inflation and industrial unrest, sales slumped and Morris's bank overdraft increased dramatically. By now Morris Motors, he had a high number of unsold vehicles stored and no room for any more. In January 1921 he decided to cut his prices (in the case of the Morris Cowley model by a fifth) and from then sales took off; the large bank overdraft was cleared by the end of May. In the next two or three years Morris bought up his component makers. By 1926 some 4,000 workers were employed at Cowley where the factory occupied 80 acres and 1,000 cars a week were turned out (he had reduced his prices again in 1922.

In 1926, with some American capital, Morris formed the Pressed Steel Company located next to his own factory. This produced all-steel bodies in panels which were then welded together into a car body. Morris Motors (1926) Ltd was formed to take on the Pressed Steel operation, although in 1930 Morris' sold its shares in Pressed Steel having realised that other companies were reluctant to use the facilities because of the Morris involvement. After this Pressed Steel flourished, carrying out work for many other manufacturers as well. During the General Strike (May 1926) the Morris's work force did not strike (Cowley was not unionised until 1943) although there would have been few, if any, trains to move their product. In 1927 Morris bought Wolseley Motors. In 1927 he decided to concentrate the packing of export cars at Cowley, and for the bulk of them to be moved to the port by rail. A special packing shop was built at Cowley and three new private sidings built (at Morris's cost). The cars were loaded (in cases) to rail trucks by overhead electric crane. In 1927 the work force had grown to 5,000, which must have been the largest employer in the Oxford area by a long way. William Morris was created Baronet in 1929.

The Thame branch ran alongside the works. In January 1928 the GWR's Traffic Committee debated the proposition that a new passenger and goods station be built at Morris Cowley (the passenger station on the site of the former Garsington Bridge Halt). 'The development of the business of Messrs Morris Motors and extension of their works has led to a very rapid growth of the Cowley district, and in order to meet present requirements and anticipate future needs it is recommended that passenger and goods accommodation should be provided . . .' Some 5 acres 1 rod and 39 perches of land were needed at cost of £2,500. The civil, mechanical and signal engineering costs added a further £19,940, making a total of £22,440 (over £936,00 at 2002 prices). The work was authorised and the new Morris Cowley station opened to passengers on 24th September, 1928 and to goods on 10th December, 1928.

Workmen put the finishing touches to Morris Cowley station prior to its opening in September
1928.   *British Motor Industry Heritage Trust*

A photograph of Morris Cowley goods shed after it had been extended in 1929. The signal box
can be seen in the background.   *British Rail*

A new signal box 'Morris Cowley' opened on 24th October, 1928. The plan attached to the signal notice issued is included as an illustration overleaf. The loop and siding shown 'above' (north) of the signal box were already in use and controlled by ground frames; these connections were coupled to the new box and the ground frames recovered. The lines shown in bold south of the signal box were new with the signal box. The loop on the north side was 426 yards long while the new south loop was 400 yards long. It was possible to cross a passenger train (which stayed on the main single line) and a goods train here, or two goods trains, but not two passenger trains.

The passenger platform was on the single line, just to the left of signal 'B' on the plan. The previous electric token* section between Kennington Jn and Wheatley was split into two new sections, Kennington Jn-M. Cowley (blue token) and M. Cowley-Wheatley (red token). The signal notice stated that the new box would be open from 6.45 am until after the 5.45 pm Taplow-Oxford and 12.1 am Oxford-Taplow goods had cleared each night, but closed on Sundays. A long section token (Kennington-Wheatley) was used whenever Cowley was switched out; this was painted yellow.

Colonel Pringle, the Ministry of Transport's Inspecting Officer, did not get round to inspecting the new layout until 15th January, 1929. The major part of his report is given below:

> The works comprise (1) a new halt for passenger service, (2) a goods yard for the Morris Cowley works, and (3) a new signal box controlling the traffic.
>
> The passenger accommodation at the halt consists of a timbered platform 400' long x 12' wide, with a height of 3' together with parcels and booking office, booking hall and conveniences for both sexes. Access is provided to the platform by a footway from an adjoining public road. The platform and the footway are lighted by three challow lamps.
>
> The goods yard arrangements include an existing loop siding on the north side of the single line and in addition a new loop siding on the south side with facing point connections at each end. The yard is controlled from a new signal box (Morris Cowley) which is situated at the south side of the railway intermediate between the loop facing points. The necessary up and down line signals have been provided, and the signal box contains 25 working and 6 spare levers, and is provided with the necessary single line instruments for the sections to Wheatley and Kennington respectively. The interlocking in the new signal frame is correct.
>
> I understand that all shunting movements outside the single line starting signal in each direction are carried out under blocking back signal and such movements are entered in the train register.
>
> The passenger arrangements at the halt are adequate for present day purposes.
>
> Subject to this reservation I recommend that final approval be given to these works.

From then on the layout at Cowley was extended regularly. In 1927 Cowley had produced 61,632 cars, from 1928-1934 (through the Depression years) an average of 53,379 cars were built, then in 1935 output shot up to 96,512 (export sales also dipped between 1928 and 1933). In March 1929 the GWR authorised expenditure of £5,570 on extended siding accommodation holding 30 wagons, also the doubling of the goods shed capacity from three to six trucks with a 60 ft extension (the plan for this work is included as an illustration on page 127). (The extensions to the Pressed Steel and Morris Motors private sidings over the years are shown in *Appendix Three*.) Also in 1929 (January) a private siding was

---

* Notice E61 describing this work states 'token' although the Working Timetable continued to state that the branch was worked by the electric staff until at least 1931. It certainly was in 1922 (*vide* 1922 Sectional Appendix).

MORRIS COWLEY.

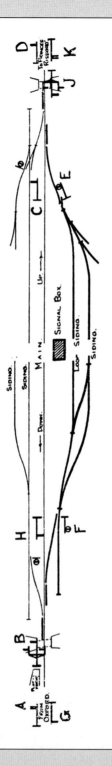

WORK TO BE CARRIED OUT ON WEDNESDAY
OCTOBER 24TH 1928.

The plan accompanying the notice issued detailing the new signal box at Morris Cowley.

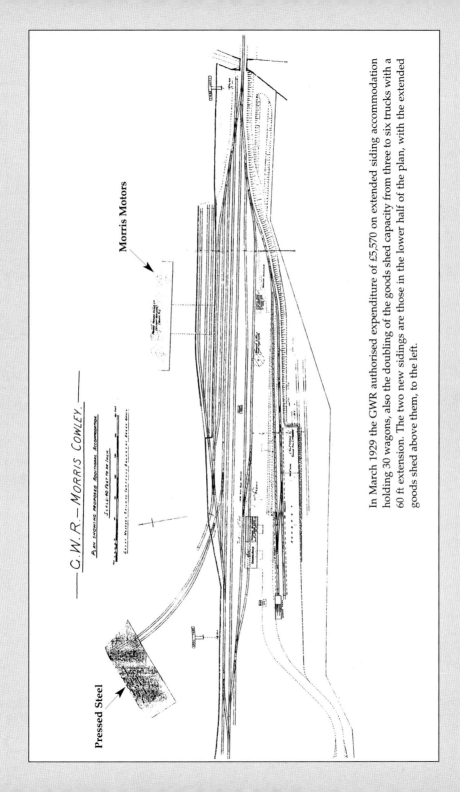

C.W.R. — MORRIS COWLEY.

PLAN SHOWING PROPOSED ADDITIONAL ACCOMMODATION

SCALE 40 FEET TO AN INCH

Pressed Steel

Morris Motors

In March 1929 the GWR authorised expenditure of £5,570 on extended siding accommodation holding 30 wagons, also the doubling of the goods shed capacity from three to six trucks with a 60 ft extension. The two new sidings are those in the lower half of the plan, with the extended goods shed above them, to the left.

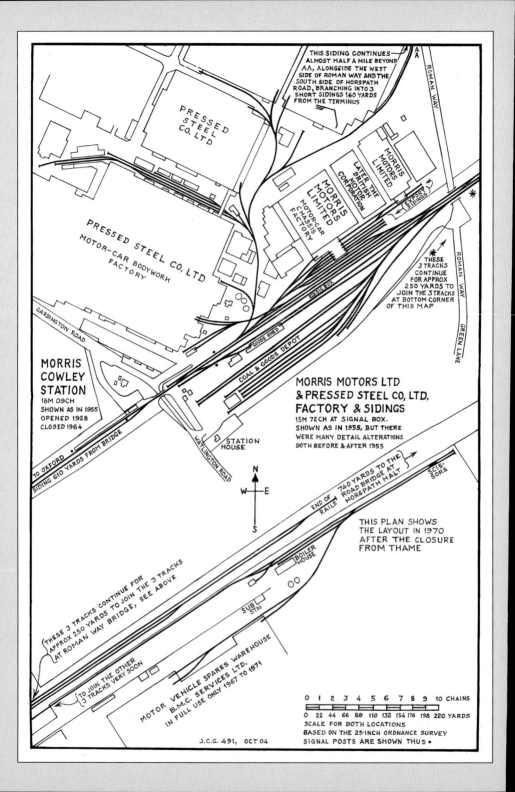

THIS SIDING CONTINUES
ALMOST HALF A MILE BEYOND
AA, ALONGSIDE THE WEST
SIDE OF ROMAN WAY AND THE
SOUTH SIDE OF HORSPATH
ROAD, BRANCHING INTO 3
SHORT SIDINGS 160 YARDS
FROM THE TERMINUS

AA

ROMAN WAY

PRESSED
STEEL
CO. LTD

MORRIS
MOTORS
LIMITED

MORRIS MOTORS LIMITED
LATER THE BRITISH MOTOR CORPORATION

MORRIS MOTORS LIMITED
MOTOR-CAR CHASSIS FACTORY

EXPORT SIDINGS

PRESSED STEEL CO, LTD
MOTOR-CAR BODYWORK
FACTORY

ROMAN WAY

GREEN LANE

* THESE
3 TRACKS
CONTINUE
FOR APPROX
250 YARDS TO
JOIN THE 3 TRACKS
AT BOTTOM CORNER
OF THIS MAP

SIG BOX

GARSINGTON ROAD

COAL & GOODS DEPOT

GOODS SHED

MORRIS
COWLEY
STATION

16M 09CH
SHOWN AS IN 1955
OPENED 1928
CLOSED 1964

MORRIS MOTORS LTD
& PRESSED STEEL CO, LTD,
FACTORY & SIDINGS

15M 72CH AT SIGNAL BOX.
SHOWN AS IN 1955, BUT THERE
WERE MANY DETAIL ALTERATIONS
BOTH BEFORE & AFTER 1955

STATION
HOUSE

WATLINGTON ROAD

TO OXFORD

SIDING 610 YARDS FROM BRIDGE

N
W E
S

END OF 740 YARDS TO THE
RAILS ROAD BRIDGE AT
HORSPATH HALT

SCIS-
SORS

THIS PLAN SHOWS
THE LAYOUT IN 1970
AFTER THE CLOSURE
FROM THAME

BOILER
HOUSE

THESE 3 TRACKS CONTINUE FOR
APPROX 250 YARDS TO JOIN THE 3 TRACKS
AT ROMAN WAY BRIDGE, SEE ABOVE

SUB
STN

TO JOIN THE OTHER
3 TRACKS VERY SOON

MOTOR VEHICLE SPARES WAREHOUSE
B.M.C. SERVICES LTD.
IN FULL USE ONLY 1967 TO 1971

0 1 2 3 4 5 6 7 8 9 10 CHAINS

0 22 44 66 88 110 132 154 176 198 220 YARDS

SCALE FOR BOTH LOCATIONS
BASED ON THE 25-INCH ORDNANCE SURVEY
SIGNAL POSTS ARE SHOWN THUS •

J.C.G. 491, OCT 04

installed at Littlemore for National Benzole, on the upside of the line west of the station, at a cost of £338.

The November 1929 *GWR Magazine* announced the appointment of R.L. A'hern from Taplow to the position of station master, Morris Cowley. He remained there until, it is thought, sometime in the 1950s. (A thorough check of the GWR/BR Magazines has not revealed the date, but station master Mr Ellwood *left there* on promotion to Princes Risborough in 1960, *see Appendix Four*.)

Before leaving the 1920s we may refer briefly to the General Strike in May 1926. This began at midnight on 3rd/4th May and was pretty complete throughout the GWR.* According to the official records there were no passenger trains over this line until an Oxford-Thame service was started on Tuesday 11th May. Although the General Strike was called off on 12th May, peace terms on the railway were not settled until 14th May. The station master at Littlemore went on strike, but it appears that he was allowed to return to his post afterwards unlike his colleagues at Kingham and Tyseley. Also, in 1928, as Oxfordshire County Council wished to widen the A40 where it passed under the railway between Tiddington and Wheatley stations, the GWR replaced the original stone-built bridge by a new one of steel girders (*see illustration page 131*). The installation took place during a 16 hour occupation on a Sunday with one up and one down train being covered by GWR road vehicles between the two stations mentioned. In 1930 the bridge over the River Thame, about ½ mile away towards Oxford, was replaced by a steel structure with one intermediate pier (*see page 132*).

In March 1930 Traffic Committee were asked to authorise £3,780 for two new sidings at Cowley, extension of a further siding and installation of electric lighting throughout the whole station:

> The traffic dealt with has shown continuous and rapid growth since the depot was opened . . . the tonnage dealt with in December being 4,700 tons and in February last 7,000 tons.
>
> The additional sidings . . . are mainly required for dealing with a valuable competitive traffic in motor cars on their own wheels destined for Scotland and Ireland, which has recently been secured from competitive routes, and upon which the carriage charges average about £3,500 a month.

The work was authorised and the sidings were in place by December.

In the 1930s the GWR rapidly introduced the Motor Trolley Economic System of Maintenance on Single lines. This rather wordy title meant that by employing a motor trolley a longer portion of track could be maintained compared with the traditional method of the gang walking their length. On the Thame branch two gangs covered the line between Risborough and Cowley - gang 135 between 0 m. 10¾ ch. and 7 m. 14 ch. (the latter mileage between Thame and Tiddington) and gang 138 between 7 m. 14 ch. and 15 m. 28¼ ch. (between Wheatley and Cowley). This rather implies that gangs 136 and 137 had been abolished as a result of the scheme. Instead of the Token, a gang using a trolley was required to carry an Occupation Key and a series of Key boxes were provided throughout the sections to enable the trolley to be removed from the line and the Occupation Key replaced in its box at various points along the line. For example in the Token section Thame-Wheatley there were seven intermediate key boxes apart from those located at the

* See the author's *The GWR and the General Strike* (Oakwood Press LP 194).

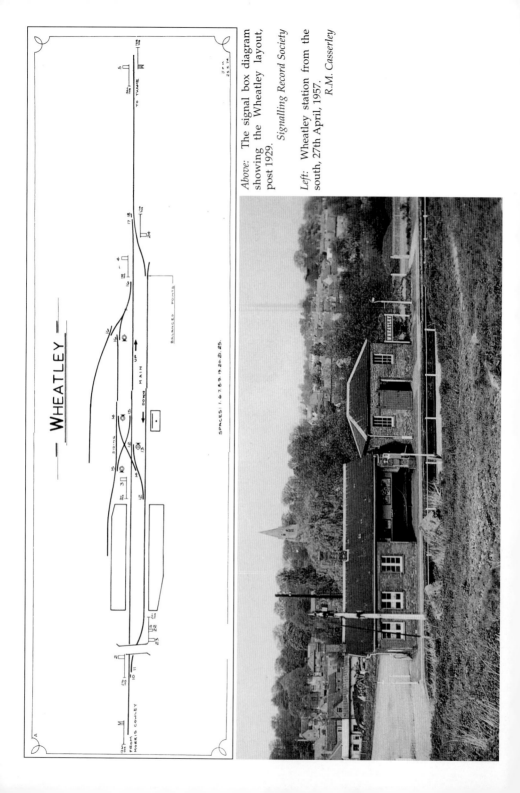

Above: The signal box diagram showing the Wheatley layout, post 1929.

Signalling Record Society

Left: Wheatley station from the south, 27th April, 1957.

R.M. Casserley

Two 1928 pictures of the bridge over the A40 near Wheatley, which was renewed in that year. The road was diverted, the old road width being 30 ft, the new width 50 ft, and the old stone overbridge was filled in with spoil. It was uncovered in 1961 when the road was widened again and a new girder bridge replaced it. In 1970, after this portion of the line had closed, the relatively new girder bridge was re-used in South Wales. *(Both) British Rail*

The bridge over the River Thame, just west of the A40 bridge, which was renewed in 1930. The Wheatley Bridge Hotel can be seen in the background. This is the hotel that was almost hit by a bomb in 1940 (*see Chapter Nine*). *British Rail*

One of a number of photographs showing the expansion of Morris Cowley between 1930-1937 (*see also photographs pages 142 and 143*). First the scene in 1930. The buildings are those of Morris Industries Exports Ltd, those of Pressed Steel are behind the camera. Note that spoil is being tipped (*right*) to extend the down yard. *British Motor Industry Heritage Trust*

Looking north at Princes Risborough *c*.1930, Watlington and Oxford bay *far left*, Aylesbury bay beyond the up platform, *right*. *Brunel University: Mowat Collection*

Looking south *c*.1930; the Watlington and Oxford bay can be seen, *extreme right*.
Brunel University: Mowat Collection

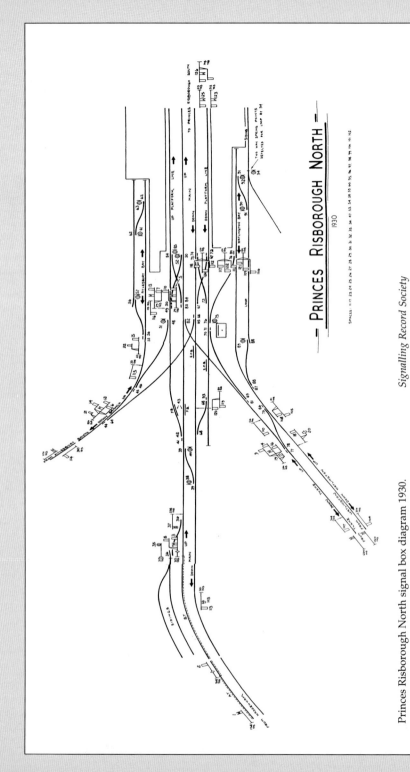

PRINCES RISBOROUGH NORTH

1930

Princes Risborough North signal box diagram 1930.

Signalling Record Society

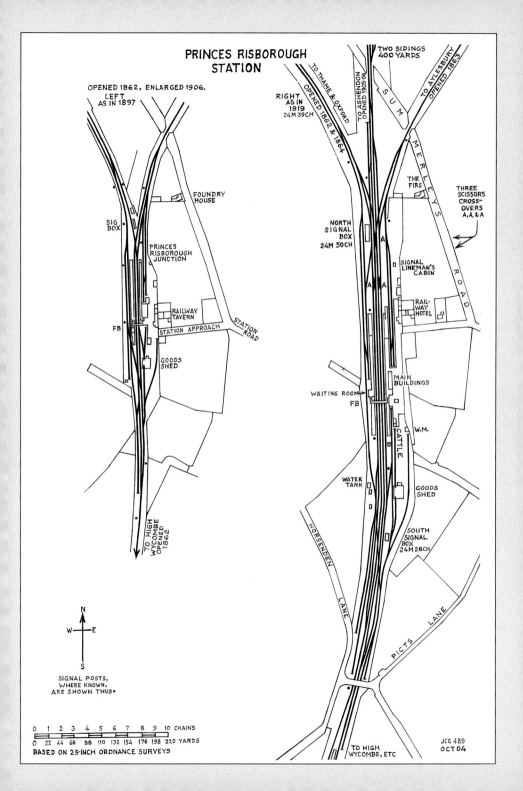

PRINCES RISBOROUGH
STATION

OPENED 1862, ENLARGED 1906.

LEFT
AS IN 1897

RIGHT
AS IN
1919
24M 39CH

TWO SIDINGS
400 YARDS

TO THAME & OXFORD
OPENED 1862 & 1864

TO ASHENDON
OPENED 1905/06

S U M M E R L E Y S   R O A D

TO AYLESBURY
OPENED 1863

FOUNDRY
HOUSE

SIG
BOX

PRINCES
RISBOROUGH
JUNCTION

NORTH
SIGNAL
BOX
24M 50CH

THE
FIRS

THREE
SCISSORS
CROSS-
OVERS
A, A, & A

A

A A

SIGNAL
LINEMAN'S
CABIN

RAIL-
WAY
HOTEL

RAILWAY
TAVERN

FB

STATION APPROACH

STATION
ROAD

GOODS
SHED

MAIN
BUILDINGS

WAITING ROOM

FB

W.M.

CATTLE

WATER
TANK

GOODS
SHED

SOUTH
SIGNAL
BOX
24M 28CH

HORSENDEN LANE

PICTS LANE

TO HIGH
WYCOMBE
OPENED
1862

N
W   E
S

SIGNAL POSTS,
WHERE KNOWN,
ARE SHOWN THUS•

0 1 2 3 4 5 6 7 8 9 10 CHAINS

0 22 44 66 88 110 132 154 176 198 220 YARDS

BASED ON 2.5-INCH ORDNANCE SURVEYS

TO HIGH
WYCOMBE, ETC

JCG 489
OCT 04

A view of Bledlow from the 1930s, looking towards Oxford. *Brunel University: Mowat Collection*

A 'County' class 4-4-2 tank locomotive waits at Oxford up platform in the early 1930s. This class of locomotive was extinct by 1935, ousted by the '61XX class 2-6-2T.   *Lens of Sutton Collection*

signal boxes. Removal and replacement of an Occupation Key required the co-operation of the signalman and withdrawal of a Token was not possible while the key was out. This system was installed on the Thame branch on 3rd October, 1932, requiring three control instruments, 21 key boxes and 17 telephones in total.

Also at this time the GWR was busily providing new halts where they thought local traffic could be obtained, and to prevent it being captured by motor buses. New halts were opened on 5th June, 1933 at Towersey and Horsepath [sic], the latter on (almost) the site of that closed in 1915. Both had short, wooden platforms, 100ft in length costing £210 and £200 respectively. Col Mount inspected them in April 1934 and his report on Horsepath read as follows:

A high level platform 100 ft long and 8 ft wide provided on west side of Horspath-Garsington Road which passes under line at this point.

The platform is built on bank of sleeper trestling with a sleeper surface. It is approached up the bank by sloping (1 in 10) fenced path from the road, where a wicket gate is provided. Shelter 12' x 8' - adequately fenced - one electric light in centre of platform and another at the gate on the road.

Halt served by 5 trains each way daily, used by 500 passengers per month. Three boards are located on each side to indicate where to stop, so that rear coach may be opposite the platform.

Halt replaces previous one on same site removed during the War.

Works in good order, approved for passenger traffic.

In March 1934, it was necessary to approach Traffic Committee again for more money to expand the goods facilities at Cowley because of the burgeoning car export business. In the commentary accompanying the application the General Manager pointed out that traffic carried for the firm had grown to 80,000 tons a year representing a revenue of over £80,000. Some 600 houses were being erected in the neighbourhood, the works was being extended and it was anticipated that the export trade would double in the next year. Extensions proposed to the layout comprised two additional and two extended sidings, two long headshunts to avoid using the single line for shunting purposes, coal wharves and a new roadway; £7,317 was requested and authorised for this work. The *GWR Magazine* for January 1936 said that 3,630 ft of additional sidings had been laid at Morris Cowley (in 1935).

Thame Agricultural Show was always a major event each September and at this time attendance would be between 20 and 30 thousand persons, with over 500 classes and over 4,000 exhibits. As the special traffic notice for 1935 has been saved, it is possible to describe its impact on the railway for that year. A special timetable operated and this is included as an illustration on pages 140/1. However, in addition to the Special branch timetable there were several pages of supplementary information 'putting meat on the bones' and these are summarised below:

Down Trains

8.10 am Paddington-Oxford.
Run in two parts, 1st part as booked, 2nd part at 8.13 am conveying passengers only between High Wycombe and Thame, calling at Risborough, Bledlow and Thame, and all parcels, fish and tail traffic for stations Ruislip to Thame. Next worked 10 40 am empty to Risborough and *11.15 am special Risborough to Thame*, thence empty to Oxford.

Two views of the very basic facilities of Towersey Halt.   *(Both) Lens of Sutton Collection*

Horspath halt from the rear, showing the pagoda hut that the Home Guard wanted to use as a pillbox! *Lens of Sutton Collection*

A close-up of the nameboard at Horspath Halt. *Brian Matthews Collection*

Special Arrangements in connection with Thame Agricultural Show, Thursday, September 19th
—continued.

TRAIN SERVICE—THAME BRANCH.
DOWN TRAINS.

	Engine and Van		Cov. Cars ex Acton.		Passenger.		1st Part 8.10 a.m. Paddington.		3.55 a.m. Slough Freight Retimed.		2nd Part 8.10 a.m. Paddington.	
	arr. a.m.	dep. a.m.	arr. a.m.	dep. a.m.	arr. a.m.	dep. a.m.	arr. a.m.	dep. a.m.	arr. a.m.	dep. a.m.	arr. a.m.	dep. a.m.
Princes Risboro'	..	..		6 40	—	8 10	9 38 X	9 48	8 15 X	9 30	10 3	10 10
Bledlow			—		8 13	8 14	9 51	9 52	—		10 13	10 14
Towersley Halt			—		8 18	8 19	9 56	9 57	—			
Thame			C S		8 22	8 23	10 0	10 5	9 47 X	10 23	10 20	X —
Tiddington			—		8 30	8 31	10 12	10 14	—	—		
Wheatley			7 12 X	7 21	8 37 X	8 40	10 20	10 22	10 43 X	10 56		
Horspath Halt			—		8 44	8 45	10 26	10 27	—			
Morris Cowley	—	7†22	7 28	—	8 48	8 49	10 30	10 31	11 5 X	12 10		
Littlemore	—		—		8 52	8 53	10 34	10 35	12 16	12 25		
Kennington Jct.	C X S		..	..	C S		C X S		12 31*	12 48		
Oxford	7†37	—			9 2		10 44		12 55			

Note (2nd Part): Leaves at 10†40 a.m. for Princes Risboro'.

	Special Passenger.		Pilot.		Special Passenger.		12.32 p.m. Paddington Passenger.		Light Engine and Guard.		Pilot retimed.		2.25 p.m. Paddington Passenger.	
	arr. a.m.	dep. a.m.	arr. p.m.	dep. p.m.	arr. p.m.	dep. p.m.	arr. p.m.	dep. p.m.	arr. p.m.	dep. p.m.	arr. p.m.	dep. p.m.	arr. p.m	dep. p.m
Princes Risboro'	—	11 15			— X	12 24	1 47	1 51					3 46	3 50
Bledlow	11 18	11 19			12 27	12 28	1 54	1 55					3 56	3 57
Towersley Halt	11 23	11 24			12 32	12 33	1 59	2 0					4 1	4 2
Thame	11 27 X	11†28			12 36 X	1 0	2 3	2 5					4 5 X	4 6
Tiddington	—	—			1†10	1†30	2 12	2 13					4 16	4 17
Wheatley	11†41 X	11†43			1†42	1†55	2 19	2 21					4 24	4 25
Horspath Halt	—	—					2 25	2 26					4 30	4 31
Morris Cowley	11†50 C X S		12†3		12 45	2†5	2 29	2 30	X	2,51		3 20	4 34 X	4 35
Littlemore	—	—			12 48		2 33	2 34	2,55	3 15	—	—	4 39	4 40
Kennington Jct.	C S		12 53*	1 37	..	..	C X S		C S		C S		C X S	
Oxford	12†18	—		1 43	..	..	2 41	—	3.22		3 38		4 47	—

	Banbury Passenger.		Special Passenger.		Retimed Auto (in place of Oil Car).		Freight.		Passenger (in place of Oil Car).		6.25 p.m. Paddington Passenger.		8.15 p.m. Freight Thame to Oxford.	
	arr. p.m.	dep. p.m.	arr. p.m.	dep. p.m.	arr. p.m.	dep. p.m.	arr. p.m.	dep. p.m.	arr. p.m.	dep. p.m.	arr. p.m.	dep. p.m.	arr. p.m	dep. p.m
Princes Risboro'					—	5 52			— X	6 37	7 35 X	7 42		
Bledlow					—	5 58			6 40½	6 41	7 46	7 47		
Towersley Halt					—	6 3			6 45½	6 46	7 51	7 52		
Thame			—	6 0	6 7	—			6 49 X	7 20	7 55 X	7 57		
Tiddington			6 6	6 8					7 27	7 28	8 4	8 5		
Wheatley			6 14	6 15					7 34 X	7 35	8 11	8 13	**Will**	
Horspath Halt			6 19	6 20					7 39	7 40	8 17	8 18	**not**	
Morris Cowley	— X	5 10	6 23	6 24			— X	7 20	7 43	7 44	8 21	8 22	**run.**	
Littlemore	—	5 13½	6 28	6 29			C R		7 47	7 48	8 25	8 26		
Kennington Jct.	C S		C X S				C7 30S		C S		C X S			
Oxford	5 20	5 22	6 36	Q			7S36	7S45	7 55	—	8 37			

Q—To be extended as necessary with horseboxes.   S—Oxford South.   Oxford North arr. 7.50 p.m.

	Military Special to Tidworth.		8.2 p.m. Auto ex P. Risboro' retimed.		Special Passenger and Poultry.		Freight to Bordesley Junction.		Special Passenger.		5.45 p.m. Taplow Freight retimed.		Special Passenger.	
	arr. p.m.	dep. p.m.	arr. p.m.	dep. p.m.	arr. p.m.	dep. p.m.	arr. p.m.	dep. p.m.	arr. p.m.	dep. p.m.	arr. p.m.	dep. p.m.	arr. p.m	dep. p.m
Princes Risboro'			— X	8 12					9†2	9 20	X 9 50		C10	30S
Bledlow			—	8 18							C R			
Towersley Halt				8 23							—			
Thame		8 20	8 27 X	—	—	8 50			9†14●	10 0	10 6	10*15	10†42	10 4
Tiddington					8 57	8 58			10 7	10 8			10 52	10 5
Wheatley	C S				9 4 X	9 5			10 14	10 15	C10	30S	10 59	11
Horspath Halt					9 9	9 10			10 19	10 20			11 4	11
Morris Cowley	C S				9 13	9 14	—	10 10	10 23	10 24	C S		11 8	11
Littlemore					9 18	9 19	—	10 27	10 27	10 28			11 12	11 1
Kennington Jct.					C S		C10	21S	C S		10 43		C S	
Oxford	8 50E	G 9 0			9 27	—	10 30S		10 35	—	10 50	—	11 20	—

The special timetable for the 1935 Thame Show.

Special Arrangements in connection with Thame Agricultural Show, Thursday, September 19th—continued.

TRAIN SERVICE—THAME BRANCH—continued.

UP TRAINS.

	Taplow Freight.		3.20 a.m. Bordesley Freight.		6.5 a.m. Banbury Passenger.		Poultry Special		Pilot.		Passenger to 'Paddington. Q		Empty Train.	
	arr. a.m.	dep. a.m.	arr. a.m.	dep. a.m.	arr. a.m.	dep. a.m.	arr. a.m.	dep. a.m.	arr. a.m.	dep. a.m.	arr. a.m.	dep. a.m.	arr. a.m.	dep. a.m.
Oxford	—	12 1	6 30	C T 6 35	6 48	6 55	—	7 30	—	7 40	—	8 18		
Kennington Jct.	C S		C6 40S		C S		CXS		C7 48S		C S			11.15 a.m. Special
Littlemore	—	—	—	—	7 2	7 3	—	—	7 53		8 25	8 26		
Morris Cowley	C12 17S		6 52	—	7 6¼	7 11	C S		7 59	—	8 29½	8 31		For Princes
Horspath Halt ..	—	—			7 14½	7 15					8 34½	8 35		ex
Wheatley	C12 25R		..	..	7 19	7 20	C7 45S		..	..	8 39	X8 42		Princes Risboro'.
Tiddington	—	—			7 26	7 27	—	—	..	..	8 48	8 50		
Thame	12 44	1 0	..	..	7 34	7 40	7 58	—	..	..	8 57	9 6	—	10†40
Towersey Halt	—	—			7 43½	7 44	Worked by		..	..	9 9½	9 10		
Bledlow ..	—	—	..	..	7 50	7 51	Thame		..	..	9 16	9 18		
Princes Risboro'	1 18	2 20	..	..	7 55		Shunting Engine.		..	..	9 22	X9 32	10†52	—

Q—Will be held at Oxford to connect with 6.40 a.m. Leamington. **Special effort to be made to regain lost time.**

	Military Special ex Tidworth.		Special Passenger and Livestock.		Empty Train.		Passenger to Paddington.		Taplow Freight.		Passenger to Paddington.		3.20 p.m. Freight Oxford to Thame.	
	arr. a.m.	dep. a.m.	arr. a.m.	dep. a.m.	arr. a.m.	dep. a.m.	arr. a.m.	dep. a.m.	arr. a.m.	dep. a.m.	arr. p.m.	dep. p.m.	arr.	dep.
Oxford	10 18E	G10 30	—	10 55			—	11 20	—	11 42	—	2 38	..	..
Kennington Jct.	10 35X	10 40	C S		For 12.24 p.m. Special ex Princes Risboro'.		11 27	11 28	C11 51S		CXS			
Littlemore			11 2	11 2½			11 31½	X11 32½			2 45	2 46		
Morris Cowley	C S		CXS				11 31½	X11 32½	C12 X2S		2 49½	X2 50	Will	
Horspath Halt ..			11 9	11 9½			11 36	11 37	—	—	2 53½	2 54	Not	
Wheatley	10 54X	10 55	11 13½	11 14			11 41X	11 42	C12 11S		2 58	2 59	Run.	
Tiddington							11 48	11 49	—	—	3 5	3 6		
Thame	11 8	—	11 27	X —		11†40	11 56	12 7	12 30	CXS 12 37	3 13	3 16	..	..
Towersey Halt			Leaves at 11†40 a.m. for Princes Risboro'.		—	—	12 10½	12 12	—	—	3 19½	3 20	..	..
Bledlow	Returns at 8.20 p.m.				—	—	12 18	12 20	—	—	3 26	3 27	..	..
Princes Risboro'					11†52	—	12 24	12 28	12 55	2 6	3 31	3 35	..	..

	Special Passenger		Freight.		Light Engine and Guard.		5. 8 p.m. Freight Oxford to Morris Cowley.		Passenger (in place of Oil Car).		Auto (in place of Oil Car).		Passenger to Paddington.	
	arr. p.m.	dep. p.m.	arr. p.m.	dep. p.m.	arr. p.m.	dep. p.m.	arr. p.m.	dep. p.m.	arr. p.m.	dep. p.m.	arr. p.m.	dep. p.m.	arr. p.m.	dep. p.m.
Oxford	—	3 30	—	4 10	—	4‖40	Coupled to 4.10 p.m. Freight ex Oxford and not to Shunt at Littlemore.		—	4 5½	..	..	—	6 35
Kennington Jct.	CXS		C4X16S		CXS				C S		—			
Littlemore	3 37	3 38	—	—	—	—			4 57	4 5½	..	..	6 42	6 43
Morris Cowley	3 41½	3 42	4 30	X	4‖55	X —			5 1½	5 ½	..	..	6 46½	6 47
Horspath Halt ..	3 45½	3 46	..	..	For 5.10 p.m. Morris Cowley to Banbury.				5 5½	5 7	..	..	6 50½	6 51
Wheatley	3 50	3 51	..	..					5 11	5 12	..	..	6 55	6 57
Tiddington	3 57	3 58	..	..					5 18	5 18½	..	..	7 3	7 4
Thame	4 5	X —	..	..					5 25½	5 26½	—	6 20	7 11 X	7 17
Towersey Halt	Forms 6.0 p.m. Special Thame to Oxford.		..	..					5 30	5 30½	—	6 24	7 20½	7 21
Bledlow			..	..					5 36½	5 37	—	6 31	7 27	7 28
Princes Risboro'			..	..					5 41	—	6 35	X—	7 32 X	7 40

	Empty Train		Special Passenger to Paddington.		Special Passenger.		8.25 p.m. Auto ex Thame retimed.		Empty Train.		Special Passenger to High Wycombe.		Light Engine.	
	arr. p.m.	dep. p.m.	arr. p.m.	dep. p.m.	arr. p.m	dep. p.m.	arr. p.m	dep. p.m.	arr. p.m.	dep. p.m.	arr. p.m.	dep. p.m.	arr. p.m.	dep. p.m.
Oxford	—	7† 5	..	..	..	..	..	..	—	8†35	..	..	—	9‖40
Kennington Jct.	C S		..	..	..	..	..	..	CXS		..	..	C S	
Littlemore	—	—	..	..	..	..	..	..	—	—	..	..	—	—
Morris Cowley	C7X18S		..	..	..	..	..	..	C S		..	..	9‖55	—
Horspath Halt ..			..	..	..	..	..	..			..	..		
Wheatley	7†28	CXS 7†36	..	..	..	..	..	..	9†0	CXS 9†6	..	..	..	..
Tiddington			..	..	..	..	..	..			..	..	..	..
Thame	7†49	—	— X	8 0	— X	8 28	—	8 45	9†18	—	9 28½	9 25	..	..
Towersey Halt	Forms 8.0 p.m. and 8.28 p.m. Specials ex Thame.		—	—	8 31½	8 32	—	8 49	Forms 9.25 p.m. Special ex Thame.		9 28½	9 29	..	..
Bledlow			—	—	8 38	8 39	—	8 56			9 35	9 36	..	..
Princes Risboro'			8 11 X	8 12	8 43	K	9 0	X—			9 40 X	9 41	..	..

K—To connect with 7.55 p.m. Brackley.

The special timetable for the 1935 Thame Show.

The second of three photographs showing the expansion of Morris Cowley between 1930-1937. The view in 1934, probably photographed on Sunday as no living soul is to be seen. The Pressed Steel sports ground is bottom right, Roman Way crosses the picture top right. The yard crane shown was moved from Littlemore in 1929/30.

The third of three photographs showing the expansion of Morris Cowley between 1930-1937. This 1937 view shows major expansion of Pressed Steel (left-hand half of picture) and still more sidings in the down yard with tipping and expansion continuing. The goods shed can be seen at bottom left of the picture. Roman Way is top right.

British Motor Industry Heritage Trust

An aerial view looking east showing how Morris Cowley had developed by c.1937. The railway runs from lower right to the centre of the picture where Horspath village can be seen. Morris Industries Exports can be seen furthest from the camera at 90 degrees to the railway line. This is where the tanks were built during the war. The massive development west of that is the Pressed Steel body plant. To its left, with the two tall chimneys is the Morris Motors northern works. The Garsington Road divides these works from the recently opened southern works (bottom) which were to play such a large part in World War II aircraft manufacture and repair. To the right of the down side sidings (*extreme right*) is the sports field that was used to store the huge pile of aircraft parts in the war (later reported to extend almost to Horspath).

British Motor Industry Heritage Trust

12.24 pm special P. Risborough to Thame.
Formed off *10.55 am special Oxford-Thame* (and empty to Risborough). After arrival at Thame, empty coaches forward to Cowley (shunting yards at Tiddington and Wheatley *en route* if required); coaches berthed (to form 5.10 pm Cowley-Banbury), then engine and guard to Oxford, shunting yard at Littlemore *en route*.
6 pm special Thame - Oxford. (2 Thirds and Brake Compo).
Formed off *3.30 pm Oxford special.*
8.50 pm special Thame-Oxford.
Worked by special shunting engine located at Thame (which had arrived with 7.30 am special from Oxford. Conveys passengers and vans (containing poultry) for Leicester, Windermere, Newton Abbot and Paddington (via Oxford).

Up Trains

7.30 am Poultry special Oxford-Thame.
Worked by engine to act as shunting engine at Thame all day until return with 8.50 pm poultry special.
7.40 am military special Tidworth-Thame.
Conveys one officer, 25 men (3rd King's Own Hussars), horses, donkey, dog, motor car and jumps. Engine returns to Oxford attached to 11.28 empty train from Thame. Engine returns attached to 6.35 pm ex-Oxford and train returns at *8.20 pm to Tidworth.*
7.5 pm empty Oxford-Thame.
Formed engine for 8 pm Thame-Paddington special, engine for 8.28 pm Thame-Risborough special, 3 vehicles for 8.28 pm, 8 vehicles for 8 pm special.
8 pm special Thame-Paddington Calls Risborough, Wycombe, Maidenhead, Slough, Southall, Ealing B, Westbourne Park, Paddington (arr. 9.37 pm). [Note 'original' route to Paddington taken].
8.28 pm Thame-Risborough.
Returns empty to Thame, then forms *10 pm Thame-Oxford special.*
8.35 pm Oxford-Thame empty (4 coaches).
Forms *9.25 pm Thame-H. Wycombe special*, returning 10.15 empty H. Wycombe-Thame (Risborough pass 10.30 pm), then *10.45 pm Thame-Oxford special.*

Note that certain trains, normally formed by diesel units ('oil cars') are on this day covered by engine and coach formations. Because of the heavy occupation of the branch certain freight trains were withdrawn, or their intermediate stops cancelled, and the notice goes into the minutiae of the altered freight working necessary, too detailed to include here. To handle all this traffic the staff at Thame was supplemented by an inspector, two clerks, six ticket collectors, two van guards, four porters, a relief porter and two permanent way men to assist in clearing cattle trucks. Some of these extra staff were also required on days before and after the actual show day (19th September). Additionally two extra lorries and their drivers were supplied by Oxford. Ever cautious, the GWR decreed that the telegraph linesman must be on duty at Thame from 9 am to 8 pm on show day.

You had to have stamina for GWR excursions. On Sunday 19th July, 1936 a half day excursion from Aylesbury to Weston-super-Mare meant leaving Thame at 10.22 am and arriving back at 11 pm, with time in Weston from 1.23 to 7.50 pm. Presumably the half day was the time at Weston! The train called at all stations and halts between Risborough and Oxford, including Morris Cowley which did not normally have a Sunday service. Mr A.D. Ayres, who was born at Horspath in 1930, says that there was an annual excursion to Southend on a Sunday.

A trainload of cars destined for Ireland is being loaded at Morris Industries Exports sidings on 18th August, 1937. The crate held by the electric overhead crane is marked 'Dun Laoghaire Kingstown Co. Dublin via Royal Edward Siding Avonmouth'. '57XX' class 0-6-0PT No. 3722 has a chalked inscription '6.15 MC' under its numberplate.   *British Motor Industry Heritage Trust*

Morris Cowley yard viewed from Pressed Steel, 1937. In the foreground is an access siding to Pressed Steel added in that year, beyond that is the gated access to Morris Industries Exports Ltd sidings. Then came the three GWR reception sidings and up loop, the up and down single line, the signal box, down loop and down yard sidings, with the goods shed out of sight to the right. Beyond the down yard can be seen the goal posts of the Pressed Steel sports ground, with Roman Way following the hedge line at its boundary.   *British Motor Industry Heritage Trust*

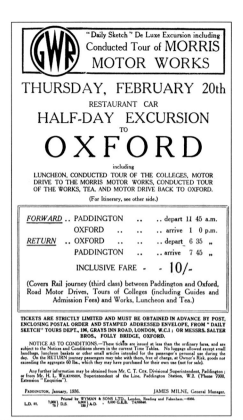

By October 1936 yet further additions were required at Cowley principally the extension of the goods shed (again) and new goods administration offices. The General Manager told the Traffic Committee that traffic had increased from 87,000 tons in 1933 to 127,000 tons in 1935, and that industrial and residential development of the locality was proceeding rapidly. Expenditure of £3,856 was authorised on 29th October (note from *Appendix Three* that the latter part of the 1930s also entailed major extension of the private siding facilities of Morris Motors and Pressed Steel Ltd).

Mr A.D. Ayres, who lived in a house with its back garden backing onto the railway until 1941, can remember Bertram Mills' circus train travelling over the line in about 1937 or 1938. He saw it emerging from Horspath tunnel, its vehicles containing all the animals and equipment for the circus later that week in Oxford cattle pens.

Mr Gordon Gresly was a schoolboy in Thame in the 1930s and used to help one of the coal merchants on Saturday mornings by holding the bags while they shovelled in coal from the rail wagons. He left school at the age of 14 in 1938:

My first job was at Risborough furniture factory next to the station. I always cycled, except sometimes in bad weather I went by train. One morning on the way to work I remember maggots kept dropping onto the seat from the overhead rack. I could see they were falling out of a dinner bag. The owner of the bag took it down, removed his sandwiches and emptied the maggots out of the window, then put the food back. He explained that he had been fishing over the weekend.

Soon after the war started sweets were put on ration but we lads discovered that the cast-iron chocolate machines on Thame station were being refilled. So we made a profit, putting in 2d. and selling them for 3d.

Some of the wartime aircraft parts piled up at Cowley. The railway line is in the background behind the trees at the edge of the scrapfield with Horspath to the right and the car works buildings visible, *left*. This illustration was included in *Calling All Arms*.

Chapter Nine

War and Nationalisation

On the outbreak of war on 3rd September, 1939, all private car production at Cowley was stopped immediately, all cars currently in production being requisitioned for the Services as they were finished. At first this led to considerable unemployment in the district but it was not long before the works were adapted to help the war effort. Its principal role was in the repair of crashed aircraft, although it continued to make vehicles for the Forces and for Civil Defence purposes, as well as assembling sea mines and sinkers, and later tanks. Its workshops were even used to train men of the SAS in industrial sabotage!

A Civilian Repair Organisation (CRO) was set up under Lord Nuffield (Sir William Morris was created Baron Nuffield in 1934), who was designated Director General of Maintenance, Air Ministry , with its headquarters at Cowley as well as its No. 1 Repair Depot (there were five in all throughout the country), known as No.1 Civilian Repair Unit (CRU). The works designed the necessary tools and produced the replacement components. A flight shed and airfield were constructed at Cowley. By Dunkirk the CRU was employing 800 workers, by August 1940, 1,200. During the Battle of Britain Cowley returned to service 150 seriously damaged aircraft, in addition to those landed at Cowley without warning for immediate repair. Between January 1940 and March 1945 75,000 aircraft were repaired there.

In addition to repairs, the CRO was responsible for salvaging usable parts from aircrafts which were beyond repair and Cowley was the home of No. 50 Maintenance Unit, RAF, which brought in crashed aircraft from all over the country. Anything that could not be repaired or reused was sent to one of the two Metal & Produce Recovery Depots (MPRD) for the aluminium to be melted down and reused. No. 1 MPRD was at Cowley, a set of sidings on the downside at the eastern end of the layout equipped with cranes.* In wartime most of the traffic for any of these processes, repair, salvage or scrap, would have been moved to or from Cowley by rail, only the large airframes coming by road. The acres of aircraft scrap lying beside the factory at Cowley were recorded in Paul Nash's dramatic war painting *Totes Meer* (Dead Sea) which could be seen in the Tate Galley. In his book *Calling All Arms*, Ernest Fairfax says that the fields full of scrap eventually stretched to Horspath (another writer says that the dump stretched alongside the Garsington Road towards Garsington!). During the war the two MPRD's (No. 2 was at Eaglescliffe) recovered 25,000 tons of aluminium, enough for 5,000 planes, and 70,000 tons of other material, rubber, steel, plastics, etc.

---

* The Pressed Steel sports ground was on the right-hand side of Roman Way (looking south) after passing under the railway bridge near 15¾ mp. This ground was used for the collecting together of the crashed aircraft and Mr A.D. Ayres, who lived at Horspath until 1941, remembers that in 1940 a siding was laid into this ground, which was rapidly filling up, for recovered aluminium scrap going out by rail. A private siding for the Air Ministry was authorized on 28th June, 1940 at £1,460; this may well be it. It is thought the MPRD site came later, in 1941.

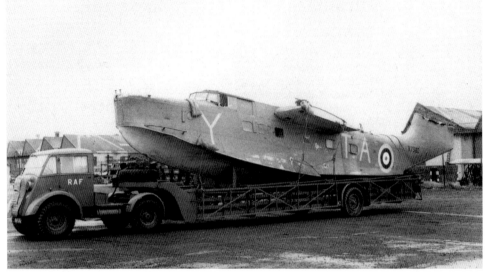

A flying boat arrives at Cowley on a 'Queen Mary' trailer for repair by the Civilian Repair Unit in 1941.   *British Motor Industry Heritage Trust*

The Crusader tank was assembled from 10,000 parts and took 12 days to put together. Here Sir Miles Thomas, Vice Chairman of the Nuffield Organisation, drives the first completed tank out of the Cowley workshops on 20th May, 1942. Note that the Exports building has been camouflaged.   *British Motor Industry Heritage Trust*

In 1940 the CRO headquarters was moved to Merton College, Oxford, as a precaution against air attack and the official responsibility for repair arrangements transferred from the Air Ministry to the Ministry of Air Production. Lord Nuffield disagreed with this change and resigned his post as Director General, but of course his factories continued with the war work. The CRO organisation was a closely guarded secret, as secret as 'Ultra' at Bletchley which was reading the Germans' coded messages. It was never mentioned in the Press or described in the official story *The Battle of Britain*.

In addition to this repair work, any remaining capacity at Cowley was filled with the manufacture of new aircraft (Tiger Moths, used for training) aero engines (for Beaufighters and Lancasters) and the tail units for Horsa gliders, plus spare parts for all these products. Additionally torpedoes, mines and sinkers (over 8,000) were made for the Admiralty (as in World War I), and shells and fuses for the Ministry of Supply. McAlpines laid a new siding into the factory in 1940 to bring out the sea mines and sinkers, etc; this ran parallel to Roman Way. Between 1942 and 1944, 650 tanks were assembled in the Morris Industries Exports buildings. After the tanks, in 1944, the giant Neptune amphibious vehicle was built. The workforce at Cowley expanded to over 10,000 people, a good proportion being women.

All of this work would have kept the GWR at Cowley exceedingly busy. The large scale extensions to the private sidings at Cowley, for war work, are listed in *Appendix Three*. The main line south between Kennington Jn and Sandford (1¼ miles) was quadrupled in 1940, and between Oxford South and Kennington (2 miles) was quadrupled in 1942. Also in 1942 a large new marshalling yard at Hinksey was opened; the combined cost of the quadrupling between Oxford and Kennington and the yard at Hinksey was about £¼ million. I think it is reasonable to assume that the wartime traffic passing to and from Cowley would have been a major factor in the decision to build a yard at Hinksey.

There was a land slip near Thame at 7 m. 11 ch. on 10th January, 1940. The slip in an embankment measured 39 ft in length and 45 ft from the top of the slip to the nearest rail. The same place slipped again on 5th February, when about 10 tons of filling slipped through the boundary fence onto adjoining property, with no effect on trains. The next day, 6th February, the 4.40 pm goods from Oxford was shunting the yard at Littlemore at 6.45 pm when two wagons became buffer-locked fouling the main line. The C&W examiner from Cowley attended and the wagons were released, with difficulty, at 8.15 pm. The 6.38 pm Oxford-Paddington passenger train was delayed 92 minutes in consequence.

The 4.40 pm Oxford goods was involved in another mishap, the first of two that took place in less than a week at Cowley in October 1940. In the first incident at 8.45 pm on 12th October, the 4.40 pm had been divided and the rear part consisting of nine 'Bocars', two open 'Bs' and brake was placed on the down loop while the remainder of the train shunted. When rejoining the train, the rear portion ran away, although the brake in the van was hard on, hitting the stop block and derailing two open 'Bs' and a 'Bocar' (but not the brake van).

On 18th October the same shunter and another man went to Station Sidings (near the passenger platform) with pilot engine No. 3722 to pick up some wagons. Once the engine was inside the points, one shunter told the driver to

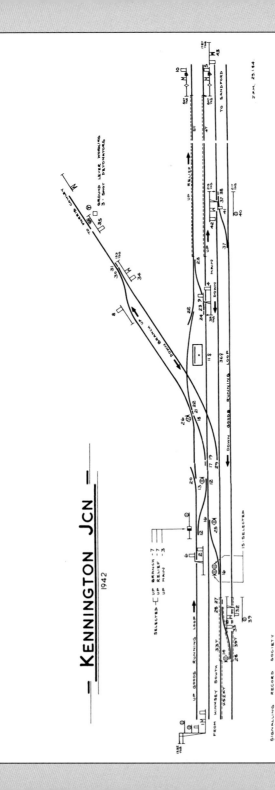

The signal box diagram showing the layout at Kennington Jn in 1942, following quadrupling of the main line.

stand against the wagons while both shunters went over to the station for their wages. On returning their happiness was short lived for they saw that the wagons they had come for were running away, and on hitting the stop block, three wagons were derailed. On this occasion, apart from the damage to the wagons and a brake van, a 3 ton case containing a motor chassis for the Ministry of Supply was badly damaged. On investigation it was found that only the brake van and one vehicle had their brakes on, two other vehicles merely having the brakes dropped, not pinned down.

On 2nd December, an alert P. Way inspector at Kennington Jn, noticed that as the 3.10 pm goods from Cowley to Oxford was drawing to a stand at the signal, the seventh vehicle from the engine parted from the remainder of the train when its drawbar broke. The train which comprised 52 vehicles drawn by 2-6-0 No. 6328 detached the defective vehicle at Kennington and continued with its journey after 20 minutes delay.

A more serious accident occurred on 23rd March, 1941. As the 7.40 am Oxford goods ran into Cowley at 8.30 am, it was noticed that the third and fourth wagons were on fire. These two vehicles contained scrap aeroplane parts from Quedgeley (Glos) destined for the No. 1 MPRD at Cowley. The Cowley staff stopped the train short of the water column, then uncoupled the first four wagons from the train and drew them under the water column. Unfortunately the heat given off was so intense that the yard foreman burnt his hand when pulling the chain of the water column. Fortunately the Pressed Steel Co.'s Fire Brigade was on patrol nearby, connected up their hoses and extinguished the fire. The two open trucks, both LNER vehicles, were badly charred and their contents (tyres, batteries, fabric, etc.) damaged. It was considered that the fire was caused either by acid leaking from accumulators in the wagons, or a spark from an engine.

At 4.43 pm on 8th August as the ganger's motor inspection trolley No. PWM 1700 entered the down loop at Thame, the signalman reversed the locking bar derailing the trolley, which suffered a bent front axle. It was said that the signalman had been attempting to prevent any delay to the 4.45 pm Thame to Princes Risborough auto-train and, under the impression that the trolley had cleared the bar, attempted to unlock the facing points; he was reprimanded.

Moreton accommodation crossing at 6 m. 19 ch. (between Thame and Tiddington) was run into by a gunner from a Searchlight Battery in a War Dept lorry on 5th September, damaging one of the gates beyond repair and breaking its concrete posts. One of the gates had been previously damaged (on 21st May, 1940) when a local from the village drove a light car into it.

On 7th November, 1942 a US Army private from Ashurst Military Hospital, adjoining Littlemore station, was for some reason on the line at 17 m. 49 ch. when he was knocked down by the 3.20 pm Hinksey-Princes Risborough freight train, hauled by pannier tank No. 3741. He was pronounced dead by a doctor from the Military Hospital.

A runaway barrage balloon caused some disruption on 28th January, 1943. At 7.10 pm all communication was lost between Thame and Wheatley and it was found that a complete span of telegraph and telephone wires at Thame had been broken. Pilot working was put into operation between Thame and

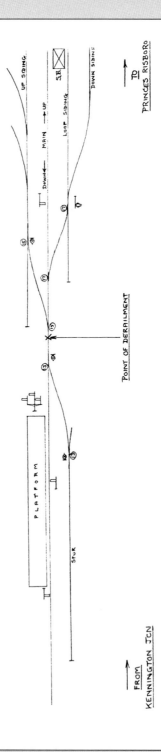

Diagram showing the location of the 18th December, 1945 derailment.

Wheatley commencing with the 6.38 pm Oxford-Paddington at 7.26 pm. This train was delayed 44 minutes, the 6.48 pm Risborough to Oxford diesel railcar 77 minutes, and the 6.25 pm Paddington-Oxford 29 minutes. Normal working resumed at 10.05 am the next day.

Between 2nd and 9th May the S&T Department was working at Cowley installing a new facing junction to sidings on the upside 300 yards Wheatley side of the signal box. A new locking frame was installed in the signal box, increasing the size of the lever frame from 31 to 43 levers.

An American Army lorry, driven by a US private in the US Army Post Office collided with the brickwork parapet of the Chinnor Road bridge at Thame (5 m. 36 ch.) on 2nd March, 1944. He demolished the parapet over a distance of 34 ft and damaging the point rodding underneath when the bricks fell down. Fortunately as it was 10.15 pm no trains were delayed.

On 1st April, the Watlington branch engine left Risborough at 5.01 pm to run to Thame for water (one wonders what was wrong with the Risborough supply). Approaching Bledlow the down distant signal was at caution and the locomotive stopped 20 yards from the gates. After hearing the engine whistle, the Bledlow porter went to open the gates, throwing the downside gate open and securing the upside one. But before he could return to secure the downside gate the engine moved forward and collided with the gate, smashing it and breaking off the iron hanging post - an expensive run for water!

Over a year later, and after the end of war in Europe, an act of vandalism had serious consequences. On 19th June, 1945 at 4.30 pm motor gang trolley No. 841 was conveying six men of Gang 138 from Horspath Key box to Wheatley when it became derailed near Littleworth bridge over the railway at 13 m. 55 ch. It had hit a rail key placed on the low rail at a point where the track was on a curve with 3½ in. cant at a speed of about 12 mph. All the men were thrown off and three were injured, two being taken to a local doctor. Further ahead more rail keys and stones were found on the rails - the police were informed. The accident report notes that the track had been laid in 1932 and was due for relaying in 1955.

On 10th October, a young lady of about 23 was cycling from Thame to her home at Moreton, at about 10.30 am, when she encountered a cow in the road adjacent to the level crossing where the branch line crossed the Thame-Moreton road. This animal had been put in a field the night before after escaping 'from our Road Transport people [i.e. GWR]'. The lady was bruised, her clothes ripped and her cycle damaged. Many months later she was still complaining of pains in her abdomen. The GWR's solicitor considered that a Court would hold the company liable for the accident due to negligence, and after copious correspondence passed, the GWR finally settled paying compensation of £150 almost a year later in September 1946.

At about 6.50 am on 18th December, 1945 the 3 am Acton to Long Marston freight train, formed engine, 40 wagons and brake van was shunted to the up siding at Morris Cowley to allow the 6.05 am Banbury-Princes Risborough to pass. After it had done so, at about 7.15 am, the freight left the siding via points 15 to proceed on its journey via Oxford (see sketch of location *opposite*). At a point on the single line, eight sleepers from the heel of points 15, the 29th and

30th wagons from the engine became derailed, the rear pair of wheels of the 29th wagon striking the buttress of the rail over road bridge at 16 m. 5¼ ch. and being torn off. The train parted between the 29th and 30th wagons, and the 30th wagon (fully derailed) and the rest of the train remained at Cowley, the 30th wagon halting on the overbridge. The front portion continued with the rear wagon being dragged along partly on its body. At Littlemore this wagon broke away and was thrown at right angles across the tracks. The engine and remaining 28 wagons continued to Kennington Jn!

The Oxford breakdown vans and the Old Oak Common crane were ordered at 7.35 am, the vans arriving at 8.57 am. The Old Oak crane was stopped at West Wycombe as it was found not to be necessary. Meanwhile a bus service was inaugurated between Oxford and Wheatley, the 6.05 am Banbury stock shuttling between Wheatley and Risborough. The vehicle at Littlemore was cleared from the line and the derailed wagon at Cowley rerailed at 11.45 am. As the breakdown vans were preparing to leave Cowley one of its vehicles was derailed at exactly the same spot (8 sleepers from the heel of points 15) at 12.20 and rerailed at 12.55 pm. After track repairs, the first train to pass over the single line was the 12.20 pm Paddington-Oxford at about 2.30 pm. Signal department equipment was badly damaged and 'it will probably be a day or two before full repairs are effected'.

It was discovered that four crossing timbers were decayed and had allowed the track to spread about two inches in the point lead. The track had been laid in 1928 and was not due for renewal until 1950. The divisional engineer inspected the defective timbers personally and stated that 'the appearance of the top and sides [of the sleepers] was deceptive, the internal condition being much worse than what would be concluded from an inspection of the surface'.

A look at a wartime working timetable may be of interest. That for passenger trains for May 1943 has been chosen but those for October 1943 and May and October 1944 were practically identical. At this time separate passenger and freight timetables were issued - the May 1943 freight one is detailed below.

Down passenger trains (weekdays)	Times at Thame
8.17 am Risborough-Oxford	8X29 - 8.32
7.30 am Paddington-Oxford	9.59 - 10.04
11.22 am Risborough-Oxford (diesel SX)	11.37
12.20 pm Paddington-Oxford	2.04 - 2.06
4.12 pm Risborough-Thame (auto)	4.27
5. 10 pm Cowley-Banbury	-
5.55 pm Risborough - Thame (diesel SX)	6.08
6.45 pm Risborough - Banbury SX (diesel)	7X0 - 7.17
6.45 pm Risborough - Oxford SO	7X0 - 7.17
6.25 pm Paddington - Oxford	8.13 - 8.13
Sundays	
9.40 am Paddington - Oxford	11.39 - 11.44
4.15 pm Paddington - Oxford	6.00 - 6.03

Up passenger trains (weekdays)	Times at Thame
6.05 am Banbury-Risborough	7.34 - 7.45
7.30 am Oxford-Risborough (diesel SX)	8X8 - 8.52

Up passenger trains (weekdays)	*Times at Thame*
8.22 am Oxford-Paddington	9.05 - 9.12
2.38 pm Oxford-Paddington	3.19 - 3.23
4.20 pm empty Oxford-Cowley (for 5.10)	-
4.45 pm Thame-Risborough (auto)	4.45
3.40 pm Chipping Norton-Risborough (diesel SX)	5.25 - 5.27
6.18 pm Thame-Risborough (diesel SX)	6.18
6.38 pm Oxford-Paddington	7.16 - 7X28

Sundays

7.15 am Oxford-Paddington	8.04½ - 8.05
5.55 am Oxford-Paddington	6.42½ - 6.43

Down freight trains (weekdays)	*Times at Thame*
10.50 pm Park Royal-Worcester	(12.12 am pass Risborough MX)
11.55 pm Paddington-Worcester	(1.36 am pass Risborough MX)
4.30 am Park Royal-Oxford RR MX	(5.51 am pass Risborough)
9.30 am Cowley-Banbury MX	-
3.15 am Slough-Oxford	10.29 - 10.50
3.10 pm Cowley-Oxford RR	-
5.20 pm Cowley-Littlemore engine SX	-
7.20 pm Cowley-Oxford SX	-
8.20 pm Thame-Oxford	8.20
10.10 pm Cowley-Oxley Sidings (terminate Oxford SO)	-
11.42 pm Cowley-Crewe RR SX	-
8.50 pm Taplow-Oxford	12.39 - 12X59

Sundays

10.50 pm Park Royal-Worcester SO	(12.12 am pass Risborough)
11.55 pm Park Royal-Worcester SO	(1.36 am pass Risborough)
4.30 am Park Royal-Oxford RR	(5.51 am pass Risborough)
9.30 am Cowley - Banbury	-

Up freight trains (weekdays)	*Times at Thame*
12.01 am Oxford-Taplow MX	12.57 - 1.15
6.05 am Oxford-Cowley	-
5.35 am Banbury-Cowley	-
11.20 am Oxford-Taplow	12.16 - 12.30
3.20 pm Oxford-Thame (Risborough if required)	6.15
4.10 pm Oxford-Cowley SX	-
4.40 pm Oxford-Cowley SO	-
6.05 pm Littlemore-Cowley SX	-
6.45 pm Oxford-Cowley engine SX	-
5.10 pm Worcester-Paddington SO	11.42 (pass)
3.20 pm Worcester - Paddington SX	(Risborough pass 12.31 am)

Sundays

12.01 am Oxford-Taplow	12.55 - 1.10
5.35 am Banbury-Cowley	-

Notes: MX Mondays excepted; SO Saturdays only; SX Saturdays excepted; RR Run if required; X Crosses another train here.

In 1943 zonal collection and delivery arrangements for goods traffic were introduced with Oxford as the main concentration point. In future traffic under one ton for Littlemore, Cowley or Wheatley would be sent to Oxford for road delivery. Truckloads for which delivery had been paid would continue to be dealt with at Cowley and Wheatley, but those for Littlemore would be delivered from Cowley. However, all three stations would continue to deal with 'S to S' truckload traffic (station to station, with no road delivery involved).

The late Harold Purser was born in Thame in 1926 and commuted from Thame to London for a year in 1944 and early 1945. He used the train weekly for one year before that and weekly for many years from the late 1940s until passenger closure. He has some valuable memories of the war years:

The first up passenger train from Thame, the 6.05 am from Banbury which I used in the 1943-1945 period was usually hauled by Banbury's 5188, but occasionally Leamington's 5187 was in charge. Once I was astonished to see Newport's 7241 in charge, my first sighting of this class on the line.

The next up train was a railcar from the mid-1930s, then followed an Oxford-Paddington which was in Thame just after 9 am. This was usually hauled by an Oxford 'Hall', often *Barton Hall* - my favourite, but occasionally a 'Grange'. This had several wagons set aside for milk churns and a lot were loaded at Thame - it was called the 'Milky Way'. In the 1930s many farm carts passed our door with milk churns for loading on this train. The 7.35 am Paddington-Oxford via Bourne End usually had a 'Castle' or 'Hall' from various sheds.

The 11.20 am Oxford to Paddington was hauled by various 'Castles', 'Halls', 'Granges' or 'Stars'. It was the best up through train to London. It was withdrawn as a wartime economy around December 1939 [actually 25th September] and shortly before its demise I was surprised to see semi-streamlined *Manorbier Castle* at its head. The 12.25 pm Paddington-Oxford was usually behind a 'Hall'. This train called at Ealing Broadway before traversing the Greenford Loop.

The 2.38 pm Oxford-Paddington was often hauled by 'Star' class *British Monarch*. The 2.25 pm Paddington-Oxford was sometimes hauled by a Mogul. I think this train was withdrawn from December 1939 [actually 25th September] as a wartime economy too. At some later period, around 1940, the Watlington branch train was sent down to Thame from Risborough soon after 4 pm returning at 4.52. For many years this train was hauled by one of three Panniers 2055, 2178 and another (2112?).

In my schooldays I often used to spend several hours in the evening in Thame signal box which was quite busy at that time of day. When there was no passenger train movement there was always the local goods which came up from Oxford and spent two hours shunting before returning to Oxford as soon as the 6.25 pm Paddington-Oxford had cleared Wheatley around 8.15 pm. It was usually a pannier tank but at times a '52XX' or '93XX' might be substituted to give it spice! There would be the movements of the railcars around 6 pm and 7 pm and then the 6.38 pm Oxford-Paddington would arrive; this could be hauled by 'Castles', Moguls or Prairies at that period. The Aylesbury auto arrived at 8.17 pm, returning to Risborough shortly afterwards [these trains were taken off in September 1939]. My father travelled down on that for years after catching the 7.10 pm express from Paddington which dropped off two slip coaches at Risborough. These coaches were picked up by the Banbury auto which took them north, one coach in front of the engine and two behind. The Aylesbury auto had a '48XX' locomotive whereas the Banbury auto in those days had a '54XX'.

On Sundays in GWR days there were two up and two down through trains to London, the first up one going via Bourne End. My only sighting of a 'Saint' on the branch I recall was *Saint Stephen* on the Sunday evening down train.

There were two middle-of-the-day goods trains through Thame. First the down Slough which shunted every yard on its way and could be seen any time between mid-morning and early afternoon depending on workload. The up Taplow goods used to pass through Thame about 1 pm but frequently did not do any shunting. Once during the war when I was watching the latter pass west of Thame from Lord William's School, it came to a halt in front of the school. It was a heavy train with a Dean goods piloting the usual '61XX'. Only the front part of the train was visible, the rear part had broken adrift and was out of sight.

The line was bombed and hit in October 1940. Two bombs fell near Wheatley Bridge Hotel (now the Harvester). One fell on the railway embankment and the other in front of the hotel on the bank of the River Thame. It was I think the night of 18th/19th October around 10 pm and the line was blocked until about midday on the Saturday. The 7.35 am Paddington-Oxford was held in Thame station until the line was cleared. It was still there around 1 pm when a solitary '61XX' arrived from the Oxford direction.

During the War the line was often used for diversions. On one such occasion when the line at Ealing was bombed I remember seeing the diverted up 'Pembroke Coast Express' passing Thame behind two 'Castles', the only time I ever saw this combination. During another diversionary period the pickup goods was derailed at the east end of the Thame loop putting paid to diversions and other trains in one stroke.

Sometime in October 1944, I arrived at Paddington to catch the 5.23 for Risborough, only to find that earlier in the day the 'Cornish Riviera Express' had derailed outside the terminus and that no trains were leaving. I hurried to Marylebone and caught an LNER train to Risborough. Meanwhile the railcar for Oxford which should connect with the 5.23 had been sent off and there was no way to get to Thame. The Watlington train was in the bay and there was a fire in the waiting room and I spent the next three hours in one or the other until at about 10.45 the 6.25 pm from Paddington to Oxford got through and I arrived in Thame nearly 4 hours late!

Mr A.D. Ayres was born in 1930 and lived in Horspath until 1941. His memories of the war years remain:

During the early years of World War II the local goods train became much longer carrying army vehicles, small tanks, etc. The Pressed Steel and Morris Motor factories at Cowley produced war items in great numbers and during the middle of the night very heavy laden and large goods trains would labour up the incline into the tunnel and on into the night. We understood from the grownups in the village that they were carrying sea mines made at Cowley.

A siding was put in at Cowley for receiving aluminium from crashed aircraft. The siding was on Pressed Steel's former playing field, alongside Roman Way immediately after the railway bridge, and descended on an incline from the downside of the single line. Parts were brought in from all over the South East of England by road in 'Queen Mary's' (low loaders). They were compressed and the aluminium removed and sent away by rail for re-use.

I can clearly remember, just after Dunkirk, a very long passenger train slowly going northwards, with all carriages painted with large red crosses on the sides and roofs. The whole train was packed with wounded soldiers, with medical personnel in attendance. It ran to Wheatley, where the patients were unloaded to ambulances and taken to Holton (services hospital).

Of an evening, the passenger train pulling away from the halt on its way to Wheatley, passed a detached house at the bottom of the embankment, by the bridge at the village green. The guard on this train was a friend of the occupants of the house and would drop that day's *Oxford Mail* - rolled up - where the owner's Labrador would be waiting to catch it.

Horspath Halt was the traditional type, corrugated iron, suspended off the bank with timbers and the platform constructed of old sleepers. During the war the local Home Guard cut slits through corrugations in the hope that in the event of invasion it could be

The opening of the military hospital at Holton near Wheatley in World War II brought long ambulance trains onto the line. In this picture GWR 'Grange' No. 6827 *Llanfrechfa Grange* heads a LNER 'B12' class locomotive and its lengthy train at Kennington Jn, with the signal 'off' for the Risborough line.   *P.Q Treloar Collection*

An ambulance train, presumably empty, comes off the Risborough line at Kennington Jn, again during World War II. GWR '43XX' class 2-6-0 No. 5303, running tender-first, heads LNER 'B12' class 4-6-0 No. 8557 as it rejoins the main line.   *P.Q. Treloar Collection*

used as a type of pillbox - some hope, as I think that a pea shooter would have penetrated the structure. The banks of the line through Horspath were a beautiful carpet of blooms from masses of cowslips and the villagers used to go along and pick them. In the summertime there would be very large embankment fires, when the local people would spend frantic hours trying to stop the spread into their gardens.

Mr Ayres recalls diesel railcar No. 4 (now preserved at Swindon) as the most regular of its type along the line during his time.

Mr P.R. Forbes was born in Princes Risborough and travelled to Thame Grammar school daily from 1943 to 1951 and has a few memories of the wartime period:

> The first two years of my commuting covered the wartime period and food was in short supply. On several occasions we looked out of the window to see why the train had almost stopped between Bledlow and Towersey and discovered the fireman had either shot a rabbit or a pheasant with a .22 rifle and was busy retrieving it from beside the line.
>
> When sitting on Thame station it was not unusual to see a goods train with wagons piled high with scrap iron and aluminium (often crashed aircraft) going to the motor car works at Cowley. Also sugar beet was often transported which we liked because we could often 'retrieve' one which we cut into slices and sucked instead of sweets.
>
> In the months before D-Day it was not unusual to see very long American supply trains, pulled by WD locomotives, going towards Princes Risborough, their ultimate destination the South Coast, ready for the invasion of Europe. We could see tanks and armoured cars on flatbed wagons, additionally there were box vans, etc. I don't know how many of these ran in those few months, I saw them only on the days we were playing cricket, maybe once a week. They were an impressive sight as they passed slowly by - I do not remember seeing any double-headed or banked trains.
>
> One loco crew in particular did not like schoolboys - probably because we enjoyed putting items, like coins, on the rails at Thame, so they hit upon a revenge plan of stopping the loco with the funnel right beneath the footbridge. So we had to run the gauntlet across and hold our breath to avoid inhaling fumes and reeking of smoke when we arrived at school.

Mr Harold Purser has some memories of the diesel railcars in the period following the war:

> One night after the war I was travelling in a diesel railcar down to Thame and the token fell out of the train while we were stopped at Towersey. The big hoop was not given to the railcars but the guard had care of the token which I think used to be put in the central doorway area. Anyway it could not be found . . . and I presume a pilotman had to be found as a substitute.
>
> Later, in the more unreliable days of the railcars, I was returning home [on Maundy Thursday] when there were of course more passengers than usual on the last train. The driver was having trouble with the gears and we crawled down to Bledlow. We eventually left Bledlow in bottom gear but came to a halt at the occupation crossing a mile or so west of the station, at the end of a narrow road off the Chinnor-Bledlow road. My father was waiting at Thame station with the car and was talking to Mr Jones (the station master) and he heard what the problem was and where we were stuck. Whilst Mr Jones organised an Oxford bus to come to our rescue, my father drove to the crossing and ferried passengers in relays to a point that the bus was able to reach.
>
> Mr Jones must have told Paddington, because in due course my father received a letter and £5 for his trouble. Mr Jones was a great character and we knew him well.

An up local trip working headed by '57XX' class 0-6-0PT No. 8767 saunters through Oxford
station at an unknown date in early BR days. Oxford Station North box is in the background,
and note the fine array of backing signals, no less than four can be seen.

M. Yarwood/GW Trust

'Metro' 2-4-0 tank No. 3589, seen at Oxford shed in 1948. This class would have worked over the
Risborough line. This particular engine, built in 1899, was scrapped in August 1948.

The end of the GWR came at midnight on 31st December 1947. One minute later British Railways (Western Region) (BR(WR)) was born, taking over the former territory of the GWR. Very little change was seen for a good number of years, apart from the gradual repainting of locomotives and rolling stock in the new BR livery, and introduction of BR 'sausage' totems at stations. There are plenty of photographs where station masters can be seen wearing their old GWR 'pillbox' uniform caps, years after Nationalisation. The Thame branch continued as part of the London District of BR (WR) as it had in the GWR era.

In December 1948 expenditure of £320 was authorised on provision of a private siding at Littlemore for the Oxford City & County Mental Hospital (there had been a private siding for Littlemore Asylum here since 1870). Work was not completed until November 1950, the actual expenditure (paid by the hospital) being £376. When the completion certificate was received in the chief civil engineer's office in January 1951, it was date stamped with a stamp marked 'GWR Paddington'! Probably because of its long life as a company (since 1835), the Western Region was the most reluctant of all the six BR Regions to forget its history as a private railway company.

Also at the end of 1950 (in December) Col Langley of the Ministry of Transport finally inspected some new works at Cowley that had been brought to his notice in 1937 (!):

> In 1937 a new siding connection was provided for the Morris Motor Works at the east end of the station platform. In 1943 another siding connection leading to the Pressed Steel Co.'s works was laid on the north side of the line near 15¾ mp. Various modifications were made to the signalling, which is now [on file]. Traffic at this busy station is very heavy for a single line and it averages 80 loaded wagons received and 200 forwarded daily, in addition to the passenger service.

On 18th/19th February, 1951 Littlemore signal box (not a block post) and all associated signalling was removed and control of the layout give over to two new ground frames. The West ground frame, of 3 levers, just Cowley side of the platform, controlled access to the up and down sidings at the station end of the layout, while the 2-lever East ground frame, nearer Cowley, released the facing points leading into the down sidings at the Cowley end of the yard. Both ground frames were released by the Cowley-Kennington Jn token. The up siding at Littlemore also gave access to the National Benzole petrol depot and the sand siding used by the Chief Mechanical & Electrical Engineer's Department.

In February 1951 Percy Smith retired after 32 years as station master at Bledlow, only the third 'man in charge' since the station opened in 1862! There must have been something special about Bledlow. It can't have been the money, though, because in 1914 the post, class 2, was paid 33s. a week, whilst his similarly graded colleague at Littlemore earned 45s.

On 30th January, 1955 a new 2-lever ground frame was installed at Morris Cowley at 16 m. 13 ch., near the Oxford end of the platform and 476 yards from the signal box. This controlled access to some new sidings and a new export packing factory for Morris Motors. The sidings, at Morris's expense, had been authorised in November 1953 at a cost of £41,066. This was the last expansion in the car works which had joined with Austin in 1952 to become the British Motor Corporation.

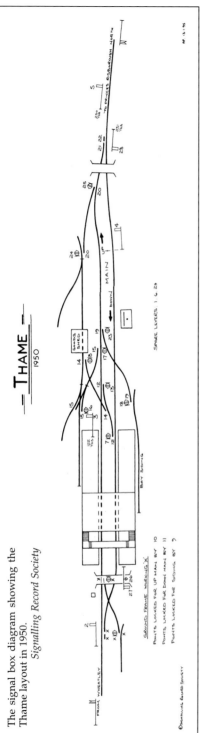

The signal box diagram showing the Thame layout in 1950.
Signalling Record Society

Photographed in September 1954, this overall view of the facilities at Thame shows what a cramped site the station had to use. *N. Simmons/Hugh Davies*

The brick-built station offices behind the up platform, viewed in September 1954. *N. Simmons/Hugh Davies*

A down freight train, hauled by a 2-6-2T, passes through Tiddington in 1950.   *Stations UK*

The downside buildings at Oxford photographed in 1953.   *Lens of Sutton Collection*

'28XX' class 2-8-0 No. 3857 heads a train of motor cars at Morris Cowley destined for the Scottish Motor Show in the early 1950s. The engine looks to have been specially cleaned. The station master, on the right of the group, is thought to be Mr A'hern.

British Motor Industry Heritage Trust

The exterior of the upside station building at Princes Risborough, viewed in 1955.
Lens of Sutton Collection

A good load for a '14XX' class 0-4-2T; on 2nd March, 1955 No. 1442 substitutes for a diesel railcar at Oxford on the 2.40 pm to Princes Risborough.

John Glanville can recall a memorable trip over the branch in 1955. John had joined the railway at Newton Abbot as an engine cleaner in January 1953, became a passed cleaner in early 1954 and in the autumn of that year was promoted to fireman at Slough. John says,

Promotion at any depot in the London area was a lot quicker than Newton Abbot, Plymouth or any of the Cornish depots, or in Wales. At any of the London depots there was a mix of Cornish, Devonshire or Welsh lads. I had a very enjoyable time at Slough at the age of 17; I was in No. 2 Passenger link.

I can't recall the exact date, but it was January or February 1955, I was 'spare' and received a call paper at Slough Hostel telling me to sign on for an afternoon duty which involved travelling passenger to Oxford to work an evening service from Oxford to Paddington via Thame and Maidenhead, six coaches plus two milk tanks detached at Princes Risborough.

My driver was Charlie Ayres, his regular fireman, Joey Abbot, had reported sick. When I reported for duty there was this driver in a GW style overcoat looking rather intimidating standing nearby. When I was pointed out as his fireman he said, 'I'm not responsible for this fireman!' This did wonders for one's confidence, to work a top link duty over a line I had no knowledge of!

As we travelled to Oxford few words were exchanged, except that he told me we would have his regular engine, No. 6133. I explained to Charlie I had little experience of picking up the single line token. On arrival at Oxford No. 6133 had been prepared to a fashion, but there was an uneven fire and large lumps of coal in the shovelling plate which had to be broken up with the coal pick. I built the fire up, trying to avoid the engine blowing off.

There was no trouble with the token at Kennington Jn or Cowley. When I had been told about this job at the Hostel, much had been made of Horspath Bank. I said, we have some severe gradients in the West Country, is it like them? However, this one turned out not to be as steep as I had been told. The worst thing was Horspath tunnel, which had a very low roof, the engine exhaust beat against the roof and was sucked back into the driving cab. 1 had been working hard keeping a good fire with large lumps of coal giving problems, having to be broken up to pass through the firehole door.

Approaching Wheatley I held the token out to put on the collection arm but failed to hold it out far enough, catching the tip of the arm and sending the token into the signal rodding. I was able to pick-up the new staff for Thame. This process was repeated at a few more change-over points, the last one being Bourne End. At which point Charlie warned me that if I failed to put the token on the collection arm he would ask for another fireman at Slough. Fortunately, I achieved the objective at Cookham and Maidenhead, probably fear helped!

I think the main reason for my errors was leaning over the cab door which is different to tender engines on which I had previously gained experience of token exchange in the West Country.

On arrival at Paddington we had less than half a bunker of coal, probably having burnt about 2½ tons of coal; very hard work for a 17-year-old. I then had to climb into the bunker to move coal forward to the shovelling plate. Much to my amazement, after I had completed this task, Charlie offered me an orange. We worked back, bunker first, to Slough, berthed the stock and I signed off, a very tired fireman.

I met Joey Abbot a few weeks later. He said, 'Did you work with Charlie over the Thame branch?' I confirmed that I had and asked why. He said that Charlie had been impressed with my efforts. This was praise indeed, particularly after my first impressions of him when signing on and the problems with the tokens.

Chapter Ten

Timetables and Operations

Passenger Timetables

After opening to Oxford in 1864 there was a passenger service of four trains each way on weekdays and, although there were variations in the timings of these trains, the four (later five) train service remained remarkably consistent over the next 70 years. In 1865 and 1866 there was a short-lived boost to five each way (4.20 pm from Oxford to High Wycombe and 11.32 am from Taplow to Oxford were the extra trains) but by 1868 it was back to four. The Sunday service of two trains each way continued throughout GWR ownership of the line. In February 1868 the 8.15 am and 5.25 pm from Oxford on weekdays were through to London and the 6.55 am and 5 pm from Paddington were through to Oxford. On Sundays all four services were through to or from London. The fastest through trains were the weekdays 8.15 am up (2¾ hours) and the 5 pm down (2 h. 35 min.).

By July 1874 a fifth down train had been introduced by again making the long-standing 5 am Taplow goods 'mixed' from High Wycombe (dept 6.55 am). By this time three down trains on weekdays were through from London, leaving there at 8.15, 11 am and 4.50 pm and all four up trains were through, leaving Oxford at 8.25, 11.15 am, 2.35 and 6.10 pm. On Sundays all except the evening down train were through to or from London. The timetable remained like this until 1885 when a sixth down train was introduced (but still only four up), being a 7.15 pm from Maidenhead, giving an Oxford arrival of 10 pm. This train did not call at Bledlow or Littlemore, and was probably a mixed train on this slow schedule; it certainly was in 1890.

This unbalanced timetable of four up and six down trains continued until 1892. In that year departures from Oxford were at 8.20, 11.20 am, 2.37 and 6.20 pm and from High Wycombe at 6.25, 10.05 am, 12.40, 2.33, 6.14 and 8.00 pm. By January 1893 the 6.25 am and 8.00 pm down trains had gone, leaving a balanced service but by June 1893 the service was improved to five each way leaving Oxford at 7.10 am (a new earlier departure), 8.20, 11.20 am, 2.37 and 6.20 pm and (down) from High Wycombe at 8.38, 10.05 am, 12.40, 2.33 and 6.12 pm. In July 1895 the (now) 6.40 am Oxford service ran through to Aldgate, calling at Bishops Road station at Paddington. Even with the earlier up train, the service was considered so 'thin' that a Thame company ran a twice-daily horse bus to Aylesbury to connect with the LNWR trains; the journey to London and back could be accomplished for 1s. 5d. less than the GWR charged! This bus continued to run until 1907 when the GWR improved the service with extra motor trains (*see below*).

The basic five-train service appears to have continued for the next 30 years (with variations in the timings of course) although there are gaps in the timetables seen by the author between 1898 and 1901 and 1907-1909.

In 1897 a 'short' train, 11.15 am Princes Risborough-Thame had been introduced on Tuesdays only for Thame market day. Later, certainly by 1906,

Additional Passenger Train

FACILITIES BY

Streamlined Rail Cars

(ONE CLASS ONLY—LIMITED ACCOMMODATION)

EACH WEEK DAY

Commencing
MONDAY, FEBRUARY 3rd, 1936.

OXFORD and PRINCES RISBOROUGH.

		a.m.			a.m.	a.m.
Train {	LONDON (Paddington) .. .. dep.	7 35	Train {	LONDON (Paddington) .. dep.	5 30	—
	HIGH WYCOMBE ..	8 57		READING	6 18	—
	BANBURY	8 35		DIDCOT ..	6 52	—
	BICESTER	8 53				
	AYLESBURY (Joint) ..	8 52	OXFORD .. .. dep.	7 30	—
	WATLINGTON ..	8M40	LITTLEMORE ..	7 38	—
			MORRIS COWLEY ..	7 42	—
PRINCES RISBOROUGH .. dep.	9 30	HORSPATH HALT ..	7 47	—
BLEDLOW	9 34	WHEATLEY ..	7 52	—
TOWERSEY HALT ..	9 39	TIDDINGTON ..	7 58	—
THAME	9 43	THAME ..	8 4	8 52
TIDDINGTON	9 50	TOWERSEY HALT ..	—	8 56
WHEATLEY	9 57	BLEDLOW ..	—	9 1
HORSPATH HALT ..	10 1	PRINCES RISBOROUGH .. arr.	—	9 6
MORRIS COWLEY ..	10 5			
LITTLEMORE	10 9	Train { AYLESBURY (Joint) .. arr.	—	9 33
OXFORD .. .. arr.	10 22	LONDON (Paddington) ..	—	10 0
WITNEY .. .. arr.	10 48			

OXFORD and WITNEY.

		a.m.	p.m.			a.m.	p.m.
Train {	LONDON (Paddington) .. dep.	8 40	6 5	WITNEY .. .. dep.	11 2	8 15
	READING	9 27	6 49	SOUTH LEIGH ..	11 7	8 20
	NEWBURY (via Compton) ..	8 28	—	EYNSHAM ..	11 12	8 25
	SWINDON	9 0	6B30	YARNTON ..	11 19	8 32
	DIDCOT	9 51	7B15	OXFORD .. arr.	11 28	8 39
OXFORD .. .. dep.	10 25	7 38	Train { DIDCOT .. .. arr.	11 53	10 21
YARNTON	10 31	7 44	SWINDON ..	12 40	10 8
EYNSHAM	10 38	7 51	NEWBURY (via Compton) ..	1 19	—
SOUTH LEIGH ..	10 43	7 56	READING ..	12 45	10 5
WITNEY .. .. arr.	10 48	8 1	LONDON (Paddington) ..	—	10 55

A—One class only. Ealing (Broadway) to High Wycombe.

B—Streamlined Rail Car, one class only (limited accommodation) Mondays to Fridays inclusive. On Saturdays, depart (by train first and third class) Swindon 6.20 p.m. and Didcot 6.52 p.m.

M—One class only.

X—Streamlined Rail Car, one class only (limited accommodation).

NOTE.—Additional services by Streamlined Rail Cars shewn in heavy type.

For complete Train Services in these Districts see Company's Time Tables.

Paddington Station,
February, 1936.

JAMES MILNE,
General Manager.

It would appear from this Notice that 3rd February, 1936 was the date when the GWR streamlined railcars began to run between Oxford and Princes Risborough.

Courtesy David Castle

there was a corresponding 4.30 pm Thame-Princes Risborough on Tuesdays only for returning market visitors. By July 1906 an 8.50 pm Oxford-Thame and back had been introduced on Saturdays only.

The opening of the additional halts in 1907/8 meant some additional (steam) railmotors on the Thame branch. In the 1909 timetable these were: from Oxford 10.25 am (to Wheatley), 1.02 and 4.40 pm to Princes Risborough and 8.35 pm to Thame. In the down direction there were: 11.00 am Wheatley-Oxford, 2.13 and 6.33 pm Princes Risborough-Oxford and 9.25 pm Thame-Oxford. These trains (or similar timings) were still running in October 1914 but the closure of the halts in March 1915 caused their withdrawal.

By October 1914 the public timetable showed the train service as 'Princes Risborough, Thame and Oxford' where previously they had been part of a composite London, Aylesbury, Oxford and Banbury table. Despite the war the branch continued with the five-train service until reduced to three each way in April 1918. Then the service from Oxford was 8.30 am, 2.30 and 6.23 pm and from Princes Risborough at 9.43 am, 4.10 and 7.40 pm, plus the Tuesdays-only services between Risborough and Thame. In May 1919 the four-train service was restored, the 11.25 am Oxford and 1.40 pm Risborough again running. These same times applied (more or less) in January 1921, but by July 1922 it was back to five each way, with the early 7 am ex-Oxford and 8.10 am ex-Princes Risborough restored. Additionally there was now an evening auto-train service each weekday between Risborough and Thame, leaving the former at 5.47 and 8 pm and returning from Thame at 6.20 and 8.25 pm. These gave connections out of the 4.40 pm and 7.10 pm ex-Paddington (the latter a slip carriage), and to cater for Saturday evening leisure traffic there was also an 8.55 pm Oxford to Risborough returning from the latter at 10.28 pm, after connecting with the 9 pm ex-Paddington. In subsequent years the 8.55 pm (Saturdays only) ran to and from High Wycombe.

This 1922 timetable was repeated (with slight variations) in 1923, 1925 and 1927 (and probably the years in between, not seen by the author). The opening of Morris Cowley station in 1928 did not really disturb the basic pattern, but additional 'short' trains were introduced to serve the new workforce:

A Banbury to Morris Cowley morning train arriving there about 7.15 am
A Midday train from Cowley to Oxford on Saturdays only
An evening return to Banbury leaving Cowley about 5.10 pm (Saturdays excepted).

(The late Saturday trains and the Sunday trains did not call at Cowley.)

This was still the position in July 1929 and September 1931: the basic service in operation since 1922 plus the Cowley trains introduced when the station opened. In summer 1932 the Cowley morning arrival had been combined with the first up train to Risborough, which now started at Banbury rather than Oxford. In June 1933 the new halts at Horspath and Towersey opened with no alterations to the timetable except that all trains called at the halts.

The introduction of diesel railcars here in February 1936 (a handbill would seem to indicate) meant some additional services for the line. In the July 1936 timetable there was a new 9.30 am Princes Risborough to Oxford (but running

An unidentified GWR streamlined railcar leaves Princes Risborough bay with an Oxford service in 1957. The lowered signal (*right*) is applicable to the down main platform.   *P.Q. Treloar*

The 2 ton hand crane and the loading gauge can be seen in this view of Bledlow looking towards Princes Risborough, September 1954.   *N. Simmons/Hugh Davies*

Looking along the platform at Bledlow towards Risborough. *Lens of Sutton Collection*

A close up view of the signal box, station master's house and waiting accommodation at Bledlow in September 1954. *N. Simmons/Hugh Davies*

Has the whole village come out to catch the 11.30 am from Oxford at Towersey Halt on 11th April, 1955? *N. Simmons/Hugh Davies*

A close up of the 10,000 gallon water tank and its pump house that pumped water from the well to the tank at Thame. At first horse driven, later oil driven, the pump was converted to electricity in 1936. *R.H.G. Simpson*

Two views of Thame goods shed. Note the grounded 'Toad' (goods brake van) body being used as some sort of store. *(Both) S.J. Dickson*

A close up view of the weighbridge in Thame yard with vintage car alongside. Note the BP oil wagons stabled in the adjacent siding. *S.J. Dickson*

A nice study of Thame up inner home signal and water crane. The little hut in the background was probably used to store material to clean the adjacent cattle pens. *S.J. Dickson*

'Hall' class 4-6-0 No. 6975 *Capesthorne Hall* heads an up through service to London at Thame on 11th April, 1955. *N. Simmons/Hugh Davies*

Thame signal box, photographed in September 1954. It would appear to have been recently repainted. *N. Simmons/Hugh Davies*

A view of Thame after closure to passengers and removal of the overall roof at the station. A 'D63XX' diesel stands alongside the signal box.   *R.H.G. Simpson*

A view across the goods yard to the front of Tiddington station building; there is one truck at the loading platform.   *N. Simmons/Hugh Davies*

only 18 minutes in front of the 8.10 am Paddington-Oxford), the 5.42 pm Risborough-Thame became a railcar (returning at 6.20 pm) and there was a new service, 6.37 pm Princes Risborough-Oxford (with a ½ hour wait at Thame). In the up direction a 7.30 am Oxford-Risborough usefully filled a gap at the Oxford end but stood at Thame from 8.04-8.52 and only left there 14 minutes in front of the 8.18 am Oxford-Paddington, which itself stood at Thame nine minutes waiting for the diesel to clear. Another big gap was filled by a new 4.50 pm Oxford-Risborough. The working timetable columns became full of symbols declaring 'streamlined car must stop dead at Kennington Jn, Morris Cowley, Wheatley, Thame and Princes Risborough North signal boxes to exchange token'. The congested state of the single line and its low number of crossing loops made these additional diesel services less useful than they otherwise might have been.

The timetable described for 1936 continued up to the war. After war was declared on 3rd September, 1939, the GWR published a National Emergency timetable from 25th September, a very slim book compared with previous editions. The Thame branch was reduced to just four trains each way: 8.10, 9.43 am, 1.49 and 7.45 pm from Risborough to Oxford and 6.55, 8.18 am, 2.38 and 6.42 pm in the up direction. Additionally the two 'short' trains ran for the Cowley workforce: 12.10 pm (SO) and 5.08 pm (SX) Cowley-Oxford. By this reduction the Thame branch lost one of its through trains to/from London in each direction.

This spartan service was probably an over reaction and by June 1940 the weekday timetable was back to a much more reasonable service:

Down
8.10, 9.47, 11.18 am, 1.52, 4.02 (to Thame), 5.50 (to Thame), 6.45, 7.50 pm (*all from Princes Risborough*) 5.8 pm SX (*from Cowley*)

Up
6.55. 7.30, 8.18 am, 2.38, 4.50, 6.38 pm (*from Oxford*)
4.45, 6.18 pm (*from Thame*)

Of these the 9.47 am, 1.52 pm and 7.50 pm down were through from Paddington, and the 8.18 am, 2.38 pm and 6.38 pm were through to Paddington. The diesel cars worked the 11.18 am, 5.50 pm and 6.45 pm down trains and the 7.30 am, 4.50 pm and 6.18 pm (from Thame) up trains, except that on Saturdays all were covered by conventional steam-hauled trains. This service continued unchanged, apart from variations in minutes, for the rest of the war.

In May 1946 the two London services, withdrawn during the war, were reinstated, 2.25 pm Paddington-Oxford splitting the previous five hour gap in afternoon services to Oxford, and the 11.22 am from Oxford to Paddington, filling the six hour gap in up trains. These extra services were withdrawn a year later in the June 1947 timetable and so the pattern of services remained for the few last months in the life of the GWR. In 1947 unadvertised workers' trains were put on from Thame to Cowley about 6.20 am and returning from Cowley to Thame at about 5.30 pm, for the benefit of car workers; these trains continued, unadvertised, until the withdrawal of passenger services in 1963.

Tiddington's compact station building, freshly painted, looking towards Risborough.
N. Simmons/Hugh Davies

This former clerestory carriage was in use as a store room at Tiddington.
N. Simmons/Hugh Davies

The freight facilities at Tiddington, including the 3 ton crane. The original timber siding is that running off diagonally behind the crane.   *N. Simmons/Hugh Davies*

Although claiming to be a signal box, this structure ceased to signal trains before 1902 and was, in reality, a superior ground frame. When this photograph was taken it had been recently repainted.   *N. Simmons/Hugh Davies*

A view from Wheatley goods yard to the up platform and station buildings. Vehicles used to inspect Horspath (also known as Wheatley or Littleworth) tunnel are stabled in the adjacent siding.   *N. Simmons/Hugh Davies*

Wheatley coal yard photographed in January 1962.   *Doug Nicholls*

Wheatley, looking from the down platform towards the goods yard with its yard crane. An up train has just left for Princes Risborough. *N. Simmons/Hugh Davies*

A nice picture of Wheatley signal box, not long repainted, with token pick-up post alongside. *N. Simmons/Hugh Davies*

A ganger's motorised trolley leaves Horspath tunnel, seen in the background, and heads towards Oxford. This tunnel was 524 yards long and trolleys passing through it had to be signalled on the block instruments and carry the token or an occupation key.   *R.H.G. Simpson*

A stopping train hauled by 'Hall' class 4-6-0 No. 4921 *Eaton Hall* near Littleworth, between Horspath tunnel and Wheatley.   *R.H.G. Simpson*

The new owner, British Railways, reintroduced the two middle day London services in May 1948 but did not otherwise alter the timetable, apart from making the evening train from Cowley to Oxford 'unadvertised'. So matters remained until September 1949 when the service was considerably improved. Marylebone became the principal London station for High Wycombe, Princes Risborough and Oxford (via Thame) services. In the down direction there were new trains at 9.27 am Princes Risborough to Oxford (with another following at 9.45 am!) and 7.31 pm Risborough to Thame; in the up direction a 12.52 pm Oxford to Risborough and 8 pm Thame to Risborough were the new trains. But the most dramatic increase was to the Sunday service, seemingly always two each way over the GWR years. There was a new down train at 4.55 pm from Risborough and the last train was retarded by an hour to 7.05 pm. In the up direction there were two extra trains at 10 am and 3.10 pm from Oxford. None of these Sunday trains called at Morris Cowley but all other stations and halts were served. This fairly lavish service continued during the following summer and a slight alteration in September 1950 was that the 7.31 pm from Risborough to Thame was extended to Oxford (but ran Saturdays excepted) and the 8 pm Thame to Risborough was withdrawn. There were now nine trains each way over the full length of the branch, one (the 7.31 pm) Saturdays excepted. From 1950 onwards the through trains to or from London were reduced to no more than one or two each way; by 1959 only one weekday and one Sunday up train ran through to London.

The fuel crisis of February 1951 caused a relatively slight reduction in services. The 1.52 pm Risborough to Oxford and 12.52 pm Oxford-Risborough were made Saturdays only and the 4.12 pm Risborough to Thame and its 4.45 pm return journey were withdrawn. The lavish Sunday service was not touched. This service was continued through the summer 1951 timetable but in September 1951, although the weekday service was unchanged, one down (the 4.55 pm) and one up (the 3.05 pm) Sunday trains were withdrawn. The summer 1952 timetable saw the withdrawal of the 9.27 am Princes Risborough-Oxford (only 18 minutes in front of the 9.45 service) and the 11.24 am Oxford-Risborough service which was rather more serious as it left a gap between 8.20 am and 2.40 pm departures from Oxford, except on Saturdays when the 12.52 ran. Both these trains were restored in the 1952 winter timetables and the 1953 and 1954 timetables saw no changes in the number of trains whatsoever.

The next change in June 1955 was relatively modest. The last up train, 6.50 pm Oxford to Risborough was made Saturdays excepted. Whereas before the war it was necessary to have a later service from Oxford on Saturdays, now it finished earlier on that day, a sign of the public's altered travelling habits so far as the railway was concerned.

There was now a further period of stability, with the timetable hardly having changed since 1949, until summer 1958 when the Western Region decided it needed to make draconian cuts in local services. Although the summer timetable, from 9th June, showed an unaltered service, a 62 page supplement from 30th June changed all that. So far as the Thame branch was concerned the alterations were these:

Horspath Halt looking towards Oxford.   *N. Simmons/Hugh Davies*

From the bridge over the Garsington Road, Morris Cowley, this view looks towards Risborough, goods office and goods shed to right.   *N. Simmons/Hugh Davies*

Morris Cowley looking towards Princes Risborough, part of the Morris car works at left.
N. Simmons/Hugh Davies

The passenger facilities at Morris Cowley, looking towards Oxford. Probably photographed on a Sunday as signals are off in both directions, meaning the signal box is switched out of circuit.
N. Simmons/Hugh Davies

A close-up of Littlemore station building, which has been recently repainted.

N. Simmons/Hugh Davies

An unusual view of Kennington Jn from the main line towards the Risborough line. A lengthy train, banked at the rear, is heading towards Littlemore. *R.H.G. Simpson*

9.27 am Princes Risborough-Oxford withdrawn
11.20 am Princes Risborough-Oxford terminates at Thame
7.31 pm (SX) Princes Risborough-Oxford withdrawn
8.16 am Oxford-Princes Risborough withdrawn
11.30 am Oxford-Princes Risborough starts from Thame

This meant that there were now five down trains (six on Saturdays) and seven up trains running the length of the branch. Also there was a gap in the service from Risborough to Oxford between 9.45 am and 4.02 pm except on Saturdays, and in the service from Oxford between 8.16 am and 2.42 pm, again except on Saturdays. The winter 1958 timetable saw the withdrawal of the 8.16 am Oxford train, further lengthening the gap in up trains from 7.50 am to 2.42 pm. The only thing that changed in the summer 1959 timetable was the extension of the long standing 5.44 pm Risborough-Thame to Wheatley, Saturdays excepted.

The only change in the winter 1959 service was the reversion back to two up trains on Sundays, as it had been in GWR days, the service withdrawn being the 7.10 am from Oxford. A year later, August 1960, the two up trains leaving Oxford between 6 and 7 in the evening became one, at 6.27 pm, there were thus now five up trains running the length of the branch (six on Saturdays), and this was the service that continued, with minor alterations in timings, until the branch closed to passengers in January 1963.

Freight Services

The first Working Timetable (WTT) found, that for March 1866, showed just one goods train in each direction. The 2 am from Taplow to Oxford ran daily, except Mondays, calling at all stations and arriving in Oxford at 7 am on weekdays and 8.05 am on Sundays. In the reverse direction the 7.45 pm Oxford to Paddington also stopped everywhere, including Penn Farm siding, and arrived in Taplow at 12.45 and London at 2.50 am. This train did not run on Sundays but the 5.40 pm passenger Oxford-Paddington on Sundays did also convey cattle. By February 1868 only the down train called at Tiddington, on an 'as required' basis, but there was now also a 2.50 am (Mondays excepted) Paddington-Thame which arrived at 8.15 am, calling if required at Bledlow. It returned to Taplow at 9 am, calling at Bledlow *en route*. The down service also ran on Sundays, but not the up train.

By June 1875 the former 2 am Taplow now started from Paddington at 2.20 am arriving in Oxford at 8.30 am (weekdays), 9 am (Sundays). A second train started from Taplow at 5 am on weekdays only and left Risborough at 7.30 am, 50 minutes behind the 2.20 am goods, calling at all stations except Bledlow, and arriving Oxford at 9.25 am. This ran as a mixed train between Wycombe and Oxford: 'A composite and third class coach to be attached'. A third down goods train left Taplow at 5.50 pm on weekdays, and this one missed out Bledlow, Tiddington and Littlemore and arrived at Oxford at 9.45 pm. Finally a 7.30 pm Paddington to Wolverhampton coal empties on weekdays left Risborough at 12.20 am and called at Thame and Wheatley, arriving at Oxford at 1.55 am. In the up direction a much expanded weekday freight service left Oxford at 11.20 am to

Taplow calling at all stations including Penn Farm if required, 6.15 pm to Paddington, not calling at Littlemore or Tiddington, arriving at London at 1.05 am, and finally a 10.30 pm (Saturdays excepted) to Taplow omitting Littlemore and Tiddington and calling at Bledlow if required. On Sundays there was a 10.40 pm Oxford-Taplow with the same calling pattern as the 10.30 pm weekdays train.

By February 1876 the down Wolverhampton coal empties had become a general goods train running just on Tuesdays between Taplow and Oxford only, leaving Taplow at 11.20 pm and Risborough at 1.40 am and after calling at Thame and Wheatley arriving at Oxford at 3.10 am. This returned at 5.15 pm (Tuesdays only) Oxford to Taplow, omitting Littlemore and Tiddington stations. The 10.30 pm (SX) up now ran two hours earlier at 8.30 pm, but reverted back to 10.20 pm in 1877.

The timetable for October 1890 showed considerable alteration:

Down
2.20 am (MX) 3 am (MO) Paddington-Oxford (arr. 8.25 am), 'Mixed' Wycombe-Oxford
4.50 am (MX) Taplow-Oxford (arr. 9.40 am)
4.15 pm (RR) High Wycombe-Oxford (arr. 7.22 pm)
6.20 pm (RR) High Wycombe-Oxford (arr. 8.55 pm)
5.55 pm Taplow-Oxford (arr. 10 pm), 'Mixed' Wycombe-Oxford
7.30 pm (RR) Taplow-Oxford (arr. 11.15 pm). Called Thame & Wheatley only on branch
9.45 pm Paddington-Oxford (arr. 2.35 am). No station stops on branch.
2.20 am (Sundays) Paddington-Oxford (arr. 8.40 am)
5.10 am (Sundays) Taplow-Oxford (arr. 9.50 am)

Up
9.40 am (RR) Oxford-High Wycombe
11.21 am Oxford-Taplow
12.40 pm (RR) Oxford-Wycombe or Taplow. When run, returned as 6.20 pm Wycombe or 7.30 pm Taplow to Oxford.
6.15 pm Oxford-Paddington
10 pm Oxford-Taplow (called only at Wheatley & Thame on the branch)
5.55 pm (Sundays) Oxford-Paddington

RR - Run as Required.

There was an interesting footnote against the 2.20 am (MX) Paddington 'Mixed' as follows: 'If this train should be running so late as to be likely to cause delay to the 8.25 am passenger train from Oxford, the engine passenger coach and van must be run to Oxford in the times of the mixed train, and the engine and van must return to work the goods trucks from the station where they were left'.

The July 1896 timetable was not greatly different although there were variations in train timings. The 12.40 pm Oxford and 6.20 pm Wycombe/7.30 pm Taplow conditional trains had disappeared from the timetable. There was an additional up goods train at 4.30 pm Oxford-Taplow and the 10 pm up had become 11.35 pm. The 9.45 pm Paddington down now started at Taplow at 10.45 pm and included calls at Thame and Wheatley.

The opening of the Joint line in April 1906 caused some revision of the goods train on the Thame branch which now practically all ran to and from London (July 1906 timetable):

Down
2 am (MX) Paddington-Oxford (via Maidenhead). *Also ran on Sundays*
1 am (MX) Crimea Yard-Oxford (via Maidenhead). (Although this train left
Risborough at 8.25 am, shunting and waiting a path at Thame & Wheatley meant that it
did not arrive at Oxford until 1.15 pm!) *Also ran Sundays arriving Oxford 10.25 am*
10.05 am Old Oak Common-Oxford (via Joint line), arrived Oxford 2.57 pm
5.55 pm (MO) Taplow - Oxford (arr. 9.50 pm)
5.00 pm Taplow-Oxford (arr. 10 pm) [?this was MX, but not so shown in timetable]

Up
4.30 am Oxford-Old Oak Common (via Joint line). Called only at Thame on branch.
11.45 am Oxford-Taplow
4.35 pm Oxford-Paddington (via Maidenhead)
11.00 pm Oxford-Old Oak Common (via Maidenhead). Called only at Wheatley &
Thame on branch.
6.05 pm (Sundays) Oxford-Kensington goods and milk (via Maidenhead).

By the next working timetable seen, July 1915, the 10.05 am Old Oak Common
and 4.30 am Oxford trains had disappeared. The 1 am Crimea now started from
Slough at 4.00 am, still arriving at Oxford at 1.15 pm. On Mondays only a 3.42
pm from Acton ran to Oxford, calling only at Thame and Wheatley on the
branch and arriving Oxford at 10.03 pm. There was only one down evening
train from Taplow at 5 pm. In the up direction a 9.35 pm Worcester-Paddington
left Oxford at 12.40 am using the line only as a through route, not calling
anywhere. This train also ran on Saturday night/Sunday mornings. The 4.35
pm up goods now ran at 3.25 pm and there was a new 5.10 pm Oxford to
Wheatley 'trip' calling only at Littlemore, which returned at 6.45 pm again
calling at Littlemore. Another through train, 3.35 pm Worcester-Paddington,
left Oxford at 11.13 pm running over the branch without stopping. Finally the
11.00 pm Oxford now left at 11.30 and terminated at Slough. The other trains
listed above in 1906 and not mentioned here were little altered.

By January 1921 the old established 2 am from Paddington had become a
through train to Worcester, leaving Paddington at 12.05 am and no longer working
at stations on the branch except Thame. It ran to a fast schedule arriving at Oxford
at 3.28 am rather than the previous 8.5 am. This train also ran on Sundays. The 3.42
pm (MO) from Acton no longer ran but there was a new daily 9.55 pm
Risborough-Oxford goods calling at all stations. In the up direction there was a
new 5.40 am Oxford-Taplow goods calling at Wheatley and Thame if required.
The afternoon 'trip' to Wheatley and back had gone as had the late night 11.30 pm
goods. Finally the two up Worcesters had become one, 5.10 pm from Worcester,
which left Oxford at 12.28 am, Monday mornings excepted. The Sunday evening
up goods and milk train also no longer appeared in the timetable.

The July 1923 timetable had almost reverted to the pre-Joint line situation
with no overnight trains, no through trains to London and a simple service of
two through trains each way on weekdays only: 4 am Slough-Oxford (arr. 1.20
pm); 4.55 pm Taplow-Oxford (arr. 10.45 pm); 5.45 am Oxford-Taplow; 11.25 am
Oxford-Taplow. In addition there was a local goods 2.50 pm Oxford-Thame and
8.15 pm Thame-Oxford. The last timetable seen (summer 1927) before the
opening of Morris Cowley was almost the same, except that the 5.45 am Oxford

PRINCES RISBORO' AND OXFORD.

Down Trains.

Single Line, worked by Electric Train Token, between Princes Risboro' and Kennington Junction. The Crossing Stations are at Princes Risboro', Thame, Wheatley, Morris Cowley and Kennington Junction. At Morris Cowley it is only possible to cross one Passenger and one Goods train, or two Goods trains. The Passenger train must be kept on the running line. "Change of Gradient Boards" (illuminated by Night) are fixed between Thame and Tiddington on the Up Side of the Line at 6 miles 8 chains, 6 miles 42 chains, and 7 miles 10 chains.

Week Days.

Distance from Paddington	Mile Post Mileage	STATIONS.	Falling Gradient 1 in		Point to point Allowances			Goods	Passenger		3.35 a.m. Acton Cov. Cars.		Engine and Van.	Passenger				Diesel Car.		Passenger		Pilot.		Banbury Pass.		3.55 a.m. Slough Goods.			Pass.		Eng'ne Tues. only.		Passenger		

Light engine leaves Morris Cowley MX at 8||40 a.m. for Oxford due 8.52 a.m.

SUNDAYS.

STATIONS.	Goods	Passenger	Banbury Pass.	Diesel Car.	Goods	Diesel Car.	Passenger	Goods	5.45 p.m. Taplow Goods.	5.45 p.m. Taplow Goods.	Bourley Junct. Goods.	5.45 p.m. Taplow Goods.	Leamington Goods.	10.30 pm Wycombe Pass.	Passenger	Passenger

M On Saturdays starts at 10.0 p.m., runs correspondingly earlier and terminates at Oxford. Q Oxford South End arr. 9.50 p.m. depart 10.0 p.m. U Kennington Junc. arrive 10.58 a.m.
V Oxford North. Oxford South arrive 7.38 p.m., depart 7.46 p.m. Z Time allowed for signal checks approaching Oxford. If late running time Littlemore to Oxford to be 7 minutes. ‡ From Paddington Goods. § Diesel Car must stop dead at Thame, Wheatley, Morris Cowley, and Kennington Junction Signal Boxes to exchange Token. Light Engine leaves Morris Cowley SX at 5‖20 p.m. for Littlemore due the 5.25 p.m. to shunt yard.

July 1939 Working Timetable - down trains.

was now back to its old time of 11.30 pm and there was an additional 'trip' 4.40 pm Oxford-Wheatley, returning from there at 7.05 pm.

The main change to the timetable after Morris Cowley opened was the inclusion of new trunk trains to move the cars produced at the Morris works. In September 1931 the following services ran from Cowley: 12.50 pm (RR) to Brentford; 8 pm (RR) to Brentford; 10.10 pm to Bordesley Jn. These trains all ran via Kennington Jn; the Brentford trains ran to the docks and carried cars for export. The basic pattern (Taplows) was little altered in July 1939, although the opening of Cowley required a new 11.30 pm Oxford-Acton goods, but as the trunk trains were altered and there were several additional trips the timetable is included as an illustration (July 1937 was very similar).

Wartime necessity entailed the use of the line as a through route again for freight trains to and from Worcester and the May 1943 book (see Chapter Nine) showed the 10.50 pm Park Royal and 11.55 pm Paddington passing over the line in the early hours on Tuesdays-Sundays inclusive. In the up direction a train which left Worcester in the afternoon entered the line at Kennington Jn just after 11 pm each weekday evening. The 5.45 pm Taplow-Oxford freight now left Taplow at 8.50 pm which meant that the residents of Thame could enjoy the sounds of shunting at 12.40 am! Otherwise the timetabled service was similar to 1939, but there were additional daily services (including Sundays) at 5.35 am from Banbury to Morris Cowley and at 9.30 am from Cowley to Banbury. By October 1943 there was a second service from Park Royal at 1.50 am to Oxford which called at Morris Cowley at 3.55 am (this had been shown 'RR' in the May timetable), and a new 6.48 pm Old Oak Common to Worcester goods which used the line as a through route, passing Risborough at 8.50 pm.

May 1946 was very similar to 1943 apart from the removal of the Old Oak Common train and the fact that all freight trains for Oxford now terminated in Hinksey yard rather than Oxford North yard. The following October the 8.50 pm Taplow had reverted to its former 5.50 pm departure, but now the 1.50 am Park Royal called additionally, except on Sundays, at Thame at 3.28 am! The final, October 1947, timetable produced by the GWR showed very little change from those operated since the commencement of war.

By June 1955 the freight service consisted of three or four trains in each direction running the length of the branch and a greater number running to or from Morris Cowley only, from the Oxford end:

Down
12.35 am Park Royal-Worcester (MX) called Thame and Morris Cowley (also ran Sundays)
2.35 am Acton-Hinksey (MX) called Morris Cowley (also ran Sundays if required)
9.18 am Morris Cowley-Hinksey (SX)
11.50 am Morris Cowley-Hinksey (SX)
2.0 pm (SO) 3.0 pm (SX) Morris Cowley-Hinksey
9.34 am Taplow-Hinksey called all stations except Littlemore
7.12 pm Morris Cowley-Hinksey
8.0 pm Morris Cowley-Three Spires Jn (SX)
9.15 pm Morris Cowley-Bordesley Jn (SX)
10.20 pm Morris Cowley-Birkenhead (SX)

Up Trains.   OXFORD AND PRINCES RISBORO'.   Week Days.

Time allowance for Freight Trains—See page 207.

STATIONS.

Oxford
Kennington J'nct'n
Littlemore
Morris Cowley
Horspath Halt
Wheatley
Tiddington
Thame
Towersey Halt
Bledlow
Princes Risboro'
Paddington

Point to point allowances — Vac'm Mins. / Expr's Mins. / Ordin'ry Mins.

Ruling Gradient in 1 in

Allow for stop. Mins. / Allow for start. Mins.

Light Engine leave Oxford MX at 6.5 a.m. for Morris Cowley, due 6.20 a.m., and at 2.30 p.m. (station pass. at 41 p.m.) SX for Morris Cowley due 2.56 p.m. J Thame arrive 8.4 a.m. P Calls at Penn Farm when required.

SUNDAYS.

§ Kennington Junc. 11.35†11.63 p.m. Morris Cowley arrive 12.0 night.   ‡ Diesel car must stop dead at Kennington Junction,
Morris Cowley, Wheatley, Thame, and Princes Risborough North Signal Boxes to exchange token.   ¶ To Watlington Bay Line.
Y—Shunts Yard at Littlemore.

July 1939 Working Timetable - up trains.

Up
12.40 am Hinksey-Slough (MX) non stop on branch
6.50 pm Washwood Heath-Morris Cowley (MX) arr. Cowley 1.40 am (also ran Sunday mornings)
12.10 am Longbridge-Morris Cowley (MX) arr. Cowley 4.05 am
6.05 am Hinksey-Morris Cowley
8.35 am Hinksey-Morris Cowley
2.25 am Three Spires Jn-Morris Cowley (MX) arr. Cowley 9.02 am
9.25 am Hinksey-Slough, non stop to Wheatley, then all stations
11.0 am Hinksey-Morris Cowley (SX)
12.05 pm Hinksey-Morris Cowley (Thame if required) the only train to call at Littlemore
4.05 pm Hinksey-Morris Cowley
3.30 pm (SX) 4.55 pm (SO) Worcester-Paddington called at Morris Cowley 11.05 pm (SX)
11.20 pm Hinksey-Slough (SO) non stop on branch
3.15 pm Birkenhead-Morris Cowley arr. Cowley 11.50 pm

A very similar timetable operated four years later in June 1959, except that the new oil terminal at Thame now warranted a 9.50 pm Thame to Acton. No inwards service was shown, the tanks probably being dropped by the 12.55 am Park Royal to Worcester. A path had been created at 1.50 pm from Morris Cowley to 'anywhere' to cater for the variations in the export car traffic. Dick Tolley, writing in his autobiography *Steaming Spires*, said that the men booking on at Oxford for this job had to have road knowledge of, and be prepared to work to, Wolverhampton, Worcester, Swindon or Acton, as required. For this reason the job was in the top goods link. In those days, before articulated car-carrying vehicles, the trains would be formed of up to 60 'Asmos', box vans with end doors, with a single car in each one. Two years later, in September 1961, the freight timetable was not significantly different.

Later developments up to the end of 1968 will be covered in Chapter Eleven.

Signal box hours

The line's signal boxes (block posts) were Thame, Wheatley and (from 1928) Morris Cowley; the first two of these dated from just before the installation of the electric train staff system in 1892. There were earlier structures during the period of train staff and ticket working but they are not those seen in the photographs, all of which were built in 1891/2. Although there were signal box structures at Bledlow, Tiddington and Littlemore these were not block posts; Bledlow appeared in the lists of 'hours of opening' because it had to be manned throughout opening hours to control the level crossing. The other two were just superior ground frames for shunting purposes.

In 1896-1898, Thame and Wheatley boxes were open continuously, except between 10.45 pm Sunday and 6.40 am Monday. In July 1906 they were continuous until about 11 am on Sundays, shut until 5.30 pm, closed again after the Sunday evening service at about 10.45 pm and reopened at 4.30 am (Wheatley) on Mondays. In January 1921 the same situation applied with altered timings to suit the current train service. In July 1923 the boxes were closing each week night between midnight and 5.45 am, and open for two short shifts on Sundays as before.

In September 1931, Thame and Wheatley were open from 6.45 am until after the passing of the 12.01 am Oxford goods train at about 1 am each weekday and for the two Sunday shifts. Morris Cowley was open from 6.45 am to 10.45 pm on weekdays and closed on Sundays, for which a block switch was provided. In July 1937 (and 1939) Thame and Wheatley were closed for little more than four hours each week night, closing after the 12.01 am Oxford (at 1.30 am in the case of Thame) and opening again at about 5 am (6.45 am on Mondays). Morris Cowley also opened at 5.15 am (except Mondays) but still closed at 10.45 pm and all day on Sundays.

By October 1942 (and probably earlier), and for the rest of the war, the three branch boxes were open continuously. By October 1945 the boxes had reverted back to being open continuously in the week, closing early on Sunday mornings (about 4 am) reopening for two short shifts on Sunday and then closing until 6 am Mondays. Morris Cowley, however, was slightly different at weekends, remaining open through Sunday morning until 1 pm, then shutting until 6 am Monday. These opening hours continued throughout the remainder of the GWR's life.

Similar hours to these were still in operation in BR days; in June 1959 the only difference was that Morris Cowley closed at 6 am on Sundays and did not reopen until 6 am Mondays; the other two, not having block switches, continued to open for two short Sunday turns. These hours were also applicable in 1961 and 1962.

After withdrawal of the passenger service, the box opening hours would be governed by the limited freight service using the line. Wheatley box closed on 12th July, 1964, Thame closed on 17th November, 1968 and finally Morris Cowley on 28th January, 1982. With the closure of Morris Cowley box, this end of the line was operated by 'No Signalman Key Token', the token being obtained by the driver from instruments located at Kennington Jn, the token being released by the signalman in Oxford Panel box which now controlled the signalling of the line up to Morris Cowley.

Both sets of token set down/pick up apparatus are visible in this view of Thame signal box looking towards Princes Risborough.   *Geoff Gamble*

Guards' Working

A snapshot of passenger guards' working at two points in the line's life can be given. In July 1924 the passenger train weekday service was covered by three Paddington guards, three Oxford guards (four on Saturdays) and the evening auto-trains between Princes Risborough and Thame by an Aylesbury guard. In addition the Tuesday-only service for Thame market was covered by a Princes Risborough porter; this was the only turn Risborough had.

In June 1958 two Reading guards, three Oxford guards and three Banbury guards covered the weekday passenger service between them. Unlike in 1924 when some guards worked to or from Paddington, in 1958 only the Reading turns worked as far as High Wycombe, all the remainder went no further east than Princes Risborough on Thame branch trains.

Gradients

The gradients on the Thame branch were quite fierce. The 1922 Sectional Appendix in a table of gradients steeper than 1 in 200 listed them as follows:

Incline Between	Length (about)	Gradient 1 in	Falling towards
Princes Risboro' and Bledlow	¾ mile	100	Bledlow
Thame and Tiddington	¾ mile	115	Tiddington
Tiddington and Wheatley	1 mile	135	Wheatley
Wheatley and Littlemore	1 mile	84	Wheatley
Wheatley and Littlemore	1 mile	83	Littlemore
Wheatley and Littlemore	¾ mile	82	Littlemore
Littlemore and Kennington Jn	¾ mile	93	Kennington Jn

Almost one-third of the branch mileage was composed of these steep gradients. As mentioned earlier, 'Change of Gradient' boards were fixed by the GWR in 1920 in the section between Thame and Tiddington, positioned at 6 m. 8 ch., 6 m. 40 ch. and 7 m. 10 ch. These indicated to traincrew that their train was about to enter a descending gradient.

Special Operating Instructions (1922)

Penn Farm siding, between Thame and Bledlow, was controlled by a lever locked by Annett's key, which formed part of the Risborough-Thame electric staff. Only those trains shown to call here in the working timetable were allowed to call, except on the authority of the divisional superintendent. By 1929, no down train was allowed to call, although as mentioned in Chapter Five, at one time they did do so. In addition to the security of the Annett's key, the points were clipped and padlocked and a shunter from Thame had to accompany any train working at the siding to unlock the points and afterwards lock them, returning the key to Thame signal box (presumably on foot). The guard was responsible for ensuring

Extracts from the 1922 London District Sectional Appendix

Engine Headlights on Branch Goods Trains

Engines working Goods trains between the undermentioned points will carry only one headlight (in centre of buffer plank):

Princes Risborough and Oxford

Ground Frames and Intermediate Sidings

Name	Where Situated	By whom attended
Bledlow	Bledlow station	Station Master
Penn Farm	Between Bledlow and Thame	Head Guard
Thame	Down platform	Foreman Porter
Tiddington	At station	Station Master
Wheatley	Down platform	Porter
Littlemore	At station	Station Master

Single Line Loops at Stations

Thame	1,249 feet long
Wheatley	959 feet long

Coupling of Goods Trains

Goods trains may be coupled as under:

Line	Points between which trains may be coupled	Combined load not to exceed
Down	Maidenhead & Oxford via Wycombe	50 wagons

Where Engines can take water

Thame	End of Down and Up platforms
Princes Risborough	South end (up platform), North end (down platform)

Public Level Crossings

Name	Situated between	Block Post?	Whether there is a gatekeeper indicators or Bells?	Signals?	Are gates interlocked with signals?
Bledlow	Bledlow Station	NO	Gatekeeper, Indicator & Bells	YES	YES
Hinton	Bledlow & Thame	NO	Gatekeeper Indicator & Bells	YES	YES

that the siding was left 'in order in every respect' on departure. The ground frames at Bledlow, Tiddington and Littlemore were also locked by Annett's key forming part of the electric train staff.

Because the points at the Oxford end of Thame station were worked by a ground frame, the operator there had to co-operate with the signalman in signalling the trains. The ground frame operator had a special bell code to communicate with the signalman or vice versa; when a down train left for Oxford he signalled 2 pause 1 to notify the signalman accordingly and in foggy weather (when presumably the signalman might not see the train leave), the latter was not allowed to send 'Train Entering Section' to Wheatley until he received this 2-1 signal from the ground frame. Other bell codes in operation were:

Up train arrived with tail lamp and clear of crossing	2 pause 2
Unbolt points for long siding	3 pause 2
Set points for up train	3 pause 4
Set points for down train	2 pause 5
Obstruction Danger	6 beats
Test signal	16 beats

Similar arrangements applied at Wheatley, including use of the 2-1 signal when a down train left for Kennington Jn. (These instructions, and those for Wheatley, dated from 1st November, 1891, which could well be the date of opening of the new signal boxes at those places.) These arrangements continued at Thame until the removal of the ground frame in 1959, but the ground frame at Wheatley closed in 1929 and the points were put on the signal box.

About ¼ mile west of Wheatley station there was an occupation level crossing serving Messrs Cooper's brickworks. The firm had a traction engine and on 25th August, 1902 a telephone was installed at the crossing connected with the signal box at Wheatley, to enable the firm to obtain permission for the engine to cross the line. (Prior to this the signalman would either withdraw a staff, or flagmen would be sent out in both directions.) The signalman could give permission if there was no train in the section between Kennington Jn and Wheatley; he had to withdraw a staff and keep his signals at danger. However, if a down train was proceeding towards Kennington Jn he could give permission, provided he could ascertain that the train had passed Cooper's crossing, complete with tail lamp. These instructions were printed in the 1922 Appendix, but by the time of the 1938 issue the firm was required to give 'notice to the station master' for authority to cross. The telephone had been replaced by an 'automatic warning device' which rang a bell at the crossing when a train approached.

Littlemore station closed at 9.15 pm each night, and traincrew of any goods trains calling after this had to do their own shunting. The Annett's key operated the lock on the 'signal box' door. These instructions were perpetuated in the 1938 Appendix.

Locomotives

As this was an important secondary route to the GWR, particularly in the case of a blockage somewhere on the main line, a wide range of locomotives could

BRANCH LINES—LONDON DIVISION

CLASS OF ENGINE

From	To	40XX	29XX 43XX 31XX	"County" 22XX 102-3-104	"Bull Dog" 44XX & 45XX 0-6-0 T. B & C Groupe (New Boilers) 4-4-0 Cam. (Belpaire).	"City," "Atbara," "Duke," 36XX & 39XX 0-6-2 T.—C. Group—Old Boilers 0-6-0 M. & S.W. (G.W. Boilers).	3521 Type 0-6-0 & 0-6-0 T. (Stand. Gds.) 0-6-2 T. A & B Groups (Sm l. Boilers) 0-6-0 Cam. (Belpaire) 0-6-0 M. & S.W. (Old Boilers).	3201 to 3205 3501 to 3520 3206 to 3225 3521 Type (Sml. Boiler) (Constituent) 4-4-0 M. & S.W. (New Boilers).	898 to 1082 Cam. 4-4-0 M. & S.W. (Old Boilers).	3232 to 3251 2-4-0 T. Metro 4-4-4 T. M. & S.W. 1112, 1118 1, 28-9 Cam.	0-4-2 T (517 Type) 0-4-4 T (M. & S.W.) 2-4-0 T (M. & S.W.)
		Tons	Tons	Tons	Tons	Tons	Tons	Tons	Tons	Tons	Tons
Princes Risboro'	Aylesbury	—	—	—	—	—	—	—	—	—	168
Aylesbury	Princes Risboro'	—	—	—	—	—	—	—	—	—	112
Princes Risboro'	Oxford	336	308	280	252	224	196	182	—	168	140
Oxford	Princes Risboro'	364	336	308	280	252	224	210	—	224	196
Radley	Abingdon	—	—	—	—	—	—	—	—	224	196
Abingdon	Radley	—	—	—	—	—	—	—	—	224	196
Reading	Basingstoke	392	364	336	208	280	252	238	—	224	196
Basingstoke	Reading	392	364	336	208	280	252	238	—	224	196
Slough	Windsor	392	364	336	208	280	252	238	—	224	196
Windsor	Slough	392	364	336	208	280	252	238	—	224	196
Southall	Brentford	—	—	—	—	—	—	—	—	196	—
Brentford	Southall	—	—	—	—	—	—	—	—	196	—
Twyford	Henley	392	364	336	308	280	252	238	—	224	196
Henley	Twyford	336	308	280	252	224	196	182	—	168	140
West Drayton	Staines	392	364	336	308	280	252	238	—	224	196
Staines	W. Drayton	392	364	336	308	280	252	238	—	224	196
W. Drayton	Uxbridge	392	364	336	308	280	252	238	—	224	196
Uxbridge	W. Drayton	392	364	336	308	280	252	238	—	224	196

Engine loads allowed over the Thame branch - 1927.

be seen unlike a dead-end branch line. In broad gauge days the only record found of a specific locomotive is of *Sunbeam* on the opening train to Thame. Built as a 2-2-2 'Sun' class tender engine by R. & W. Hawthorn of Newcastle in 1840, it was altered to a saddle tank around 1850. Already old by the time of the extension to Thame, it is perhaps no coincidence that it was withdrawn in July 1870, just before the 'narrowing' of the Thame branch. Others of this early class of 21 locomotives will have been used on the Thame branch, 12 of which were withdrawn in 1870. From 1865 onwards these engines, together with other 2-2-2s rebuilt as tank engines, formed the 'Wolf' class. Other locomotives of a similar age, no longer front rank, such as the 'Leo' and 'Hercules' classes may have been used on the line, also the later 4-4-0ST 'Bogie' class.

The only other references found to specific locomotives used on the branch before the turn of the century are those in Chapter Six. In 1878 engine No. 1020 worked the Taplow goods - this was a '1016' class 0-6-0ST built at Wolverhampton in 1867 weighing 37 tons and with a boiler pressure of 140 psi and a tractive effort of 13,540 lb. Tank capacity was a modest 880 gallons so a water stop at Thame was probably obligatory on any train over the Thame branch. Out of a class of 60 locomotives, No. 1020 was one of 11 never fitted with pannier tanks and was withdrawn in 1928. In 1881 locomotive No. 951 was working the Taplow goods - this was a '1076' or 'Buffalo' class 0-6-0ST similar in appearance to the '1016' class. No. 951 was slightly more modern, built at Swindon in 1874 and weighing 38 tons with boiler pressure of 140 psi and a tractive effort of 15,288 lb. Only 860 gallons of water was carried. Fitted with pannier tanks in 1920, No. 951 was withdrawn in 1930. Other locomotives that might have been seen on the line at this time were the 'Metro' 2-4-0 tanks, 2-2-2 and 2-4-0 tender engines, and the Armstrong and Dean goods 0-6-0 tender engines.

In 1921 the following classes of locomotive were shedded at Oxford and will have worked over the Thame branch:

2-4-0T 'Metro'	0-6-0T '1813' class	0-6-0 Standard goods
0-6-0 Dean goods	4-4-2 De Glehn Compound	2-6-0 'Aberdare' class
0-4-2T '517' class	4-6-0 'Saint' class	0-6-0T '1076' class
2-4-0 'Stella' class	0-6-0T '1016'class	2-4-0 '3232' class
0-6-0T '1661' class	4-4-0 'Bulldog' class	0-6-0T '1854/1701' class
4-4-0 'City' class	4-4-0 '41XX' class	

Neighbouring depots held other classes of 0-6-0T, 2-4-0 and 4-4-0 types which would have worked over the line as would the '28XX' 2-8-0, 'ROD' 2-8-0, '3100' 2-6-2T, 'Star' class 4-6-0 and '43XX' 2-6-0 all held nearby. The loads allowed for different classes of engine over the branch (passenger, parcels and fish trains) from the 1927 loads book is included as an illustration opposite.

By the 1930s successor classes of those mentioned above and all types of 4-6-0 would be seen on the line except the 'King' class which was prohibited, as was the '47XX' class 2-8-0. The '56XX' class 0-6-2T, based at Slough, were regular performers on freight trains. Some of the actual locomotives seen on the line in the 1940s are mentioned in Chapter Nine, which include No. 7241 a '7200' class 2-8-2T. Additionally there were the diesel railcars from 1936 which were operating half of the services on the branch during most of the 1950s. The 1950s BR-built dmus were not employed on the line, but occasionally traversed it when diverted from the main line.

Oxford shed yard on 24th April, 1955 with various engines in steam and two of the GWR streamlined railcars in the background.   *N. Simmons/Hugh Davies*

Class '14XX' 0-4-2T No. 1420, which worked over the Risborough line, seen at Oxford shed on 5th May, 1957.   *Philip Kelley*

On 31st August, 1957, a '51XX' class 2-6-2T and a single brake third substitutes for a diesel railcar on the 2.42 pm train to Princes Risborough, waiting to leave Oxford. *Dr G.D. Parkes*

'Hall' class locomotive No. 6975 *Capesthorne Hall* heads a Risborough and London service in Oxford's up platform, 11th April, 1955. *N. Simmons/Hugh Davies*

Traffic dealt with Thame Branch - 12 months ending May 1957

	FORWARDED		RECEIVED		Parcels Forwarded	Parcels Received	Wagon Accommodation
	Wagons	Tons	Wagons	Tons			
Littlemore							
No. 1	-	-	1,606	17,747	2,864	633	36
No. 2	11	60	81	741			
No. 3	343	1,000	130	956			
Cowley							
No. 1	-	-	2,385	28,868	-	-	100 Nuffield Exports
No. 2	315	2,556	1,444	12,144			200 BMC
No. 3	53,898	74,591	8,330	33,577			100 Pressed Steel
							350 BR*
Wheatley							
No. 1	-	-	446	4,654	1,459	4,159	30
No. 2	1	8	35	304			
No. 3	36	108	147	412			
Livestock			24	72			
Tiddington							
No. 1	-	-	19	215	1,111	243	35
No. 2	75	815	51	381			
No. 3	84	80	219	817			
Livestock	1	3	105	315			
Thame							
No. 1	-	-	700	7,059	17,959	14,657	90 in position
No. 2	7	80	162	1,236			122 out of position
No. 3	444	1,247	1,191	3,666			
Livestock	53	159	19	57			
Bledlow							
No. 1	-	-	7	32	115	461	20
No. 2	-	-	15	140			
No. 3	17	139	178	204			

Notes: No. 1 - coal or coke or patent fuel, No.2 - other minerals, No.3 - general merchandise * includes 100 'Old Tip' temporarily closed for relaying.

Chapter Eleven

Closure as a Through Route

Closure of the Thame branch was considered well before Beeching. In January 1956 the district operating superintendent at Paddington wrote to Regional Headquarters with a list of 18 services that would be examined under the 'Unremunerative Passenger Services' procedure. They were listed in order of priority, Princes Risborough to Oxford being twelfth.

On 13th February, 1957 the chief operating superintendent at Paddington HQ wrote to the district as follows:

Oxford - Reconstruction of station

The above scheme provides for additional freight running facilities through Oxford Station in addition to other forms of modernisation, and the cost of the complete scheme is estimated at between two and three millions pounds.

Certain amendments to a plan prepared by the Chief Civil Engineer are proposed but before the matter is taken any further it is necessary to know what the prospects are of withdrawal of the existing passenger services as follows:

> Oxford-Fairford
> Oxford-Thame etc.
> Oxford-Didcot (Local)
> Oxford-Banbury (Local)
> Oxford-Worcester (Local)
> Oxford-Bletchley (LMR)

It is felt that if these services were withdrawn there would be a very considerable reduction in line occupation at Oxford and a modified scheme of improvement may be possible at much less cost.

I shall be glad if you will say what stage has been reached in regard to investigations regarding these services and let me know as far as can be seen, when the passenger facilities under notice are likely to be dispensed with.

Had *all* these local services been withdrawn, it is doubtful that more than a single platform would have been required at Oxford station!

In an internal memo, following receipt of the above letter, the district staff considered that bus replacement of trains on the Thame branch would be very costly, but that a preliminary examination revealed that a *prima facie* case existed for withdrawal of the majority of the passenger trains, or alternatively the introduction of light weight diesel cars. It was envisaged that a steam-hauled parcels service would continue and there would not be any alteration to freight services, although the question was asked whether freight facilities were necessary at all of the stations on the branch.

A full examination of the freight and parcels traffic levels was carried out in 1957 and some interesting statistics obtained. These are summarised in the table opposite. Note that Cowley dealt with about 66,000 wagons in a year which on the basis of a 6 day week of 50 weeks is 220 wagons a day on average. In addition to the traffic figures, some other interesting facts were detailed, as follows:

A prairie tank takes this Oxford-bound train over the Kennington viaduct.   *R.H.G. Simpson*

Diesel shunter (later class '08') No. D3804 heads this engineering train on the Risborough line near Kennington Jn.   *R.H.G. Simpson*

Littlemore
3 ton fixed hand crane
20 ton cart weighbridge, rented by Morris & Beecham Fuel Service
Parcels forwarded were racing pigeons and rose trees
Coal merchants - Morris & Beecham and R. Taylor
Staff - one station master (class 3) and two porters (one vacancy)

Cowley
6 ton fixed hand crane, 6 ton mobile crane, gantry crane in shed
20 ton cart weighbridge
Operating staff - 18 including station master (class 2)
Passenger commercial staff - 2
Goods commercial staff - 18

Out of this total of 38 staff, there were eight vacancies, five in the operating and three in the goods commercial departments.

Wheatley
6 ton fixed hand crane
Cattle pens
Coal merchants -W. Tombs & Son, J. Reid & Sons, C. Hempsted
Staff - 7 including station master (class 3)

Tiddington
3 ton fixed hand crane
Coal merchant - E. Walters (Oakley, Bucks)
Staff - 4 including station master (class 3)

Thame
6 ton fixed hand crane
30 ton cart weighbridge
Cattle pens
Parcels forwarded - live chicks S.G. Brown - Chearsley
Coal merchants - H.W. Lovell, T. & R. Bambrook, J.A. Freeman & Son
Staff - 12 including station master (class 2), eight of which were goods commercial staff.
SM covers Bledlow

Bledlow
2 ton fixed hand crane
Staff - 3

Although all this information was produced, no further steps were taken at this stage to introduce any economies.

Further expansion of the Cowley facilities took place in March 1957 with two new long sidings and extension of a third, authorised in December 1956 at a cost of £13,857.

A new private siding for Shell Mex and BP Ltd was opened just west of Thame, between 5¾ and 6 mp, in 1958, the private siding agreement dated 24th October, 1958, at a cost of £7,344. The sidings were on the down side of the line, two discharge sidings each capable of holding 13 tank cars and a holding siding for 22 tanks. Access to the sidings was by means of a 2-lever ground frame, 592 yards from Thame signal box, released by the token for the Thame-Wheatley section. It

The driver opens up his '61XX' class tank for the climb to Littlemore, as it crosses the Kennington viaduct with a Princes Risborough train.

R.H.G. Simpson

The signal box diagram showing the Morris Cowley signalled layout, post 1956.

Signalling Record Society

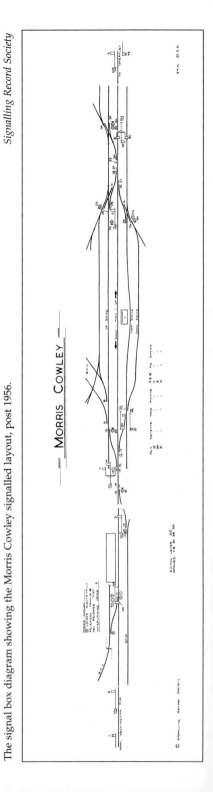

An overhead view of Littlemore station and yard, after removal of the signal box, on 16th June, 1956. Note the yard crane. *R.M. Casserley*

'61XX' 2-6-2T No. 6124 enters Littlemore with a Princes Risborough train on 11th August, 1962. Note the fixed distant signal at the platform end, this applies to Kennington Junction. *F.A. Blencowe*

An up stopping train, hauled by '14XX' class 0-4-2T No. 1420 pauses at Wheatley to unload passengers on 27th April, 1957. Note the steep steps leading to the road overbridge, there was no footbridge, as such, here.   *R.M. Casserley*

A close-up of the Oxford end of the station after closure to passengers (1964); note the 'Wheatley' running-in sign has been removed. The standard GW cast-iron sign requesting passengers to cross the line by the bridge is still present, however!

J.M. Neville courtesy G.A. Carpenter

View from the 11. 30 am Oxford as it approaches Risborough on 11th April, 1955, with a fine array of semaphore signals to be seen and the North signal box in the distance. The line on the right is the Watlington branch.   *N. Simmons/Hugh Davies*

On 18th May, 1959 '41XX' class 2-6-2T No. 4148 arrives at Princes Risborough with the 2.42 pm from Oxford.   *Michael Hale*

A rare sight at Wheatley. On Sunday 20th April, 1958 'Dukedog' class 4-4-0 No. 9017 stands at Wheatley with a Railway Enthusiasts' Club excursion. This had left Windsor at 8.44 am and run via Maidenhead and High Wycombe. It was destined for Cheltenham (St James) via Oxford and Kingham. Here the party would change to a push-and-pull train and travel via Gloucester dock lines and Forest of Dean branches to Severn Tunnel Jn, where they would rejoin this train for the return journey via Badminton.   *John Spencer Gilks*

'14XX' class 0-4-2T No. 1437 leaves Oxford with a Princes Risborough service *c.*1958.
                                                                                      P.Q. Treloar

was permissible for a train working at the siding to return to Thame station, and if the movement was propelled, at a speed not exceeding 20 mph, the guard's brake van must be the leading vehicle. A special 'Ceag' hand lamp was kept in Thame signal box for use in the sidings after dark (remember at this time staff used paraffin hand lamps normally). As Dick Tolley recalled in his memoirs *Steaming Spires* with some surprise, steam engines were allowed into the oil sidings. However, 'BR locomotives must not pass this point' boards were erected in 1968.

In December 1958 the General Manager authorised expenditure of £7,250 to relay and slue the Old Tip sidings at Cowley.

It may be remembered that the chief mechanical engineer (at Swindon) was the 'owner' of a sand quarry at Littlemore. This sand was mainly used for furnace bottoms in the works and, with the decline in building and repair of locomotives at Swindon, and with a problem of trespass at Littlemore, it was decided to investigate another source of supply. A source was found in Swindon, which, although of slightly lower quality, was considered suitable. It was therefore decided to 'abandon' the quarry in 1960. The correspondence reveals some interesting information: the quarry was 140 yards long and between 44 and 88 yards wide and there remained 33,200 cubic yards of sand available. It was anticipated that the land, which had poor road access, would rise in value as the County Council intended to build a By-pass nearby.

On 31st May, 1959 Hinton level crossing, a mile west of Bledlow, at 2 m. 50 ch., was reduced to accommodation crossing status, its gates replaced by field gates and its signals removed. This work had been authorised the previous November at a cost of £731 and was an economy to enable withdrawal of the crossing keeper.

In November 1959 a new locking frame was installed in Thame signal box. At the same time the opportunity was taken to abolish Thame ground frame which controlled the facing connection off the single line at the Oxford end of the station and put the connection on the signal box. The new locking frame was destined to have a short life at Thame.

A meeting was held at Paddington in April 1960 to discuss ways of speeding up the supply of new high density diesel multiple units (dmus) to the London division, to combat a shortage of footplate staff to keep steam engines going. The meeting took into account lines that were 'suspect' under the unremunerative passenger services procedure and there was a telling paragraph dealing with the Oxford-Risborough line:

> In view of the situation prevailing in regard to the Fairford branch [which was being progressed for withdrawal of passenger services] and the fact that both lines converge at Oxford it was considered unwise and therefore agreed not to dieselise any of the services on the Oxford-Princes Risborough section at this juncture. The Commercial Officer will urge forward the Oxford-Princes Risboro' line enquiries under the URS procedure.

The shortage of staff caused the withdrawal of one evening up train from Oxford as from 8th August, 1960.

The Area Board of the Western Region authorised expenditure of £45,640 (£48,800 at 'private party' prices, which the County Council would be charged) in September 1960 for provision of an additional span to the underbridge near

BRITISH RAILWAYS

MORRIS MOTORS ATHLETIC & SOCIAL CLUB
MUSICAL FESTIVAL
AT
OXFORD

SATURDAY, SEPTEMBER 26th

FIRST AND SECOND CLASS
CHEAP DAY RETURN TICKETS

WILL BE ISSUED

TO

OXFORD

FROM ALL STATIONS AND HALTS WITHIN A RAIL DISTANCE OF

80 MILES

**TICKETS WILL BE AVAILABLE FORWARD AND
RETURN BY ANY TRAIN ON DAY OF ISSUE**

As certain trains are Second Class only, First Class passengers should, before booking, ascertain which trains are provided with First Class accommodation.

Notice as to Conditions.—These tickets are issued subject to the British Transport Commission's published Regulations and Conditions applicable to British Railways exhibited at their stations or obtainable free of charge at station booking offices. Luggage allowances are as set out in these general notices.

Tickets can be obtained in advance at Stations and Agencies

Further information will be supplied on application to Stations, Agencies, or to Mr. E. FLAXMAN, Commercial Officer, Paddington Station, W.2 (Telephone: Paddington 7000. Extension "Enquiries": 8.0 a.m. to 10.0 p.m.), or to the Commercial Officer, Euston Station, N.W.1.

Paddington and Euston Stations,
August 1959

L.D. 528 D.   Printed by W. A. SMITH (Leeds) LTD., Carlton Printeries, Leeds.

Wheatley looking towards Oxford . . .

. . . and towards Princes Risborough, *c.*1960.   *(Both) Lens of Sutton Collection*

An Oxford-Paddington dmu diverted via Thame passes Morris Cowley platform in September 1961.   *John Hubbard*

The same dmu passing the Morris Works, looking towards Princes Risborough.   *John Hubbard*

Wheatley at 11 m. 49 ch., the one renewed in 1928. This was to enable a dual carriageway to be provided underneath, at that time the A40, now part of the M40 where it links with the A40.

Closure moved a step closer when, on 23rd November, 1960, the divisional manager wrote to the regional accountant saying that it was intended to withdraw all passenger services over the line, except workers' trains to Cowley, and freight would be withdrawn from Wheatley, Tiddington and Bledlow. The workers' trains would run as unadvertised passenger/parcels services. The accountant was asked to provide 'shot' estimates of the train movement cost savings likely to be achieved.

The accountant replied speedily on 9th December with an estimate of annual savings of £20,656, based on 69,954 annual train miles saved. The savings were made up as follows:

Staff (2 drivers, 2 firemen, 2 guards)	3,768
Repair of rolling stock (locomotives & coaches)	6,675
Train movement costs (coal, water, lubricants)	10,213
	£20,656

Interestingly, the coal allowed for was 1,590 tons at £6 4s. 7d. per ton (pit price).

In July 1961, the station master at Cowley was asked to give the number of passengers alighting and joining the 'workers' trains' for a week in July, and this survey gave the following total figures for each train (5 day week):

Alighting
6.17 am from Thame	259
5.50 am from Banbury	72

Joining
4.45 pm from Oxford	193
5.15 pm from Cowley (to Oxford)	39
5.31 pm from Cowley (to Thame)	38

Some freight figures recorded in July 1961 for Wheatley and Tiddington (only) for the previous 12 months are interesting as they show that the traffic had held up reasonably well, when compared with those for 1957 shown earlier in the chapter:

Wheatley

Forwarded
81 tons

Received
Coal 4,470 tons
Other 490 tons
Livestock: 3 wagons

Tiddington

Forwarded
746 tons
(practically all sugar beet)

Received
Coal Nil*
Other 496 tons

*No longer a coal merchant here, but Mobbs of Wheatley bringing coal by road from there and put to ground at Tiddington.

'61XX' class 2-6-2T No. 6138 approaches Horspath Halt with a train for Oxford on 20th March, 1960.   *Brian Matthews Collection*

On the last Saturday of the winter service, 10th June, 1961, and running some 24 minutes late, '61XX' class 2-6-2T No. 6123 arrives at Towersey Halt with the 4.02 pm Princes Risborough to Oxford.   *Michael Hale*

On Saturday 10th June, 1961, '61XX' class 2-6-2T No. 6129 waits acceptance into the yard at Morris Cowley. *Michael Hale*

The 12.52 pm (Saturdays only) Oxford-Princes Risborough arrives at Littlemore on 10th June, 1961. The motive power is '61XX' class 2-6-2T No. 6138. On the right in the sand siding are some empty former coaching stock underframes now used to carry cars. *Michael Hale*

Right: Class '9F' 2-10-0 No. 92220 *Evening Star* waits to leave Morris Cowley with a car train in March 1963; goods shed to the right. *John Hubbard*

Below: BR Standard class '9F' 2-10-0 No. 92005 waits for the road to the shed at Oxford Station North on 23rd July, 1961; a service is signalled out of the down platform. Running light, the locomotive had possibly returned from Morris Cowley.
Philip Kelley

Next the Region wrote to the postal authorities asking if alternative arrangements could be made for the bags of mail put on trains at Thame which were as follows:

4.02 pm P.Risborough-Oxford (4.15 at Thame) 2 bags forwarded
6.48 pm P. Risborough-Oxford (7.07 at Thame) 4 bags (SX), 10 bags (SO) forwarded
6.27 pm Oxford-P. Risborough (7.05 at Thame) 2-6 bags forwarded, 2-3 bags received

The Post Office replied within a couple of days pointing out that there was no suitable alternative as the local bus service was restricted to two bags only, and that '[they] look forward to receiving your proposals for the conveyance of mails, either by freight train or railway road services operating in the current train timings'.

Some long standing freight train arrangements were altered from 8th January, 1962 when the 8.30 am Slough to Hinksey and 9.22 am Hinksey to Slough were both altered to terminate at Princes Risborough. The 8.30 am from Slough was due to arrive at Risborough at 11.24 am and return to Slough at 1.10 pm; the 9.22 am Hinksey was due at Risborough at 12.11 pm and returned to Oxford at 12.45 pm. Doubtless intended to exchange traffic at Risborough (although only 10 wagons for beyond Risborough were allowed on the 9.22 service, except by special arrangement), sometimes delays would have meant these trains did not meet with inevitable extended transit times. As it was, empty box vans from Oxford for High Wycombe, previously conveyed by the 9.22 service, were diverted via Reading and Slough.

Another, longer, step towards closure took place on 17th January when the General Manager submitted the following memorandum to the Area Board:

A case has been established for the withdrawal of the passenger train service operating between Princes Risborough and Oxford, a distance of approximately 21 miles.

The proposal is set out in the attached memorandum, which is required to be submitted to the East Midland Area Transport Users' Consultative Committee [TUCC], and provides for the complete closure of two halts and one station, and withdrawal of passenger facilities from five other stations, one of which would also be reduced to an unstaffed goods siding. Other main features are:

1. The advertised passenger train service to be withdrawn comprises eight trains in each direction on Mondays to Fridays, nine on Saturdays and two on Sundays. One unadvertised train operating in each direction between Thame and Morris Cowley and one service from Morris Cowley to Oxford on Mondays to Fridays would also be discontinued.

2. A number of road services provided by City of Oxford Motor Services, Limited, in conjunction with the Thames Valley Traction Company, Limited, already operate in the area, and it is considered that these facilities would afford a reasonable alternative means of transport for the majority of passengers at present using the rail services between Thame and Oxford.
    While there are no comparable alternative public transport facilities between Thame and Princes Risborough, approximately half of the regular passengers travelling by rail between these points are schoolchildren, for whose transport arrangements the local education authority is responsible, and the provision of any additional road services to cater for the remainder of the displaced passengers would not be a remunerative proposition.

3. Arrangements for the collection and delivery of parcels and goods 'smalls' traffic in the area would be maintained, whilst facilities for the handing in and/or collection of this traffic by the public would continue to be available at Thame, Wheatley, Morris Cowley and Littlemore stations.

Right: Looking from the down platform towards Thame goods shed and signal box in the last year of passenger operation, 22nd April, 1962.   *Geoff Gamble*

Below: Looking west towards the oil depot at Thame. The first wooden hut is a P. Way store (12 ft x 9½ ft), the second one is that used to house the P. Way motor trollies (29 ft x 16 ft); note the rails outside.
                    R.H.G. Simpson

Alternative facilities for freight traffic in full truck loads at present dealt with at Bledlow would be available at Thame and Princes Risborough stations.

4. Two of the passenger trains are already operated by diesel traction and, while complete dieselisation of the service would enable further economies to be achieved, it is clear that, with the most economical working arrangements and rationalisation of the cheap fare facilities in the area, the potential passenger receipts would be insufficient to justify retention of the passenger train service.

5. After allowing for loss of receipts and additional cartage costs, the net annual savings to be secure from the proposal are estimated at not less than £26,000.

There are no legal objections to the proposal, which is recommended for approval by the Board.

S.E. Raymond
General Manager

Note that the 'diesel traction' referred to was ex-GW diesel railcars. The station proposed for complete closure was Bledlow and the 'unstaffed goods siding' would be Tiddington.

The Board approved and the memorandum to the TUCC was duly issued. After detailing the proposal and giving the location and description of the line, a table listed train services proposed for withdrawal, as were the alternative bus services available. Parcels and freight would continue to be dealt with at Thame, Wheatley, Cowley and Littlemore and full load traffic (only) at Tiddington.

A count of passengers during the week ended 4th November, 1961 had disclosed a daily average number of 263 passengers joining the branch trains and 261 alighting, and 61 joining and alighting on Sundays. The busiest station was Cowley with 50 joining and 73 alighting each weekday, Thame next, just beating Risborough, with 50 joining and 39 alighting. On Sundays, Risborough was top with 23 joining and 14 alighting. The report stated that there was no knowledge of any industrial or housing development which would lead to increased passenger traffic.

Next came the estimated savings (per annum):

	£
Staff costs (station staff)	6,873
Staff costs (train staff)	4,056
Other staff costs	4,080
Repair of rolling stock	6,430
Train movement costs	11,140
Day to day repairs (buildings etc.)	450
Provision for renewal of rolling stock saved	1,343
	£34,372

From this figure had to be deducted the estimated loss of gross receipts, which were given as £7,822 passenger and £116 parcels, plus it would cost an extra £400 in cartage costs giving a total of £8,338 to be deducted from the savings. The report concluded therefore that it would be possible to save £26,034 each year (£34,372-£8,338) if the passenger services were withdrawn. Additionally a further £5,400 would be saved between 1962-1966 in not undertaking renewals of 'bridges, buildings and other assets' (not detailed).

While the closure proposal was in the queue for rubber stamping (TUCC approval), Thame show was held for the last time that it would be served by rail. Instead of the 10 pages detailing the event in a properly printed notice as in 1935, described in Chapter Eight, the railway arrangements for 20th September, 1962 could be described in 1½ pages of a poorly produced roneo notice. Most of the details concerned strengthening by one or two coaches of the normal timetabled trains, but there a few additions as follows:

5.10 am empty stock Oxford to Thame to convey empty vans for 7.50 pm Thame special
4.45 pm Oxford-P. Risborough. To be double-headed to Thame, assistant
engine to shunt Thame as required and return with 7.50 pm special.
5.44 pm P. Risborough-Wheatley. Retimed to leave Thame at 6.10 pm and extended to Oxford.
7.50 pm Thame-Oxford special van train conveys parcels and poultry exhibits.

As in 1935 extra staff were needed, comprising one divisional inspector, one relief clerk (from 19th to 21st September), one relief clerk (20th September only), two ticket inspectors and two porters. Altogether much reduced from the 1930s when probably nearly all passengers and poultry etc. went by rail.

Finally on 5th November, it was reported (internally): the passenger service would be withdrawn on and from 7th January, 1963; Bledlow and the two halts would close completely, Tiddington would become an unstaffed siding. (Ironically, livestock traffic arriving here from Fishguard, Holyhead and Birkenhead had increased from 49 trucks in 1961 to 81 trucks containing 946 head of cattle up to September 1962. Concern was expressed locally that adequate arrangements would exist at an unstaffed siding to deal with this. Revenue was approximately £4 per animal, paid by the consignee.) The other stations would continue to deal with parcels and freight. The public were advised before the end of the month. Details of the proposed parcels service were issued internally on 14th November:

7.45 am Oxford-P. Risborough calling at all stations
10.15 am P. Risborough-Oxford calling at all stations (Littlemore if required)
4.45 pm Oxford-P. Risborough calling Cowley and Thame (plus Wheatley if required)
5.50 pm P. Risborough-Oxford calling Thame and Cowley

The division had been trying to make the afternoon services a road vehicle but had been defeated by Oxford's inability to cover the work, plus the fact that the TUCC had been assured that a twice daily parcels service would be provided. As the commercial officer put it: 'I feel we should honour this, at least in the initial stages of implementation. After experience has been gained the matter can be reviewed but I cannot see any prospect of improvement of the cartage position in the area'.

The *Thame Gazette* of 4th December, 1962 said that several councillors would travel from Thame to Risborough and back on the last train on Sunday 6th January. The paper said that councillors had expressed concern that no arrangements had been made for the 60 or so workers who caught the 6.20 am from Thame to Cowley each morning, and that the early morning bus could not possibly take these extra people. Some councillors intended to meet City of Oxford Motor Services and the Thames Valley Company with a view to obtaining bus service improvements.

The last up train of five coaches, hauled by '61XX' class 2-6-2T No. 6111, left Oxford at 5.50 pm on 6th January. The Oxford station master, Mr J. Ainsworth, and the shedmaster, Mr Joe Trethewey, travelled on the train which was thronged with enthusiasts and locals, arriving at Princes Risborough 15 minutes late. Mr R. Cox, Risborough station master, met the train wearing his GWR station master's cap. The very last train of all left Risborough at 7.20 pm for Oxford, just over 100 years since trains first ran from Risborough to Thame. The Thame branch was left with just its freight and parcels traffic to sustain an 18½ mile line, but as we shall shortly see, one of these rail flows was quickly terminated.

During the winter of 1962/3 the bridge over the Garsington Road at Morris Cowley was reconstructed with its width increased to take a double track 'because of an anticipated big increase in traffic from the BMC car works' as the *Western Region Magazine* put it. This doubling never happened but later the vacant span was used to run cars (on their own wheels) to the BR freight yard for loading, after British Leyland had built a bridge from the car works over the branch line at a cost of £34,000.

On 28th March, 1963 the firm of Stanley Brown & Son of Chearsley, nr Aylesbury (established 1910), wrote to Ernest Marples, Minister of Transport expressing grave concern at the future of rail transport following the issue of the 'Beeching Plan':

> For the past 50 years many thousands of birds have been despatched weekly [from Thame] to customers in all parts of England and Wales and, unless we can continue to get our birds delivered from the trains as before, this firm will have to close. To convey stock by road has always been impracticable owing to the widespread destinations involved.

Despite enclosing an s.a.e. all the firm got back was the information that TUCCs did not deal with closure of freight-only lines, and that Messrs Brown's letter had been referred to the British Railways Board (BRB) drawing their attention to the firm's anxiety for the future.

It was not long before the next nail was hammered in the coffin. From the start of the summer train service, 17th June, 1963, the special parcels trains were withdrawn. Parcels could still be accepted at the branch stations but they were all sent by road for loading to rail, and conversely, inwards parcels came by road from Oxford. The parcels for Haddenham had only been transferred to Thame for collection and delivery the previous January, which indicates the lack of strategic thinking at the time. In a letter to Messrs Pursers of Thame, dated 18th June, Regional HQ said that it was never the intention that the trains run in perpetuity and no guarantees had been given to that effect. It had always been the intention to introduce road conveyance of parcels but it had not been possible to arrange this before the passenger trains were withdrawn. The writer closed his letter by saying that '[he has] no reason to believe that the present service will prove in anyway inferior to that provided by rail transport'.

On 29th October the divisional manager issued a six page detailed list of 'redundant assets' for disposal on the branch. Most items were for sale or scrapping but it was intended to re-use the cranes at Tiddington, Wheatley and Littlemore and sell or lease the buildings at Bledlow, Tiddington, Cowley and

A snowy scene at Wheatley, quite possibly just before closure in January 1963.

The last Saturday of operation: on 5th January, 1963 in the thick of Britain's bleakest winter since 1947 a prairie-hauled service heading for Oxford approaches Morris Cowley platform.

Doug Nicholls

In March 1963 BR Standard class '4' 4-6-0 No. 75022 runs through Morris Cowley platform (now closed) with the Littlemore tanks, prior to running round and returning to Oxford.

John Hubbard

In June 1964 a steam-hauled car train from Morris Cowley to North Mersey or Bathgate passes Hinksey North's home signal, Oxford-bound, unfortunately the motive power details not recorded. *John Hubbard*

The rather splendid footbridge at Thame could only really be admired from the road overbridge. The building in the foreground in this 1964 view is the pump house.

J.M. Neville courtesy G.A. Carpenter

The cramped position of the footbridge at Thame is obvious in this view of the steps leading from the up platform (1964).   *J.M. Neville courtesy G.A. Carpenter*

A view through Thame station from the Oxford end looking towards the goods shed and signal box (1964). *J.M. Neville courtesy G.A. Carpenter*

A detailed look at the up platform inside the train shed (1964). The sign at left reads 'Way Out', the sign (*centre*) reads 'Gentlemen'. *J.M. Neville courtesy G.A.Carpenter*

　　　　BRITISH RAILWAYS　　　　NOTICE NO.82
　　　　　　　　　　　　　(WESTERN REGION)　　　　(EIGHT TWO)

　　　　　　　　　　　　　Office of Divisional Manager,
　　　　　　　　　　　　　PADDINGTON STATION.

　　　　　　　　　　　　　3rd March, 1964.

　　　　　　　　SUNDAY 8th MARCH.
　　　　SPECIAL ARRANGEMENTS FOR ENGINE DRIVING
　　　　　　OXFORD UNIVERSITY RAILWAY SOCIETY.

　　　　　　　A special train consisting of 61XX Class engine, SK and
BSK to be provided on the above date to work as shown below.

　　　　　　　Members of the Society will be afforded engine driving
facilities under the supervision of a locomotive Inspector.　36
members of the Society will take part and they will join and leave
the special train at Oxford Station.　Not more than two members
of the Society to be on the footplate at any one time.

　　　　　　　Morris Cowley, Wheatley and Thame signal boxes to be
opened.

　　　　　　　Inspector Mackie, Didcot to arrange.

　　　　　　　Mr. Ainsworth, Oxford to provide coaches.

　　　　　　　Messrs Luckett, Morris Cowley and Lewis, Thame
to provide staff as necessary in connection with engine running round
at Morris Cowley and Thame.

SCHEDULE.

	a.m	a.m	a.m	p.m	p.m	p.m
Oxford	9.20					
Kennington Jcn.	9/24					
Littlemore	9C29					
Morris Cowley		10.40	11.50	1.10	2.20	3.30
Tiddington	9C43	10C53	12C 3	1C23	2C33	3C43
Thame	9.52	11. 2	12.11	1.32	2.44	3.52
			p.m			
Thame	10. 5	11.15	12.35	1.45	2.55	4. 5
Tiddington	10C16	11C26	12C46	1C56	3C 6	4C16
Morris Cowley	10.28	11.38	12.58	2. 8	3.17	
Littlemore						4C32
Kennington Jcn.						4/36
Oxford						4.40

PLEASE ADVISE ALL CONCERNED AND ACKNOWLEDGE RECEIPT BY WIRE.

FOR G.A.V. PHILLIPS.

*I don't like this on
a line from which
passr. service have
been withdrawn.*

The 1964 Notice setting out arrangements for Engine Driving.

Littlemore and convert the upside ladies room at Thame to a messroom/store. Tiddington closed completely on 30th December, 1963.

It is difficult to imagine that British Railways ever allowed amateurs to drive steam engines on its lines, but the notice reproduced opposite (No. 82, dated 3rd March, 1964) is proof that it did. The Oxford University Railway Society was allowed a pretty free hand between Cowley and Thame, entailing special opening of three signal boxes, on Sunday 8th March. Note the comment by Mr Squelch, who was at Divisional HQ: 'I don't like this on a line from which passenger services have been withdrawn'. Harold Purser recalls that the public were allowed to travel on this train. Wheatley box closed permanently on 12th July, 1964, a 2-lever ground frame being provided to work the connection to the up sidings. The long section working Wheatley-Kennington Jn was withdrawn and the distant signals at Cowley fixed in the caution position; the latter box was no longer able to switch out. The existing Thame-Wheatley occupation key system was extended to Cowley, the Wheatley-Cowley system being taken out of use.

Further contraction came on 19th May, 1964 with the withdrawal from Thame of all parcels and sundries traffic and through loads entailing collection and/or delivery (C&D). Thame was left with through load station to station traffic (S to S) including coal and that to private sidings. At Wheatley parcels and through loads (C&D and S to S) were withdrawn leaving just coal traffic. The traffic previously collected or delivered from Thame and Wheatley would in future be dealt with at Oxford. Cowley passenger station, which had continued to deal with parcels until now, also closed on 19th May.

On 2nd November, 1964, a new oil siding opened at Littlemore for Shell Mex & BP Ltd. It was 480 ft in length and controlled by a ground frame, released by the Kennington Jn-Cowley token, at 17 m. 57 ch. This was on the site of the old sand siding. The previous siding for National Benzole Ltd (later Shell Mex & BP), opened in 1929, had fallen out of use some time previously. The work, including recovery of the old National Benzole sidings, cost £4,185. The traffic to the new siding did not begin until early 1965. The level crossing at Bledlow was converted to automatic half barriers, and the ground frame (one time signal box) closed on 15th September, 1965. This work cost £4,835.

The through freight service over the line at this time (June 1965-April 1966 timetable) was as follows (weekdays only):

Down

10.25 pm (SX) Paddington-Wellington parcels 3M09 (P. Risborough pass 12.03 am MX)
12.45 am (WFO) Cowley-Tyseley 4M69
12.58 am (MX - Q) Acton-Cowley 7A23 (Cowley arr. 3.15 am)
4.20 am (MX - Q) Cowley-Hinksey 0A28 (engine + brake van)
2.15 am (MX) Thames Haven-Thame 4V07 (Thame arr. 5.45 am)
6.25 am (MX) Thame-Oxford OZ25 (engine + brake van)
8.25 am Thames Haven-Thame 4V08 (Thame arr. 12.21 pm)
1.15 pm (MWFO) Cowley-Johnstone 3S49
9.15 pm (SX) Thame-Oxford OZ25 (light engine)
10.20 pm (SX) Cowley-North Mersey 4M54
11.50 pm (SX) Cowley-Oxley Sidings 5M65

A fine study of the up inner home signal at Wheatley in the year the signal box closed (1964). The black shed close to the signal box was where the P. Way motorised trolley was stored.

J.M. Neville courtesy G.A. Carpenter

Looking north from the up platform in May 1964, Princes Risborough North signal box (*centre*) with the Oxford and Chinnor (formerly Watlington) branches curving off left behind it and the Aylesbury branch veering off to the right from the upside.   *C.W. Judge Collection*

Princes Risborough looking southwards, viewed from the up platform in May 1964.
                    C.W. Judge Collection

A '61XX' class 2-6-2T runs through Princes Risborough with an up unfitted freight in May 1964. By now all the semaphores visible are lower quadrant.   *C.W. Judge Collection*

On Sunday 15th August, 1965 the LCGB's 'Western Ranger' excursion leaves Thame on its return journey to Waterloo via Kensington Olympia. Leaving Waterloo at 9.37 am, its itinerary included Swindon Works, Abingdon, Witney and Swanbourne before reaching Thame via Oxford. As well as BR Standard class '4' 4-6-0 No. 75075, seen here hauling a set of SR coaches, the tour used '38XX' 2-8-0 No. 3863, '57XX' 0-6-0PT No. 9773 and a LMR class '4' 2-6-4T.

John Spencer Gilks

Up
12.55 pm (TThO) Johnstone-Cowley 3V38 (Cowley arr. 12.18 am)
12.05 pm (MWFO) Oxford-Cowley 0A41 (light engine for 3S49)
12.08 pm (WFO) Tyseley-Cowley 4V27 (Cowley arr. 2.23 pm)
1.38 pm Thame-Thames Haven 4E08
6.29 pm (SX) Oxford-Thame 0A76 (engine + brake van (for 4E07?))
8.18 pm (SX) Oxford-Thame 0A76 (light engine)
9.10 pm (SX) Thame-Thames Haven 4E07
10.45 pm (SX) Hinksey-Paddington 5A64 (called at Cowley 1057-11.20)
10.55 pm (SX) Oxford-Cowley 0A41 (light engine for 5M65)

Q - runs if required

The main traffic being dealt with was cars from Cowley on five outward trains (4M69, 3S49, 4M54, 5M65 and 5A64) and the twice daily oil trains from Thames Haven to Thame. There were only four down and three up movements on the section of line between Thame and Cowley. This was the basic service; at the back of the working timetable were a number of 'ghost' schedules for special car trains run if required from Cowley (e.g. to Harwich, Dover, Southampton, Hull, etc.) but only one in each direction ran over the section between Thame and Cowley. Early in 1966 new private sidings, known as BMC Service sidings, were brought into use on the downside at the eastern end, the gated access being near the 15½ milepost. Regrettably this spare parts traffic only went by rail until 1971.

A letter from the divisional manager, Paddington dated 10th November, 1966 said that a policy decision had been taken at a meeting on 4th November to close the section of line from Thame to Morris Cowley. It is considered that the poor state of Wheatley tunnel played a big part in this decision; a figure of £37,000 for repairs has been mentioned to the author. The only facilities remaining at Thame would be the oil sidings, the goods yard had already closed on 10th October. The signal box at Thame would be closed and access to the oil sidings would be by hand points, normally padlocked. However, this latter decision was quickly rescinded insofar as a new connection to the oil sidings at 5 m. 73 ch. was concerned, where a ground frame was installed. This new connection two chains to the west of the existing connection allowed the stabling sidings to be lengthened. The ground frame was brought into use on 19th December.

As from 6th March, 1967 there were no trains scheduled between Thame and Cowley except a twice weekly trip from Cowley to Wheatley with coal which had to run to Thame to run-round following closure of Wheatley box. This ran at 3.50 pm from Cowley to Wheatley and 4.15 pm Wheatley to Cowley via Thame on Tuesdays and Fridays only. The date for closure of the section from Thame to Cowley was set at 1st May, 1967, after which it was intended that:

(a) Princes Risborough to Thame would be worked as a long siding and Thame box would be redundant.
(b) The motor trolley system of maintenance would be withdrawn (a 1966 letter stated that it was seldom used as there were no longer any resident length gangs).
(c) Wheatley station would be completely closed, its coal traffic (over 2,000 tons yearly, about 3/4 wagons a week) being dealt with at Cowley.

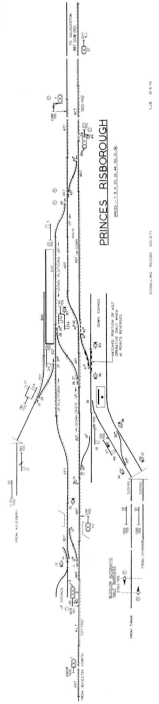

The layout at Princes Risborough after the rationalisation of 1968 until the resignalling, controlled by Marylebone, of 1991. The down platform was reinstated in the 1998 re-doubling between Risborough and Bicester.

Signalling Record Society

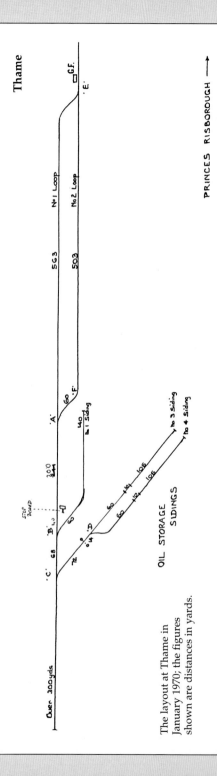

The layout at Thame in January 1970; the figures shown are distances in yards.

Morris Cowley

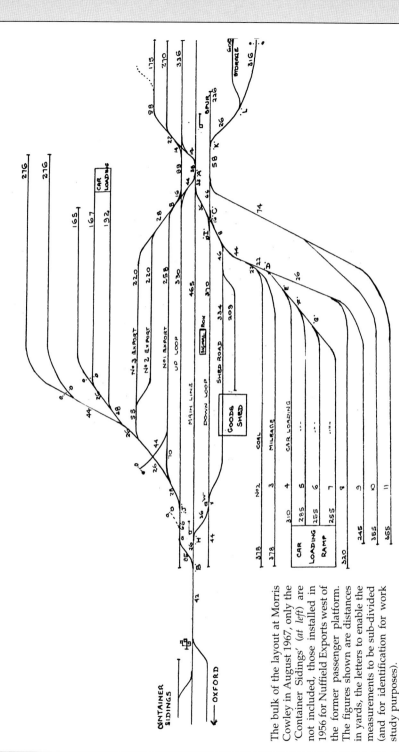

The bulk of the layout at Morris Cowley in August 1967, only the 'Container Sidings' (*at left*) are not included, those installed in 1956 for Nuffield Exports west of the former passenger platform. The figures shown are distances in yards, the letters to enable the measurements to be sub-divided (and for identification for work study purposes).

It had initially been agreed that the track and structures between Thame and Cowley could be removed immediately after closure, but publication of the Map of Railway Networks in March 1967 which showed the Thame branch in place caused this agreement to be postponed for the time being (letter from divisional manager, now at Reading, dated 21st March, 1967). Although the section was shut on the 1st May, Thame signal box did not close at that time and the signalling and track between there and Cowley remained available in emergency. Harold Purser thought that a buffer stop was placed west of Thame oil depot one weekend in August 1967.

A letter from the divisional manager dated 6th May, 1968, said that it had now been agreed that the permanent way could be lifted between Thame (6 m. 15 ch.) and Cowley (15¼ mp). From 1st July, 1968, Cowley ceased to accept coal traffic as the ground concerned was required for development as car standing space 'so that loading and unloading of car trains could be accomplished without difficulty'. The two Cowley coal merchants were relocated at Becket Street, Oxford, while the three merchants, only recently relocated (at Cowley) from Wheatley, had to go to Littlemore for their coal, which they removed to their stacking ground at the former Wheatley station.

Between 15th and 23rd September a major rationalisation of the layout took place at Princes Risborough, restoring it to something like the layout before the new works at the turn of the century. (This was a prelude to British Rail unpicking all the good work of the Great Central and Great Western railways and singling the 27 mile section of line between Princes Risborough and Aynho, south of Banbury, which was carried out between 27th October and 4th November, 1968.) Princes Risborough was left with one through platform and a bay (the former up platform) and only one signal box, the South box closing. Thame signal box should have closed during this work at Princes Risborough but had a short reprieve. Finally on 17th November Thame box closed, replaced by new ground frames at 5 m. 35 ch. (the loop facing points at the Risborough end) released by Annett's type key carried by the driver and at the connection to the two petrol sidings at the Cowley end which were not locked by this key. Thereafter the section Princes Risborough to Thame was worked as a long siding. Consideration had been given to taking out the automatic half barriers at Bledlow but it was considered that train crews would object to this, in view of the weight of the oil trains and the variations and steepness of the gradients.

The line was officially taken out of use between 6 m. 15 ch. and 15 m. 20 ch. on 1st January, 1969, and the following month the Region's Estate Surveyor reported that 'clearance' had been received from the Ministry of Transport, presumably for the land to be disposed of. The track was lifted later that year. Thus ended the life of the Thame branch as a through route. However, signifying that Morris Cowley still had a future, there was some extension of the car sidings on the downside at the Thame end of the layout there during 1969.

Chapter Twelve

Only a Stub remains

In May 1969 the Regional Board approved the construction of a new bridge over the B4009 road near Princes Risborough (at 1 m. 1½ ch.) on behalf of Buckinghamshire County Council. If this was the original bridge, it would have been over 100 years old. The tenders received from six contractors were higher than expected and the County Council was asked to obtain another four tenders, but the lowest of these was similar to those previously received. It was necessary to raise the previous estimate by £11,300 to £44,800 and in January 1970 the tender of Messrs Caffin was accepted, the total cost to be paid by Buckinghamshire County Council (outside party prices) being estimated at £47,530.

The *Oxford Mail* of 25th October, 1971, reported that 'a massive campaign to re-open the Thame to Princes Risborough rail link has been launched by the Thame Ratepayers' Association'. Every household would be asked to sign a petition calling for the line to be 'reinstated' and all the surrounding villages would be approached. The petition would be presented to Richard Marsh, Chairman of BR. One of the campaign organisers, a local Councillor, said 'This is something we badly need, especially in view of the ever increasing development, both private and industrial in the town. The bus services have been cut, isolating Thame, and if we are not careful this could become a dead town'. The Thame Urban District Council would be asked to support and subsidise a new service. Unfortunately, the massive campaign had no immediate effect and the isolated town had to wait another 15 years for Haddenham & Thame Parkway, a new station on the Chiltern line, to reconnect them with a rail service.

In February 1972 all the station sidings at Littlemore were taken out of use, leaving just the oil siding in current use, the station having officially closed on 21st June, 1971.

During the 1960s BR had been giving thought to an improved station for Oxford. Because the railways were starved of cash at this period they had come up with a scheme involving the redevelopment of the area but this had been turned down by the City Council, as had an appeal. Finally, in 1969, it was apparent that a large sum would have to be spent on repairs and renovations and it was decided to go ahead with a minimal reconstruction scheme. This was approved by the BRB at an estimated cost of £187,000 in December 1969. The new station was opened by the Lord Mayor of Oxford, Alderman A.B. Conners, on 1st August, 1972, the final cost having been £250,000.

On 7th October, 1973 the manually-operated semaphore signalling at Oxford was swept away when a new panel signal box at Oxford opened. This eventually entailed the closure of eight conventional lever frame boxes, including Kennington Jn which closed in the second stage on 15th December, 1973. The new Oxford box then controlled the main line between Radley and Heyford, the Worcester line as far as Ascott-under-Wychwood, and access to the Bicester and Morris Cowley branches. So far as the latter was concerned, a

The automatic half-barriers at Bledlow, seen from the 1Z18 railtour heading towards Thame on 25th April, 1970. *John C. Gillham*

On 24th June, 1976, 'Western' class diesel No. D1053 *Western Patriarch* hauling the last train of Chryslers to Linwood, passes Blackbird Leys on its way to Oxford. *John Hubbard*

signal box remained at Morris Cowley and the electric token working remained in force, tokens being obtained from new token instruments sited in huts at Kennington Jn, these being released by Oxford Panel.

In October 1973 Oxford City Council asked BR to look at the possibility of restarting a passenger service between Oxford and Cowley, to service the Minchery Farm and Blackbird Leys estates, in addition to the British Leyland works, but again this came to nothing.

Also in 1973/4 pressure started coming from Haddenham Parish Council for the reopening of Haddenham station. They pointed out that the catchment area included a present population of about 12-15,000 persons, expected to grow to 20,000 within five years. BR's initial response (in 1974) was to turn down the proposal and suggest improved bus links with Princes Risborough station, also that the Parish Council should approach the new County Councils (following 1974 Boundary changes) as they had added responsibilities for transport.

At the end of the 1970s the Cowley end of the erstwhile Oxford-Princes Risborough line was open from 5 am to 10 pm on Mondays to Fridays. Cowley had become the centre for all wagon load traffic for the Oxford area and an articulated delivery lorry was based there. It was also an International freight terminal and, apart from export car traffic, dealt with traffic for other destinations loaded in Continental Ferry vans or open vehicles. In 1979 some large consignments of tree trunks for France were dealt with.

The oil tanks for Littlemore came up from Oxford South Yard at about 7.15 am. The engine berthed them and then went light to Cowley and picked up the previous day's empty tanks from Littlemore and any other non-car traffic from Cowley for forwarding and took them to Oxford. After working to Bicester and back, the engine again left Oxford South Yard at about 2.15 pm with any further tanks for Littlemore and other general traffic for Cowley which had arrived in the morning (there had been an earlier service for Cowley only at about 6 am). On arrival at Littlemore the loaded tanks were berthed and any tanks delivered earlier in the day, now empty, were cleared to Cowley. The engine returned to Oxford with any general non-car traffic for the evening departures from Oxford at 3.40 pm northbound and 6.38 pm southbound, also the empty tanks, if room; if not they were left for the next morning.

The most important traffic dealt with was, of course, the car traffic. At this period there were departures of complete trains, loaded with cars, at 3.50 pm on Tuesdays and Thursdays for Bathgate (Scotland) and at 9.30 pm daily for Harwich, Parkeston Quay with export cars. This also conveyed Continental vans for Germany loaded at the Central Ordnance Depot, Bicester. Mid-afternoon the engine which had earlier worked the Littlemore tanks and Bicester trips would bring down any car traffic for the North or North East which would leave Hinksey at about 6 pm. Finally the engine would return to Cowley for cars for an 8.35 pm 'as required' train from Hinksey Yard with export vehicles, its destination dependent on where the boat had docked. To carry out any necessary shunting at Cowley, including forming up the car trains, an air braked class '08' pilot was available at Cowley from about 12.30 pm until 7 pm.

Cars to be moved by rail were driven from the car factory to the rail yard for loading. Any traffic for British Leyland (as it then was) was delivered by road,

On Saturday 18th September, 1976 L435 unit forming the 'Oxfordshire Rambler' railtour stands outside Morris Cowley signal box. This railtour, organised by Oxford Publishing Co., starting from Oxford, visited Bicester, Morris Cowley and the end of the line near Horspath, Wallingford and Abingdon before returning to Oxford.   *John Hubbard*

Class '31' No. 31156 standing at Cowley on 12th June, 1986 with the 'Torbay Express'; the nameboard had been placed by the staff as a joke. F.C. Bennett's warehouse in the background.
                                                                                      John Hubbard

from the rail yard if it had come in by rail, but most supplies were moved entirely by road.

In the 1980s and early 1990s the branch was open overnight to deal with a daily (Tues.- Fri.) service to Longbridge which left Cowley about 4 am. This conveyed 20 cargowagons loaded with car components which had been pressed at Cowley but destined for models produced at Longbridge. It was loaded in Nuffield Exports low level sidings (opposite the signal box), six wagons at a time. The empty train returned to Cowley at about 7 pm. Sometimes, at busy periods, the train ran on Mondays, involving Sunday night loading.

On 28th January, 1982 Morris Cowley signal box was closed and the method of operation of the branch changed to 'No Signalman Token'. The existing token huts at Kennington remained in use but the token instrument at Cowley was sited in the chargeman's office at the Kennington Jn end of the layout. The signals at Cowley were removed (except the up distant) and replaced by stop boards where necessary or the movements handsignalled. Two new ground frames were provided, a 3-lever one at the Kennington end controlling access to the former up and down loops, and a 1-lever frame at the east end, approximately 15¾ mp, controlling a catch point in the single line to prevent any runaway from the Horspath end of the layout travelling towards Kennington. The layout was also much simplified and connections to now redundant British Leyland sidings were abolished. The automatic half barrier crossing at Bledlow was converted to an open crossing on 11th October, 1982.

On 9th May, 1984 David Mitchell, Under-Secretary of State for Transport, opened a new 'Cowley Freight Terminal' to be managed by F.C. Bennett an Oxfordshire-based road haulage group. This was a road-rail freight transfer terminal, built on the site of the old goods shed on land leased from BR at a cost of £380,000, of which £185,000 had been provided by the Dept of Transport as a grant under Section 8 of the Railways Act, 1974. Facilities included a 20,000 sq. ft warehouse, a lengthy siding with provisions for loading/unloading under cover, two 1,200 ft sidings with loading ramps and a 40 ton travelling crane. Traffic would be moved by rail on Speedlink's fast air braked freight trains, with distribution from Cowley by road. On opening day passenger trains ferried VIP's to the terminal, a class '58', seen for the first time on the branch, providing the motive power (*see cover illustration*). The Freight Terminal was in operation for 13 years until Rover needed the ground for further expansion, when the 1984-built Bennett warehouse was demolished. Over the years traffic dealt with had been chipboard (from Austria), Perrier water (from France), gearboxes from Germany, paper, Scotch whisky; about 8 wagonloads daily. By the time Rover wanted the ground there had been a change in ownership of the company and rail traffic was diminishing.

In connection with a new link road being built at Thame, the B4012, it was necessary to construct a new automatic open crossing, locally supervised (AOCL) at 5 m. 16 ch. with a 30 mph speed restriction in the down direction, 20 mph in the up. This opened on 7th July, 1985 and was destined to have a very short life.

In the 1986-7 timetable there were weekday departures from Cowley at 4 am (Speedlink to Longbridge), 4.20 pm (Speedlink to Bescot), 8 pm (to Parkeston

Class '31' diesel No. 31260 approaches Kennington Junction with its load of cars and vans.

A pilot's-eye view of Horspath village. The railway used to follow the embankment now surrounded by trees in the centre right of the picture. Where the trees end (*top*) was the entrance to Horspath tunnel. The halt was just this side of the road crossing from left to right in the bottom third of the picture. Under a magnifying glass the distinctive house alongside No. 6138 in the picture on page 218 can be picked out to the right of the wooded area just above the road mentioned. *C.W. Judge*

Quay), 8.55 pm (to Bathgate) and 9.55 pm (to Didcot). Arrivals were at 11.25 am (from Washwood Heath) and 6.52 pm (from Longbridge).

The residents of Thame and its hinterland were again to be reconnected to the rail system (in a way) by the opening of Haddenham & Thame Parkway station, between Princes Risborough and Bicester, at 30 m. 25 ch. This was a simple platform on the downside of the single line, just 210 yards long. It opened on 3rd October, 1987. An operating notice issued the same weekend reported the closure of the terminal platforms at Birmingham (Moor Street) and their replacement by new through platforms on the line leading to Birmingham (Snow Hill). Some 16 years later, the reinvigoration of traffic over the 'Chiltern Railways' would cause these platforms and buildings to be restored to their former glory, although unfortunately the terminal platforms will not be reopened until 2005 due to delays with resignalling.

A new, and much grander, Oxford station was opened by the Chairman of the BRB, Sir Bob Reid, on 3rd October, 1990. A greatly enlarged main building on the upside houses ticket office, waiting area, toilets, refreshments and some shops, and the dingy subway between the platforms was replaced by a footbridge and, later, lifts. A much improved bus interchange was provided. At the opening ceremony locomotive 47547 was named *University of Oxford* and 47587 *Ruskin College Oxford*.

Resignalling of the Chiltern line from Marylebone commenced in 1990 and the section between High Wycombe and Bicester North was dealt with between 1st and 6th March, 1991. This involved the closure of High Wycombe and Princes Risborough signal boxes and the introduction of Track Circuit Block working between High Wycombe and Aynho Junction (south of Banbury) and between Princes Risborough and Aylesbury, all controlled from Marylebone.

The current station at Oxford, viewed from the upside, officially opened by Sir Bob Reid on 3rd October, 1990.

Class '33' diesel No. 33114 on Southern Electric Group's enthusiasts' special leaving Thame oil terminal on 12th November, 1988. The terminal is behind the wire fence.   *John Hubbard*

Haddenham & Thame Parkway station nearing completion in 1987. A second platform was provided in 1998 when the line was re-doubled.

The Thame branch was worked 'under the control of a person in charge' (official title), in this case the signalman at Marylebone. The Chinnor (former Watlington) branch had closed on 15th July, 1990. The former North box at Risborough remains *in situ* as it is a listed building.

However, Marylebone's involvement with Thame did not last long as the oil traffic finished in 1991. The Thame end of the former Oxford branch was taken out of use beyond the ¾ milepost in October 1991. This just left the stub between Kennington Jn and Cowley in use, for the oil traffic to Littlemore and, of course, the cars from Cowley.

Further track rationalisation took place at Cowley in the early 1990s. In February 1990 the down loop was made into a dead-end siding, and shortened by 160 yards, with its new buffer stop at the Oxford end. In September 1992 the up loop and two of the three parallel up sidings were taken out of use, leaving just No. 4 up siding, which was a through siding, to take the place of the up loop. Additionally the Rover Group siding, behind No. 4, and thought to be the only remaining siding into the old Nuffield Exports works, was taken out of use. These sidings and the up loop were in poor condition and the traffic now being dealt with could all be handled in Nos. 4-11 sidings on the downside.

The last regular oil train to Littlemore ran in 1993 but the traffic came back for about 18 months 1996-8, running on an 'as required' basis. When this finally ceased the depot was demolished and the site cleared within three months, although the heavy concrete bases remain in the undergrowth.

Initially 'Chiltern Lines' (from 1994), from 24th June, 1996 'Chiltern Railways' a new rail franchise obtained by M40 trains, the line from Marylebone to Birmingham (Snow Hill) via Princes Risborough has been one of the definite success stories of railway privatisation. In 1997 the company announced that it had seen a 17 per cent rise in passenger numbers since privatisation and that it would run out of space in peak times unless it could increase service frequency. It had persuaded Railtrack to redouble the 18 mile section between Princes Risborough and Bicester at a cost of £13 million, in a novel revenue-sharing deal which would compensate Railtrack for its outlay. The new track would be ready for the summer 1998 timetable, together with four new 3-car diesel units which had been purchased.

To enable one of the platforms (on a new alignment) of a new two platform station to be constructed at Haddenham and Thame Parkway, and other major work, the line between Risborough and Bicester was closed from 17th-25th January, 1998. *Railnews* stated that the total project required 53,000 sleepers, 40 miles of long welded rail and 60,000 tons of ballast. Although the physical work was completed on time, in May, the signalling was not ready and the new timetable, with more and faster trains, was eventually introduced on Sunday 19th July. The *Oxford Times* had previously reported that bus services would be timed to coincide with arrivals and departures at the Parkway station.

In 2000 as part of its preparation for applications for a new 20 year franchise, Chiltern Railways announced that it was investigating the possibility of reopening the Thame branch through to Oxford. The cost would be around £250 million and there would be an intermediate station near the Wheatley junction of the M40. It envisaged at least three trains an hour between Oxford and Marylebone, but it could take up to 10 years before the line was open. The *Oxford Times* reported that the County Council was generally in favour and would be likely to ask for a new station to serve the new Oxford United football stadium at Minchery Farm and the nearby Oxford Science Park at Littlemore. The old track bed would be used as far as possible. The company also announced that the remaining single track main line section between Bicester and Aynho Junction would be re-doubled.

The 9 mile single line section between Bicester and Aynho Park was doubled in 2002 at a cost of £60 million, the new line opening for traffic on 5th August. In the same year a new footpath for walkers, cyclists and horse riders, the Phoenix Trail, opened on the formation of the old Oxford branch between Thame and Princes Risborough. This is part of the National Cycle Network and was a project partnership between the charity Sustrans, the South Oxfordshire District Council and other local councils and businesses. Although at the time of writing (late 2003) no more has been heard of reopening the railway line, this cycle path would be a problem if it ever came about.

At the beginning of 2004 it was reported that the Chinnor & Princes Risborough Railway had bought the former Princes Risborough signal box and planned to turn it into a visitor centre and observation area. The Chinnor Railway had opened in 1995, and hopes to reinstate trains to Princes Risborough, running to the former Watlington bay line, by 2006.

With Cowley works concentrating on production of the new, very popular BMW Mini, there is still a (weekday) daily train from Morris Cowley to Purfleet with export cars. This is hauled by a class '66' locomotive and comprises eight tunnel wagons holding about 264 cars. The empty stock goes up to Cowley about 7 am and the loaded train leaves Hinksey around 5.40 pm each evening. These cars are loaded in a new car terminal on the downside at the Thame end of the layout, three sidings stretching between 15 m. 25 ch. and 15¾ mp, opened about 2000 it is thought (although nothing was ever published to this effect). Let us hope that the car traffic remains with rail (it is about 50 per cent of Cowley's output at present); while it does there is always the possibility that some or all of the branch will again see passenger trains.

Appendix One

Coaches in Through Narrow Gauge Trains - June 1880 (extract)

8.25 am Paddington-Oxford
1 x 1st, 1 x 2nd, 1 x 3rd, 1 Bk 3rd, 1 x 1st /2nd compo, 1 x van = 6
Milk vans for Wycombe branch. An extra 3rd on Saturdays.

11 am Paddington-Oxford
1 x 1st, 1 x 2nd, 2 x 3rd, 1 x 1st/2nd compo, 1 x van   = 6 Oxford (via Thame)
1 x 1st, 1 x 2nd, 1 x Bk 3rd   = 3 Windsor

1.10 pm Paddington-Oxford
1 x 1st, 1 x 2nd, 1 x 3rd, 1 x Bk 3rd, 1 x 1st/2nd compo, 1 x van   = 6 Oxford (via Thame)
1 x 1st, 1 x 2nd, 2 x 3rd, 1 x van   = 5 Reading
1 x 1st, 1 x 2nd, 1 x Bk 3rd   = 3 Windsor
Extra 3rd (Windsor) on Saturdays. Also milk vans.

4.50 pm Paddington-Oxford
2 x 1st, 2 x 2nd, 1 x 3rd, 1 x Bk 3rd, 1 x van   = 7 Oxford (via Thame)
1 x 1st/2nd compo (Marlow), 1 x 1st/2nd compo (Maidenhead)   = 2 Maidenhead
Extra 3rd on Saturdays

8.25 am Oxford-Paddington
2 x 1st, 2 x 2nd, 1 x 3rd, 1 x Bk 3rd, 1 x 1st/2nd compo, 1 x van = 8
Extra 1st from Wycombe Mondays, extra 3rd from Oxford Mondays. Also vans for milk.

11.15 am Oxford-Paddington
1 x 1st, 1 x 2nd, 2 x 3rd, 1 x van   = 5 ex-Oxford
1 x 1st, 1 x 2nd, 1 x Bk 3rd   = 3 ex-Windsor
Extra 3rd Saturdays

2.30 pm Oxford-Paddington
1 x 1st, 1 x 2nd, 1 x 3rd, 1 x Bk 3rd, 1 x 1st/2nd compo, 1 x van = 6 ex-Oxford
1 x 3rd, 1 x 1st/2nd Compo   = 2 ex Windsor

6.05 pm Oxford-Paddington
1 x 1st, 1 x 2nd, 1 x 3rd, 1 x Bk 3rd, 2 x vans   = 6 ex-Oxford
1 x 1st, 2 x 3rd, 1 x van   = 4 ex-Windsor

compo = composite 1st/2nd class vehicle
Bk 3rd = 3rd class vehicle including guard's brake compartment

Authorised Staff Establishment - 1925
Paybill and Traffic Receipts

			Paybill £	Receipts £
Princes Risborough				
Station Master	1 (Class 2)			
Booking Clerks	2	1913	?	7,385
Goods Clerk	1	1922	4,309	17,284
Station Foremen	2	1923	3,882	16,739
Ticket Collector	1	1924	3,442	16,676
Parcel Porter	1	1925	4,152	14,555
Porters	4	1926	3,913	20,448
Goods Porter	1			
Number Takers	3			
Goods Shunters	3			
Signalmen	6 (3 North 3 South)			
Lampman	1			
Total	26			
Bledlow				
Station Master	1 (Class 4)	1913	200	1,361
Porters	2	1922	616	2,445
Gatewoman	1 (Hinton Crossing)	1923	591	2,137
Total	4	1924	607	2,804
		1925	568	2,056
		1926	528	2,214
Thame				
Station Master	1 (Class 3)	1913	886	14,839
Booking Clerk	1	1922	2,308	31,079
Goods Clerk	1	1923	2,145	27,404
Station Foreman	1	1924	2,265	24,745
Parcel Porter	1	1925	2,246	25,563
Porter Signalman	1	1926	2,209	25,889
Porter	1			
Horse Parcel Vanman	1			
Goods Carter	1			
Goods Porter	1			
Goods Shunter	1			
Signalmen	2			
Total	13			
Tiddington				
Station Master	1 (Class 4)	1913	180	5,099
Porters	2	1922	541	9,941
		1923	528	9,476
Total	3	1924	529	8,232
		1925	537	8,551
		1926	?	?

Wheatley

Station Master	1 (Class 4)	1913	461	6,875
General Clerk	1 (Junior)	1922	1,095	8,962
Porter Signalman	1	1923	1,040	9,606
Porters	2	1924	1,015	8,213
Signalmen	2	1925	1,027	9,255
		1926	922	8,353
Total	7			

Littlemore

Station Master	1 (Class 4)	1913	261	10,437
General Clerk	1	1922	908	21,474
Leading Porter	1	1923	906	20,515
Porters	2	1924	921	19,440
Goods Porter	1	1925	914	22,344
		1926	992	29,113
Total	6			

Oxford (summary only)

Station Master	1 (Special class)	1913	13,824	120,375
Clerks	21 (+ 1 summer only)	1922	35,727	218,878
Inspectors/Foreman	17	1923	32,941	197,314
Ticket Collectors	13	1924	34,178	203,220
Porters, etc.	46 (+ 2 summer only)	1925	36,488	213,277
Shunters	26	1926	35,326	197,565
Signalmen	22			
Guards	46			
Others	4			
Total	196			

Morris Cowley (1929 census)

Morris Cowley did not exist in 1925 but these figures were shown in the 1929 census, which, regrettably, did not include any financial information.

Station Master	1 (Class 2)
General Clerk	1
Goods Clerks	6
Working Foreman	1
Goods Checker	1
Goods Porters	4
Ldg. Parcel Porter	1
Porters	2
Goods Shunters	2
Signalmen	2
Motor Drivers	3
Total	24

By 1929 the staff at Littlemore was now reduced to five, Oxford to 191, Risborough had increased by one to 27 and Tiddington by one (a motor driver) to four.

Appendix Three

Private Sidings for the car trade
at Morris Cowley

Authority
Date

25.3.1926   Two new sidings for Pressed Steel Co. (PrS). Connection with main line at 15 m. 74 ch. PSA 17.11.1927. Authority £1,826.

28.7.1927   Three reception sdgs for GWR and three sidings for Morris Motors Ltd for export traffic ('Exports high level sidings'). All on the upside opposite the (later) signal box. PSA 11.7.1928. (Total) authority £6,100.

26.3.1931   Additional sidings for PrS. Thought to be two sdgs leading off those authorised in 1926. Authority £668.

27.6.1935   Additional sidings for PrS. Authority £2,530.

26.3.1936   Ditto. Authority £525.

30.7.1936   Additional sidings for Morris Industries Export Ltd. To enable them to load export cars in the works rather than at M. Cowley station. Two sdgs north of those authorised in 1927 ('Exports low level sidings'). PSA 8.5.1937. Authority £1,160.

18.3.1937   Additional facilities for PrS. Authority £1,765.

7.10.1937   Extension of siding facilities for PrS. Authority £747.

28.10.1937   Further extension of siding at PrS. Authority £158.

16.12.1937   Extension of siding accom. at PrS. Authority £638.

25.5.1939   Additional accom. for PrS. Authority £492.

23.11.1939   Ditto. Authority £660.

4.10.1940   Additional facilities for PrS on behalf of Air Ministry. Authority £575.

24.10.1941   Additional facilities for PrS [? this was actually Govt work.] Authority £5,249.

29.1.1943   Ditto with the same query. Authority £3,730.

28.9.1945   Additional siding accom. for PrS. Authority £1,371.

26.10.1945   Ditto. Authority £452.

25.11.1953   Provision of private sdg facilities to serve new export packing factory of Morris Motors ('Q' block). These were west of the stn platform, access at 16 m. 13 ch. PSA 12.10.1956. Authority £41,066.

In addition the following work was undertaken on behalf of the Govt:

28.6.1940   Private siding for Air Ministry. [May have been the first aircraft scrap siding.] Authority £1,460.

23.7.1943   Private siding for Ministry of Aircraft Production. Authority £421.

Notes

(a)   PSA = Private Siding Agreement (date).

(b)   Unfortunately it is not possible to locate precisely where some of these sidings were in the Cowley complex, bearing in mind that they were in the customer's premises, not in the GWR territory. Although the Traffic Committee authority dates are known, the files seen did not have plans attached. Furthermore plans located at BR's Estate Records office at St Pancras by Tony Cooke have PSA dates but not authority dates and it is difficult to reconcile the two. Finally the difficulty in unravelling wartime authorities will doubtless be understood.

Appendix Four

Station Masters on the Line
(Recorded in the pages of the *GWR Magazine*)

1893
A.J. Noble appointed SM Thame, remained there 9 years.

1904
E.C. Phillips, Tenby, appointed SM Wheatley (reported Dec.)

1905
W.T. Ashley, SM Wheatley, appointed to Burnham (Bucks) (Feb.)

1907
W. Peace, SM Tiddington to Melangoose Mill (Cornwall) (Sept.)
J.O. Lawrence, SM Midgham to Tiddington (Sept.)

1910
J. James, SM Loudwater, to Thame (Jan.)

1913
Presentation to Waiter Cripps, SM at Littlemore for last 15 years (Mar.)
Reports promotion of Mr Cripps to relief station master Paddington DSO (July)
F. Jacques, SM Alvescot to Littlemore (July)
S.C. Chesterman, clerk Ealing, to Wheatley as SM (Aug.)

1917
S.C. Chesterman, SM Wheatley to Paddington DSO as relief clerk (Apr.)
H.H. Turner, clerk Oxford, to Wheatley as SM

1918
P.J. Molyneux, SM Bodmin to Thame (May)

1919
A. Wrighton, SM Bledlow, to Aynho and P. Smith, SM Brill, to Bledlow (Mar.)
J.O. Lawrence, SM Tiddington retired; he had spent 37 years on the branch (June)

1923
A.J. Clark, W. Drayton, to Wheatley as SM (Jan.)
C. Salmon, chief goods clerk Newbury, to Thame as SM (Dec.)

1929
R.L. A'hern, Taplow, to M.Cowley as SM (Nov.)

1930
C. Salmon, SM Thame, to Uxbridge (Vine St) (July)
G.R. Bishop, chief clerk Southall, to Thame as SM (July)
W.G. Woolford, SM South Leigh, to Littlemore (Sept.)

1933
W.G. Woolford retired as SM Littlemore (15th Nov.)

1934
W.C. Williams, Reading, to Littlemore as SM (Jan.)

1936
W.C. Williams, SM Littlemore to Beaconsfield (Mar.) H.W. Bateman, Uxbridge (Vine St), to Littlemore as SM (May)

1939
J.E. Jones, SM Kidlington to Thame (Apr.)

1940
H.W. Bateman, SM Littlemore, to Langley (Dec.)

1941
R.E. Arnold, Paddington DSO, to Littlemore as SM (Jan.)

1947
H.E. Carpenter, SM Hampstead Norris, to Wheatley (July)

1948
R.E. Arnold, SM Littlemore, to Loudwater (June)

1951
Percy Smith, SM at Bledlow for last 32 years, retired (Feb.)

1960
C.R. Hall, clerk Paddington DTMO, to M. Cowley as SM (Oct.)
J.M. Ellwood, SM M. Cowley to Princes Risborough (Dec.)

1962
(Taken from files)

Thame - Mr Lewis
Wheatley - Mr Kimber
Morris Cowley - Mr Hall
Littlemore - Mr Constantine

Note
These details are not complete, only those that have been found in a full trawl from 1904-63 of the GWR (and BR/WR) magazines. Retirements are not always reported, explaining why some appointments in the list are apparently to stations already having a station master. There were no reports at all for the London Division in the 'Staff Changes' column for 1943-5 (except for one month in 1944), nor any for 1952. No replacement for Mr Smith, who left Bledlow in 1951, has been found and one suspects that the post was discontinued then. It was certainly covered by Thame in 1957.

'61XX' class 2-6-2T No. 6129 waits at Thame with the two-coach passenger service for Princes Risborough.   *Photomatic*

Bibliography

A Country Branch Line by Karau & Turner (Wild Swan Publications)
Calling All Arms by Ernest Fairfax (Hutchinson, pub. *c.*1945)*
GWR and The General Strike by C. R. Potts (Oakwood Press)
History of the GWR by E. MacDermot (GWR & Ian Allan reprint)
History of Thame by Brown & Guest (Castle, pub. 1935)*
Making Cars at Cowley by Bardsley & Laing (Sutton Publishing)
Memoirs of a Station Master by Hubert Simmons (Adams & Dart reprint)*
Princes Risborough-Thame-Oxford Railway by R. Lingard (OPC)*
Rail Centres: Oxford by L. Waters (Ian Allan)
Steaming Spires by Dick Tolley (David & Charles)*
The Life of Lord Nuffield by Andrews & Brunner (Blackwell, pub. 1955)*
The Locomotives of the GWR (RCTS)
Track Layout Diagrams of the GWR and BR (WR) Sections 26 & 27 (R.A. Cooke)
Wheatley Records 956-1956 by W.O. Hassall (Oxfordshire Record Society)*

Bradshaw's Manual
BR (WR) Magazine
Bucks Advertiser & Aylesbury News
GWR Magazine
Oxford Journal
Oxford Mail
Oxford Times
Railnews
Railway Gazette
Railway Magazine
South Bucks Free Press
Thame Gazette (A most useful source of information)

Various WRC/GWR files held at the National Archives, Kew (RAIL and MT series, particularly RAIL 768).
Various WRC/GWR/BR files held at the BR Record Centre, Porchester Road, London W2 (now closed)

---

* Out of print, but probably most can be obtained through the library book ordering service, or a second-hand book dealer.

Index

Abingdon Road (halt), 99
Accidents (train), 59, 61, 69-70, 76, 77, 81-3, 155-6
Acts of Parliament 7 et seq., 14-5, 24, 38, 43, 50, 65, 69
Aylesbury, 32 et seq., 42, 47 et seq., 67, 68, 71, 72, 82, 83, 89, 99, 106, 145, 169, 197, 225, 245
Aylesbury & Buckingham Rly, 71, 72
Beale, S. & Co., 30, 37
Bledlow, 35, 40, 44 et seq., 52, 77, 81, 89, 91, 105, 106, 107, 110, 137, 145, 155, 161, 163, 169, 189, 195, 197, 199, 207, 213, 217 et seq., 238, 243, 250, 253, 254
Brotherhood, Rowland, 43, 47, 51, 53, 54, 63
Brunel, I.K., 7, 10 et seq., 23 et seq., 29, 31, 39
Bulkeley, Captain, 11, 16, 17, 25, 27, 31, 38-9
Buses introduced, 106
Closure, Princes Risborough-Thame, 247
Closure, Thame-Morris Cowley, 235, 238
Cookham ballast pit, 35 et seq., 55
Cooper's Crossing, 117, 199
Crutwell, Messrs, 18 et seq.
Cutting the first sod, 29
Diesel railcars, introduction, 171, 179
Electric Train Staff, installation, 90
Eiton, Revd E., 33, 50, 51, 53-4, 55, 57
Fowler, John, 35, 36
Garsington Bridge (halt), 99, 105, 123
General Strike, 123, 129
Griffin, Edward, 25, 26, 37, 66, 110
GW & GCR Joint Committee, 95, 97
Haddenham & Thame Parkway, 239, 241, 245, 247
Hicken, Philip, 49
High Wycombe, 7, 12, 24, 28. 30, 31, 35 et seq., 42 et seq., 48, 50, 52, 54, 55, 57, 62, 63, 68, 70, 73, 74, 77, 84, 89, 95, 97, 145, 169 et seq., 197, 221, 245
Hinksey (halt), 99
Hinksey Yard, 151, 193, 195, 221, 231, 235, 241
Hinton Crossing, 110, 213
Horspath, 32, 50, 51, 57, 85, 99, 117, 137, 147, 149, 155, 159, 168, 171
Iffley, 32, 99
Inspections (BoT/MoT), 19, 44, 61, 62, 72, 125, 137, 163
Kennington Jn, 72, 76, 89, 91, 99, 106, 119, 125, 151, 153, 168, 179, 193, 196, 197, 199, 231, 239, 241, 243, 247
Kennington viaduct, 57, 62, 99, 106-7
Last train, 224-5
Littlemore, 65, 66, 76, 77, 79, 83 et seq., 89, 91, 97, 105, 119, 151, 153, 156 et seq., 163, 169, 189 et seq., 207, 213, 221 et seq., 238 et seq., 247, 248, 251, 253, 254
Littlemore sand quarry, 97, 105, 213
Locking & Block Telegraph, introduction, 89, 90
Maidenhead, 7, 13, 16, 17, 19, 24, 27, 29, 34, 42 et seq., 48, 50, 54, 55, 63, 66, 67, 72 et seq., 76, 83, 84, 89, 97, 145, 168, 169, 189

Military manoeuvres, 99
Morris Cowley, 111, 117, 119, 123 et seq., 149, 151, 153, 155 et seq., 163, 168, 171, 179, 185, 191 et seq., 205, 207, 213, 217, 221 et seq., 239, 248, 251 et seq.,
Morris, William Richard (Lord Nuffield), 123, 149, 151
Motor Trolley track maintenance, 129, 137, 235
Murray, E.F., 18, 19, 26, 29 et seq., 46, 52
Narrowing of Gauge to Aylesbury, 71, 72
Narrowing of Gauge to Oxford, 72-5
Opening of GW & GCR Joint Line, 97
Opening to Aylesbury, 54
Opening to High Wycombe, 19
Opening to Oxford, 63
Opening to Thame, 44-5
Oxford, 7, 22, 25, 32 et seq., 47 et seq., 65 et seq., 72 et seq., 89, 91, 95, 97, 125, 129, 137, 145, 147, 151, 155 et seq., 168, 169 et seq., 205, 213, 217, 221 et seq., 239 et seq.
OWWR, 11, 12, 37
Peniston, William, 14 et seq., 20, 21, 68 et seq.
Penn Farm, 22, 37, 52, 66, 67, 110, 189, 190, 197
Princes Risborough, 7, 22 et seq., 31, 33, 35, 40, 44, 46, 54, 55, 57 et seq., 63, 65 et seq., 71 et seq., 76, 77, 79, 81 et seq., 89, 90, 95, 107, 129, 137, 145, 147, 155 et seq., 168, 169 et seq., 221 et seq., 235 et seq.
Sandy, James, 59, 61
Simmons, Charles, 33, 48
Simmons, Hubert, 48, 58-9
Stanley, Joseph, 79, 80
Taplow (pre-1872), see Maidenhead
Taplow (post 1871), 81, 84, 85, 91, 125, 129, 169, 189, 190, 191, 193, 201
Thame, 7, 21 et seq., 45 et seq., 65 et seq., 70, 73 et seq., 79, 81, 83 et seq., 89 et seq., 95 et seq., 129 et seq., 151 et seq., 168, 169 et seq., 207, 213, 217 et seq., 239 et seq.
Thame Agricultural Show, 137, 145, 224
Tiddington, 32, 65, 66, 69, 75, 85, 89, 91, 105, 106, 111, 115, 129, 145, 153, 189, 190, 195, 197, 199, 207, 217 et seq., 250, 253
Towersey, 24, 25, 30, 35, 49, 59, 110, 117, 137, 161, 171
Train Staff & Ticket Working, 55-6, 58-9, 89
Tredwell, Thomas (and Tredwells), 22, 25 et seq., 29, 31, 35 et seq., 46, 47, 50 et seq.
Ward, F.R., 15, 17, 20, 21 et seq., 53, 63, 68 et seq.
Ward, R.J., 38, 39, 41, 51
Watlington & P. Risborough Rly, 75-6
West Midland Railway, 37
Wheatley, 32, 34, 35, 38, 47, 50, 51, 53, 57, 61 et seq., 66, 73, 75, 77, 83, 85, 89, 90, 99, 115, 117, 125, 129, 137, 145, 153, 155 et seq., 168, 171, 179, 189 et seq., 207, 217 et seq., 247, 251, 253, 254
Wilson, W.H., 7, 8, 16,17, 22 et seq., 39, 42, 54, 62, 68